Southern Living ®

Microwave Cooking
Made Easy

Southern Living.
Microwave Cooking
Made Easy

Audrey P. Stehle

Oxmoor House, Inc.
Birmingham

Library of Congress Catalog Number: 78-55871
ISBN:0-8487-0485-1

Manufactured in the United States of America
Ninth Printing 1984

Microwave Cooking Made Easy

Managing Editor: Ann H. Harvey
Food Stylist: Marilyn Wyrick
Photographers: Charles Beck: cover, pp. 59, 91,
    123, 154, 187; Arnold, Romedy, and Sullivan,
    Inc.: pp. 58, 90, 122, 186; Jerome Drown: p.
    155; Bob Carter: p. 109; Bert O'Neal: p. 108.
Designer and Illustrator: Carol Middleton

Many recipes have been tested and reproduced courtesy of the Home Service Committee of the Georgia Electrification Council, Athens, Georgia 30602.

ISBN 0-8487-0485-1

In *Microwave Cooking Made Easy* we describe microwave cooking in 10 simple, related steps and give basic rules to follow for cooking all different types of food in the microwave oven. Each recipe gives you simple directions to follow, and where possible, a visual test to observe for doneness. For example, in some recipes, we give a range of times and also specify "until boiling" or "heated through." Many of our recipes come from microwave oven owners and some of them are even prize winners from the Georgia Electrification Council Microwave Cook-Off. And all recipes have been kitchen-tested.

The microwave oven as it is most often used today was introduced in the late 1960s as a portable microwave cooking unit with a single power level. Since that time microwave oven manufacturers have added many features and changes, so that today's ovens will likely have two or more power level settings and may have temperature probes, browning elements, and numerous other features from which to choose. At this time these are available to microwave oven owners—but many more special features are being designed by the microwave oven manufacturers.

Audrey Stehle

10 STEPS TO EASY MICROWAVE COOKING

If you are among the millions of microwave oven owners, you may be like most of them in your need for useful information about:
- *Microwave cooking techniques*
- *Selecting microwave utensils*
- *What foods to microwave*
- *What to expect when microwaving certain foods*
- *Ways to use a microwave oven effectively*

Or, you may be looking for useful information before becoming a microwave oven owner.

In the following pages we hope to answer all your questions about the proper microwaving techniques. We have provided 10 basic steps we believe necessary to understanding the full range of microwave cooking; so if you are a first-time user, begin here. If you are an experienced microwave cook, go on to the more than 400 recipes and "Special Uses" section. There is something for everyone in Microwave Cooking Made Easy.

1

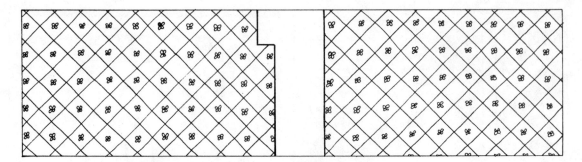

KNOW YOUR MICROWAVE

The first step in understanding microwave cooking, or microwaving, is to know what the microwave oven is and understand what makes it work.

The basic components of a microwave oven are these:

Magnetron tube, which converts electrical energy into a form of electromagnetic energy called microwaves.

Wave guide, which serves as a channel for the microwave energy to enter the oven cavity. There will usually be a stirrer of some type to cause the microwave energy to be distributed evenly inside the oven cooking area.

Oven cavity, where the dish or bowl containing food is placed for the food to cook by absorbing the microwave energy.

When microwave energy enters food, the liquid or moisture cells vibrate against each other millions of times per second and create heat. This heat is conducted through the food and microwave cooking results.

WHAT IS MICROWAVING?

When microwave cooking is discussed, you will often hear the term microwaving. Simply defined, microwaving means to *use microwave energy to defrost, heat, or cook food.* There are foods which microwave well in each of these categories. Some examples of each are listed:

- **Foods to cook by microwaves** are ground meats, vegetables, fish, chicken, fruits, eggs, desserts.
- **Foods to heat by microwaves** are frozen entrees, canned soups, pre-cooked foods or leftovers, baby food.
- **Foods to defrost by microwaves** are meats, poultry, fish, breads, baked goods, casseroles.

WHAT A MICROWAVE OVEN NEEDS

In order for the microwave oven to work effectively and properly, you must be sure that you do certain things.

- **Provide a separate grounded electrical circuit.** A countertop microwave oven must be connected to a 115/120 volt grounded electrical circuit. No other appliance should be connected to the circuit with a microwave oven. It is important that microwave ovens not be operated on extension cords.
- **Provide the proper treatment and care** necessary to keep the oven working well and safely. The oven door, seal, and interior should be wiped frequently with a clean damp cloth. Should food harden on the walls or tray, place a glass bowl containing water in the oven. Microwave at HIGH several minutes or until the water boils and creates steam. The steam will soften the hardened food, which can then be wiped off easily with a clean damp cloth, paper towel, or sponge. Wash the oven interior with warm water and a small amount of baking soda to keep it smelling fresh.
- **Use the right type utensils.** Select glass or microwave plastics for cooking, or use paper, glass, or plastic for heating and defrosting. Small amounts of metal (foil for shielding) can be used *if the manufacturer's directions are followed.*

A CHECKLIST OF GOOD MICROWAVE HABITS

- If small children might be able to reach the oven controls, keep a glass measure or bowl containing water in the oven.
- Use only the proper thermometers and other accessories when microwaving.
- Keep the oven clean, especially the door and inside parts.
- Be sure that only the microwave oven is connected to its circuit—or do not use other appliances on the circuit when the microwave oven is being used.
- Mark any utensils which are not suitable for microwave containers so that they will not be used accidentally.
- Encourage everyone in the family to read the instructions and a good cookbook, so that they, too, can enjoy the advantages of hot treats, warm desserts, and really fresh vegetables, plus all the other good foods that can be cooked in the microwave oven.

KNOW MICROWAVE OVEN WATTAGE

When microwave ovens first became available, they all had only one power level; thus in their early days, it seemed that fast cooking would become their only advantage. But more recently, manufacturers have introduced multiple and variable power settings. As a result, many foods can now be microwaved with better results.

Throughout the recipes in *Microwave Cooking Made Easy* you will see HIGH, MEDIUM-HIGH, MEDIUM, MEDIUM-LOW, and LOW. We tested all our recipes using 600 to 700 watt ovens with variable power level selections. We give what we feel to be the most suitable power level for each step of the recipe. If you have a 400 to 600 watt microwave oven, it may be necessary to increase cooking time about 20 percent. Sometimes one recipe will call for several power settings. Many food companies now recommend using two power levels, HIGH to start and a lower power to complete cooking many microwaved foods. We recommend this technique throughout our recipes. If possible, use the recommended power setting.

If your microwave oven does not have variable power, you will need to do more turning, rotating, or stirring to get similar results. Some of the more delicate foods, like rice pudding and custards, cannot be microwaved at HIGH power settings.

If your oven has only a HIGH power setting, place a 2-cup glass measure filled with water in one of the back corners of the oven. This technique makes the oven "slower" and works well when microwaving foods such as eggs, cheese, and delicate foods which do not microwave well at HIGH power.

OVEN WATTAGE AFFECTS MICROWAVING TIME

Changes or fluctuations in power coming into the house (voltage) will affect exact microwaving times. These changes

Microwave Oven Wattage

occur during very hot or cold weather and in periods of high electrical use, such as afternoons and early evenings when cooking is taking place. If you are not sure about the wattage rating of your particular microwave oven, there are simple test procedures to help you determine oven wattage.

These simple steps will help you know whether or not your oven is in the 600 to 700 watt category.
- Measure 1 cup of tap water into a glass measure. Microwave at HIGH 2½ to 3 minutes.
- If the water boils in that time, your oven is 600 to 650 watts.
- If it comes to a boil sooner than 2½ minutes, your oven is probably higher than 650 watts.
- If longer than 3 minutes is required for the water to boil, your oven is probably less than 600 watts.

Although no wattage test conducted in the home can be 100% accurate, the one below has been recommended for the microwave oven owner. However, remember that size of oven, time of day, house voltage, and even the temperature of the tap water can cause any home-conducted test to be inaccurate.

TO DETERMINE APPROXIMATE WATTAGE OUTPUT OF YOUR MICROWAVE OVEN
- Measure 4 cups of tap water into a 4-cup glass measure.
- Measure the temperature of the tap water with a reliable kitchen thermometer.
- Record the temperature in the blank below labeled temperature #1.
- Microwave the water at HIGH 2 minutes.
- Remove the water from the oven.
- Promptly record the second temperature in the blank labeled temperature #2.
- Multiply the difference by 17.5. This will give you the approximate wattage output of your oven.

Temperature #2 _____
Temperature #1 _____

Difference _____ Multiply by 17.5
Approximate _____
Oven Wattage

5

KNOW SPECIAL FEATURES
OF THE MICROWAVE OVEN

Since microwave ovens first became available, they have gone through several stages of improvements. Early models, which many people still use, have a single power setting. Defrosting, cooking, and heating are all done at HIGH power. However, in the past decade, microwave ovens have changed a great deal in style and in the features they offer consumers.

Some features available on present-day microwave ovens and a description of these follows.

MULTIPLE POWER SETTINGS

Many ovens have a HIGH or FULL power setting and a LOW or DEFROST setting. The lower setting varies among manufacturers from 25% to 50% of full power and can be used for microwaving delicate foods, reheating, and defrosting. In this system the magnetron tube cycles on and off frequently during the time the oven is operating; in other systems a special control lowers the power output of the magnetron tube. Slower cooking will result with either system.

VARIABLE POWER LEVELS

Variable power control adds additional flexibility to microwave cooking by providing multiple power settings. Depending on the manufacturer, the power output at various settings ranges from 100% at HIGH or FULL power to 10% at LOW or WARM. Power levels between HIGH and LOW are usually in 10% steps and may be numbered or named by the cooking processes (sauté, roast, bake) best done at that particular power level.

Power settings do vary from oven to oven. All our recipes were tested in 600 to 700 watt ovens, using variable power settings. Because each manufacturer uses different terms for power levels, we selected HIGH, MEDIUM-HIGH, MEDIUM, MEDIUM-

LOW, and LOW for use in our directions in an attempt to help microwave oven owners learn to use microwave ovens with variable power.

The following chart gives our power level names and some other names used by various manufacturers for similar levels:

Our Terms	Manufacturers' Terms For Same Setting
HIGH (100% power)	High, Normal, Full Power, Setting 10
MEDIUM-HIGH (70% power)	Roast, Reheat, Sauté, Flash-Defrost, Bake, Medium-High, Setting 7
MEDIUM (50% power)	Simmer, Defrost, Low, Simmer-High, Setting 5
MEDIUM-LOW (30% power)	Low-Defrost, Sauté, Low, Defrost, Keep Warm, Medium-Low, Setting 3
LOW (10% power)	Warm, Keep Warm, Setting 1

TEMPERATURE PROBES

Measuring the internal temperature of foods being microwaved is considered a very accurate way to gauge doneness. Foods which should be cooked to a specific degree of doneness, like meat, or a specific temperature for serving, like casseroles, beverages, and other foods, will cook with better results if temperature cooking is done. Many ovens are equipped with a *temperature probe* which is inserted into the center of the food and connected to the oven's electrical system through the wall of the oven. When the selected temperature is reached, the probe sensor relays the message to the microwave oven control and the microwave energy is cut off. On some microwave ovens the additional control the temperature probe offers makes it useful to time for simmering or long, slow cooking of foods which need time to develop flavor or tenderize.

Food temperature may also be measured with regular oven thermometers, which can be used *only when the food is outside the oven*. Throughout the meat cooking section, we give instructions on how to use a standard oven thermometer to measure temperature of microwaved food.

Several manufacturers are making thermometers which are designed to be left in the food while it is in the microwave oven. These have a very small amount of metal and a special plastic covering over the dial. They may be instant registering and some are designed to be used in conventional ovens as well as microwave ovens.

BROWNING ELEMENT

Some countertop microwave ovens have an electric browning element which can be turned on after the microwave cooking is completed to brown the tops of certain foods like baked goods. These ovens work off a 115/120 volt grounded circuit. Built-in or combination microwave ovens may operate at 230/240 volts and may have electric browning elements that can be operated at the same time as microwave cooking is being done.

MICROPROCESSOR OR COMPUTERIZED CONTROLS

One of the most recent additions to the microwave oven, and available on many models, microprocessors are the most sophisticated way to control microwave energy. The advantage of this device is its flexibility. A microprocessor can be designed to contain specialized instructions frequently used in microwave cooking. It can be used to control power level, monitor frequently used functions, provide memory capability, and repeat regularly used processes like defrosting or keeping foods warm. It also provides a time-of-day, and some models have a vocabulary to tell you when cooking is complete or if you have made a mistake in programming.

SPECIAL ACCESSORIES

Many microwave ovens now have special cookware available.
- **Browning grill** or dish made of a glass ceramic material. The bottom is coated with a metal oxide. As it is preheated at HIGH power in the microwave oven, the dish becomes very hot and is used for browning meats quickly as in stir-fry foods, chops, meat patties, or grilled sandwiches.
- **Dish and rack combination** may be made of glass ceramic or plastic. One manufacturer recommends using a metal rack and glass ceramic dish, but this microwave cookware item will usually be a special plastic rack and either a plastic or glass ceramic dish or tray.
- **Simmer and cook pot** designed with a slotted opening in the lid to hold the temperature probe. This pot is made of pottery and is recommended for use with soups, stews, and other foods requiring moist, steamy, slow cooking.
- **Clay pot cooker** similar to the popular clay pot used for conventional cooking. It is made of a porous clay and is glazed inside to make cleaning easier. A 10 minute soak in water is recommended before each use.
- **Popcorn popper** designed to fit into the microwave oven. Made of plastic, the cone-shaped bowl sits inside a base which acts as a concentrator for the microwave energy.

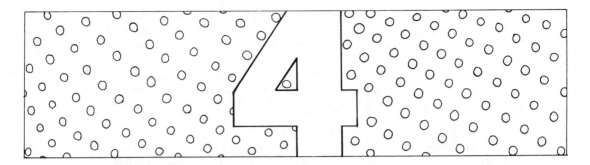

KNOW MICROWAVE FOODS

These are among the foods most suitable for microwaving:
• Ground meat
• Fish
• Chicken and other poultry
• Vegetables and fruits
• Bacon
• Brownies and other bar cookies
• Puddings, sauces, and gravies
• Candies
• Coffee cakes, upside-down cakes

There are some foods which should not be microwaved. Do *not* use the microwave to do the following:
• Cook eggs in shells.
• Fry deep fat foods.
• Pop popcorn, unless you have a specially designed popcorn popper or popcorn packaged just for microwave ovens.
• Home can foods, because a prolonged high temperature is required around the jar to create a vacuum seal. This condition cannot be achieved by microwave energy.

PROPER POWER LEVEL SETTINGS
FOR VARIOUS FOODS

Because there are many similarities between microwaving and conventional cooking, it is simple to think in terms of these heat settings when choosing a microwave power level. Just as most foods cooked conventionally should not be cooked at a high heat setting, many foods will microwave with better results if a lower power setting is used. Our descriptions of the power levels available on many microwave ovens will help you decide which settings to use for particular foods.

HIGH power is best used for fast cooking and for microwaving foods which can withstand the vigorous action produced by microwave energy at HIGH power. Usually, these will be foods high in moisture content. Some examples of foods which micro-wave well at HIGH are vegetables, ground beef, fish, sauces without eggs, gravies, soups, candies, bar cookies, and chicken pieces. HIGH is also used to bring water to a boil quickly, to pre-heat microwave browning trays and dishes, and to start foods cooking or to quickly achieve a high temperature, much as you would use the high surface unit setting on the top of the range.

MEDIUM-HIGH is usually about 70 to 80 percent of the power at HIGH and is used for foods which might not be able to tolerate the higher power settings. It will be used for heating cooked foods and casseroles, and for cooking TV dinners, large vegeta-bles, and frozen convenience foods.

MEDIUM is used for cooking many meats and mixtures con-taining delicate ingredients such as eggs and cheese. It will be about 50 to 60 percent of HIGH power. Some foods which micro-wave best at MEDIUM are egg dishes such as soufflés and quiches, dessert and vegetable custards, sour cream, tempera-ture probe cooked meats, sandwiches containing cheese, and cheese-base dips and appetizers.

MEDIUM-LOW provides slow gentle action and is almost al-ways used for easy defrosting and for microwaving foods with a delicate texture. In some recipes HIGH power will be used to start cooking and MEDIUM-LOW will be used to complete cooking. Some foods which microwave best at MEDIUM-LOW are cus-tards and puddings, cheesecakes, some soups and stews, and dried beans and peas.

LOW is the gentlest setting on microwave ovens and is a very good setting to use to hold foods at serving temperatures after they have been cooked at higher power levels. It is also used for softening cream cheese and butter, melting chocolate, making yogurt, warming cheese, softening ice cream to serving consis-tency, and proofing yeast breads.

KNOW WHAT AFFECTS
MICROWAVE TIME

One of the first steps to understand when learning to microwave food is what affects microwaving. It is necessary that you understand these factors in order to achieve good results. There are several factors to keep in mind when microwaving.

SHAPE

The shape of food will determine the final cooking results of foods being microwaved. Because of the way microwave energy enters food, thin, irregular-shaped items like chicken pieces will cook differently than meat loaf or other evenly shaped foods. The shapes which are good for microwaving are thin, evenly shaped foods such as a rounded meat loaf or a pineapple upside-down cake. These are just the right depth to take full advantage of the microwave energy as it enters the food; and they have no corners to absorb too much energy, the factor that causes overcooking. However, chicken pieces can be arranged so that they will microwave with good results. Arrange meats with the thicker parts toward the outside edge of the dish and the thin, bony parts in the center.

DENSITY

A compact food which is more dense, such as a sweet potato, will take longer to microwave than a lighter-textured porous one, such as a cake.

QUANTITY

Almost everyone who has used a microwave oven for any length of time understands that quantity influences microwaving time because he has probably microwaved one potato with good results, but has found that eight potatoes take a great deal more time than one. Remember, as the quantity increases, microwaving time increases. Depending on the size and moisture content of each potato, cooking times per potato could double or triple when the quantity is increased from one to five or six servings.

MOISTURE

Foods naturally high in moisture are among the best foods to select for microwaving. Fresh juicy vegetables, fruits, fish, poultry, and sauces all microwave very well. Popcorn, paraffin, old

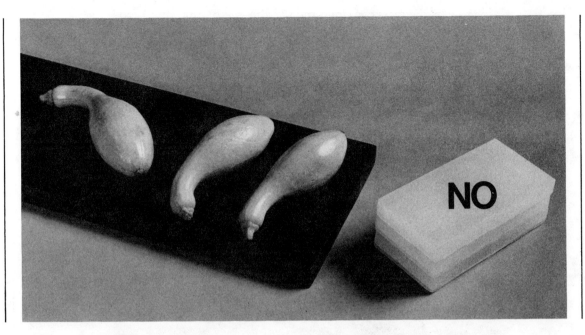

potatoes, and other over-mature or old vegetables are not good choices of foods to microwave because they are low in moisture.

SIZE

Because the amount of available microwave energy is the same on a given power level, the size of the food item that is being

microwaved affects cooking time. As the size or amount of food increases, the microwaving time increases. A good example of this is the amount of time to cook a very large turkey or ham. It will take less time in minutes per pound to microwave a small turkey than a very large one, because the amount of energy is being used more efficiently when microwaving the smaller item. A general rule about the size foods to select for microwave might be "individual portions or average family-size quantities." Four to six servings of fruit, vegetables, meats, fish, poultry, and desserts can all be microwaved in reasonable amounts of time while ten to twelve servings will take a great deal more time to microwave. In fact, these larger quantities of food probably should be cooked in a conventional way, either on the surface unit or in the conventional oven.

STARTING TEMPERATURE

Foods which are taken from the refrigerator will take longer to microwave than foods which are at room temperature. All our

recipes were tested with foods taken from their normal storage place. For example, meats, milk, cheese, and vegetables were started from their refrigerator temperatures for recipe testing purposes.

HEIGHT IN THE OVEN

Because of the way microwaves are bounced around inside the oven cavity, the best location for food placement is near the center

of the oven. Foods which are too tall, like a large turkey, may receive too much energy at the top and overcooking can occur. Cakes and other thin-type foods may cook more evenly when the dish they are being microwaved in is placed on another dish, like a glass pie plate, turned upside down. This technique raises the food nearer to the oven's center.

FAT AND SUGAR CONTENT

Foods containing high fat and sugar levels heat rapidly, reaching higher temperatures. Foods with lower fat and sugar levels require longer cooking times.

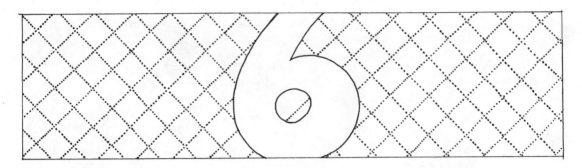

KNOW THE TECHNIQUES FOR MICROWAVING

As in all other cooking methods, there are certain techniques which, if followed, can make microwaving simpler and will assure better results with foods that are being microwaved.

COVERING

This procedure is useful for several purposes. Depending on the type covering selected, it may prevent spattering, hold in

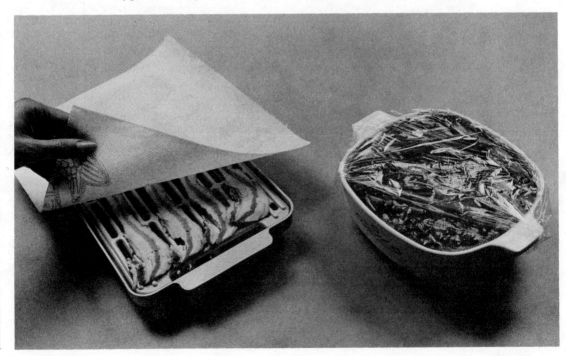

heat, or steam and speed cooking.

- **Loose coverings** like paper towel and waxed paper prevent spattering.
- **Tight coverings** of plastic wrap, casserole lids, cooking bags, frozen food packages, and sealed freezer bags trap heat and thereby steam and speed cooking.

FOOD ARRANGEMENT

Because many foods depend on the proper arrangement within the dish in order to cook properly, this technique is critical to the finished results of microwaved foods.

Chicken pieces should be arranged so that the thicker, meatier portions are around the outside edges of the dish and the thin, bony parts are toward the center of the dish.

Tender, flower ends of broccoli should be placed toward the center of the dish and the stalk ends toward the edge, where microwave energy first enters the food.

PRICKING

This technique is absolutely necessary to use with certain foods with thick skins (potatoes and squash) or membrane coverings

(chicken livers and egg yolks) to allow steam to escape. If not pricked, these foods may burst when the heat builds up and creates steam inside the food. Never microwave eggs in the shell.

STANDING TIME

Many microwaved foods require standing time to allow for further cooking to occur. Because heating continues after food is removed from the microwave oven, allow time for this additional

heat conduction. Microwave recipes will usually give range of time, 5 to 7 minutes for example. Check for doneness at the minimum time, and allow for cooking to continue during standing time.

ROTATING

This is a frequently used technique. Because the nature of microwave energy is to "clump" in spots in a microwave oven,

foods will microwave more evenly if rotated during microwaving. Rotate means to turn the dish ¼ or ½ turn and this term will be frequently used in our recipes.

Although some oven manufacturers do not specify for you to rotate foods being microwaved, it is important to the finished results that you follow recipe instructions to rotate.

STIRRING

When you stir foods being microwaved, you move and combine the heated portions of food with unheated portions. Usually foods like puddings, sauces, and custards, which require constant stirring when cooked conventionally, will need to be stirred only once or twice during microwaving. Other foods like chili,

soups, stews, and some vegetables may also need to be stirred once or twice during microwaving.

SHIELDING

Athough not used frequently, shielding is necessary when microwaving unevenly-shaped foods like poultry, or portions of

thin foods like fish. Thin strips of lightweight foil are placed on legs and wings of poultry and over thin or bony parts of roasts and other foods to prevent overcooking. Shielding with strips of thin foil may also be used when thawing some foods like small poultry.

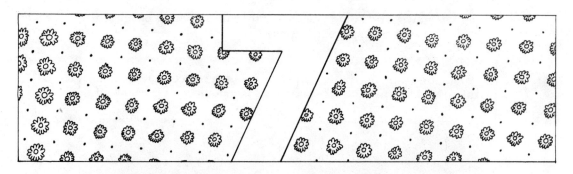

KNOW MICROWAVE CONTAINERS

A variety of materials work well in each of the different processes for which a microwave oven can be used. These processes are defrosting, heating, and cooking. The utensil selected should be of the proper material and design for use with that particular process. Some utensils work just for defrosting or heating while others can be used for any of the microwave processes.

Consider these factors to guide you when choosing containers to be used for microwaving:
• Material from which container is made
• Utensil size, shape, and design
• Type glaze or trim applied to container

Microwave cookware, containers, and utensils should have these properties:
• Be able to transmit microwave energy
• Be heat-resistant
• Be non-absorbent
• Be non-flammable

Ask these questions before you purchase microwave cookware:
• Does the cookware have handles which make hot food removal, stirring, and rearranging easier?
• Will it store easily?
• Is it a functional shape and style?
• How heavy will it be when it is filled?
• Can it be used for cooking several types of food?

SOME CONTAINER MATERIALS AND SUGGESTED USES

Paper

Paper can be used when defrosting, heating snacks, sandwiches or beverages, or cooking bacon.

Facts: Disposable, lightweight. Avoid items made from recycled paper or products containing nylon, as they may ignite when heated. Use plastic-coated items for moist foods.
Some brands: Chinet, Dixie, International, St. Regis

Paper

Glass

Glass containers are made from several types of materials and in a variety of shapes.

Oven Glass can be used for all microwave processes (defrosting, heating, and cooking).

Facts: May be heavy when filled with food. Can be used for storing unused food. Available in many styles, sizes, and shapes.

Some brands: Anchor Hocking, Fire King, Glassbake, Heller, Jena, Pyrex

Ceramic, Porcelain can be used for all microwave processes.

Facts: Some items may be difficult to store if used infrequently; can be heavy when filled with foods.

Some brands: Corning, El Camino, Marsh, Masonware, Pfaltzgraff, Serena, Shafford

Dinnerware is easy to use for defrosting and reheating; check carefully before using as a cooking container.

Facts: Avoid pieces with metal trim. Look for tags or labels indicating "Safe-for-Microwave."

Some brands: Corelle, Dansk, Franciscan, International Stoneware, Lenox, Mikasa, Pfaltzgraff, Temperware

Oven Glass

Ceramic, Porcelain

Dinnerware

Plastic

Plastics are not all of the same quality. Some can be used only for defrosting and heating, while others are excellent as cooking containers.

Foam plates and cups are used for defrosting, heating, and short-term cooking.

Facts: Distorts or melts when used with food containing fat or cooked in sauces. Lightweight and disposable.

Food storage bags and containers can be used for defrosting or short term heating.

Facts: Can distort when food is heated in them. Also they absorb color from food and fat. Avoid metal twist ties.

Some brands: Baggies, Glad Wrap, Kordite, Republic, Rubbermaid, Tupperware, Ziploc

Wrap, cooking bags, sealable freezer bags are excellent for use as a container when microwaving vegetables, frozen entrees, or foods which need steam to cook evenly.

Facts: Puncture or pierce to create a vent.

Some brands: Cooking Magic, Dazey, Glad Wrap, Handiwrap, Oster, Reynolds, Saran Wrap

Microwave utensils are those utensils which have been designed just for microwaving and can be used for heating and cooking baked goods, meats, bacon, frozen entrees, casseroles.

Facts: Lightweight, easily shaped into specialized designs. Easy to handle when filled with food. Some microwave utensils can be used for all microwave cooking; others should be used for short term cooking or for foods which do not reach high temperatures. Look for labels giving specific microwave uses.

Some brands: Anchor Hocking, Bangor, MCE, Micro-Cook, Micro-Masters, Microware, Mirro, Mr. Microwave, Nordic Ware, NUPAC, Rubbermaid, Tara

Foam plates and cups

Food storage bags and containers

Cooking and sealing bags

Microwave utensils

Miscellaneous

Items in this category can be used only for defrosting, short term heating, or specialized cooking.

Facts: Disposable and lightweight.

Some items: Wooden skewers for kabobs, appetizers; baskets for breads (no metal cores), wood for appetizers and sandwiches; and seafood shells for escargot, oysters, clams, or scallops.

27

Miscellaneous

Metal

Metals can be very helpful to use as a shield to prevent cooking while defrosting or overcooking thin parts of food. Shallow metal trays (less than ¾ inch) are also recommended by many manufacturers. (Check your user's manual before cooking in these trays.)

Facts: Foil can be used in thin small pieces, firmly pressed against food. Do not allow metal or foil to touch oven walls. Avoid twist ties which act as antenna and cause arcing.

Some brands: Alcoa, Reynolds

MICROWAVE CONTAINERS AND ACCESSORIES

When you acquire or select microwave cooking utensils, start with the basic items you will use frequently for primary cooking, then add specialized items that may be used less often.

Some basic items which can be used for microwaving may already be in your kitchen. Others may be needed to fill specific microwave cooking jobs which you plan to do often.

Basic Microwave Accessories include the following:
• Several heat-resistant 2- and 4-cup glass measures
• Two flat 12- x 8-inch casseroles
• Two or three 1½- or 2-quart casseroles
• A microwave plastic or glass trivet roasting rack
• One 3-quart casserole or a large, heat-resistant glass mixing bowl
• Several 5- or 6-ounce custard cups
• Heat-resistant 8- or 9-inch glass pie plates
• Small bowls, cups, or plates (dinnerware, if safe-for-microwave)

- Two 9-inch heat-resistant glass or microwave plastic cake pans
- A microwave oven thermometer to use with food in the oven, or a standard thermometer to use with food outside the oven

Optional Microwave Accessories you will also find useful:
- One ring-shaped baking dish
- One fluted tube pan, probably plastic
- One microwave plastic muffin ring
- One flat plastic or glass tray

Basic Accessories

HOW TO KNOW IF A DISH IS SAFE FOR MICROWAVING

You probably have dishes, bowls, or containers which will work as microwave containers; but before you use them for microwaving foods, perform this simple test to see if they are made of a material or glazed with something which is not suitable for microwaving.

Microwave Dish Test requires the following steps:
- Pour 1 cup of water into a glass measure.
- Place the measure containing the water on, in, or beside the dish being tested inside the microwave oven.
- Microwave at HIGH power 1 minute.
- If the dish being tested remains cool and the water is warm, the dish is safe for microwave use.
- If the dish being tested is slightly warm and the water is warm, the dish may be used for heating food, but should not be used for cooking.
- If the dish being tested is warm and the water is cool, the dish is not designed for microwave and should not be used as a microwave container.

Do remember *not* to test any dishes containing metal decor.

CONTAINER SIZE AND SHAPE

In addition to the proper material, size and shape are two more important factors in microwaving containers. Many new "designed for microwave" containers have a donut shape which allows the best microwave cooking to take place since microwaves can enter the food from several angles. When selecting containers, choose round casseroles or rings, tube pans, or bowl-shaped utensils. Larger containers than are normally used for conventional cooking are necessary for microwaving to allow for the increased expansion of baked products and the vigorous action of foods which have a great deal of liquid.

MATCHING CONTAINERS AND FOODS FOR MICROWAVING

Container	Use For
Deep Casserole	Foods which require stirring and/or long slow cooking like chili, goulash, stews
Shallow Casserole	Layered foods which microwave without stirring or rearranging like lasagna, macaroni and cheese, chicken pieces, fish, sausage, or vegetables such as corn-on-the-cob, asparagus, or broccoli which cook best in a thin layer
Round Baking Dish	Baked goods, rolled fish fillets, upside-down and layer cakes, bar cookies
Ring-Shaped Dish	Meat loaf, bar cookies, quick breads, coffee cakes, poached eggs
Fluted Tube Pan	Cakes, vegetable casseroles, meat dishes
Glass Measures (2- and 4-Cup)	Sauces, gravies, scrambled eggs, puddings, cream pie fillings
Muffin Rings	Individual servings of ground meat or fish, muffins, eggs, fruit (like apples), cupcakes
Custard Cups	Reheating small portions, softening or melting butter or chocolate, cooking muffins, individual custards, single servings of fish or ground meat
Small Bowls, Cups, Plates	Reheating individual servings of cooked foods, beverages, and soups
Flat Plastic or Glass Tray	Heating appetizers, holding custard cups arranged in a circle, cooking large, whole vegetables or combinations of vegetables, or for baking cookies

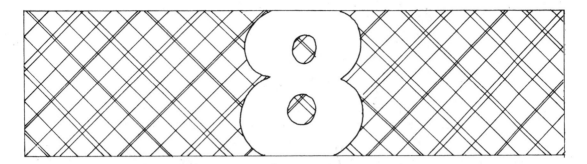

KNOW MICROWAVE COVERS

One of the key techniques to follow for good microwaving results is to cover foods. There are several materials which work well as microwave covers. Each of them meets a specific need and should be used for a particular purpose. A description of various materials and how each is used follows.

PAPER TOWELS, NAPKINS

These absorb grease when cooking bacon, absorb moisture when heating sandwiches and breads, prevent spattering, promote even heating, and softens tortillas when damp.

WAXED PAPER

This holds in heat when cooking meats, chicken, fruits, and some vegetable casseroles.

HEAVY-DUTY PLASTIC WRAP

It is used to hold in steam and heat when cooking vegetables and fish. Useful for bowls or dishes which have no cover.

Micronote: Place loosely over the container or fold back a corner to make a vent for steam to escape.

UTENSIL COVER

It covers foods and casseroles cooked in a sauce and other foods which require long, slow cooking.

OVEN COOKING BAGS

These hold in steam when cooking poultry, pork roast, ham, and other meats which need steam for even cooking.

Micronote: To make a tie, cut a strip from the open end of these bags. Avoid metal twist-ties. Slash to vent.

FREEZER BAGS AND BOXES

Products such as these hold in moisture and steam for cooking purchased frozen foods or those you package at home. Boxes should not have metal or foil trim.

Micronote: Pierce or puncture to vent and place on paper plates in oven.

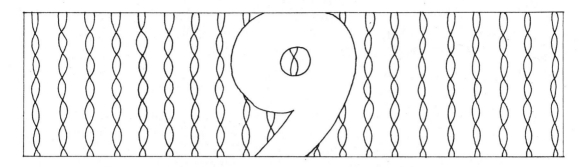

KNOW MICROWAVE MEAL PLANNING

Now that you are to this step you probably realize that a change in meal preparation sequence will likely be required for microwave meals. It is just as necessary—or maybe even more necessary—to plan and organize these meals as it is to organize conventionally prepared meals.

Perhaps the very first step in microwave meal preparation should be to set the table. Because microwave cooking is done in relatively short time spans and requires rearranging and standing time, you may not have time to set the table after you start cooking.

Until you become familiar with microwave cooking and know how much cooking and standing time various foods will require, it will help to make a list of cooking and standing times for each of the menu items you plan to cook. Consider also whether the food will cool quickly, whether it can be reheated easily, and if the cooking time can be divided into segments.

Here are some basic tips to help you get organized in your microwave meal planning:

- Make foods ahead when possible. Remember that foods re-heated in the microwave taste fresh-cooked.
- Simplify by using convenience foods and mixes for foods which require a long mixing time. It seems ridiculous to take 30 or 40 minutes to mix a food which cooks in 10 to 12 minutes.
- Use the microwave oven for the parts of cooking it does best, and complete cooking using conventional methods. Foods cooked on the surface unit and oven-prepared foods can often be partially prepared in the microwave.
- Plan to cook foods which have the longest cooking times first.
- Meats and casseroles will hold heat longer, and flavor will improve as these foods stand. Thus plan to cook these dishes before cooking vegetables and other side dishes.

The chart below can help you gauge the cooking time for certain foods often included in your menus. In addition, you may wish to create your own such chart for handy reference.

FREQUENTLY MICROWAVED FOODS

Item	Amount	Time	Microwave Power
Chicken Parts	1 to 3½ pounds	7 to 9 minutes per pound	HIGH
Ham Slice	1 slice	3 to 4 minutes	HIGH
Meat Loaf	1 to 2 pounds	14 to 16 minutes per pound	MEDIUM or HIGH
Baked Apple	1 to 4	1 to 1½ minutes	HIGH
Cabbage	1 medium head	10 to 12 minutes	HIGH
Corn-on-the-Cob	2 to 4 ears	5 to 8 minutes	HIGH
Carrots, Frozen	10-ounce package	5 to 7 minutes	HIGH
Peas, Frozen	10-ounce package	4 to 5 minutes	HIGH
Potato, Baked	1 medium	3 to 5 minutes	HIGH
Squash, Yellow or Zucchini	3 cups, sliced	7 to 8 minutes	HIGH
Fresh Tomatoes	2 medium	3 to 4 minutes	HIGH

YOUR FIRST MICROWAVE MENUS

Let's take two sample menus made up of some popular microwave favorites and give the proper cooking sequence to follow when microwaving these menu items.

Microwave Dinner To Serve 4
(See Index *for specific recipes)*
Meat Loaf
Whole Cauliflower
Wilted Greens
Pineapple Upside-Down Cake

Steps: Early In The Day

1. Wash the spinach and other greens for the salad. Drain and refrigerate until serving time.
2. Prepare the cauliflower. Place the cauliflower and a small amount of water in an 8- or 9-inch glass pie plate. Cover with plastic wrap.
3. Prepare the batter for the upside-down cake. It can be chilled until ready to cook. In the baking dish prepare the butter, sugar, and fruit topping.

Steps: At Serving Time

4. Cook the bacon for the wilted greens salad. Crumble the bacon and combine the fat and other seasonings in a glass measure or bowl. Set aside.
5. Prepare and cook the meat loaf, since it will take the longest time. When about three-fourths cooked, remove meat loaf from the oven and allow to stand covered.

6. Microwave the cauliflower while the meat loaf is standing.
   . Vegetables will stay hot 10 to 12 minutes if the cover is left on.
7. Complete cooking the meat loaf. Let it stand, covered, while continuing with the sequence.
8. Heat the salad dressing mixture. Toss with the greens.
9. Serve and enjoy a hot microwave meal.
10. Cook the dessert while eating dinner, or reheat it, if you cooked it earlier in the day.

Microwave Breakfast To Serve 4
(See Index *for specific recipes)*

Hot Applesauce
Bran Muffins
Bacon
Scrambled Eggs
Coffee

Steps:
1. Prepare the coffee to perk if not using instant coffee.
2. Place bacon on cooking rack and microwave (¾ to 1 minute per slice on HIGH) while preparing muffins. Set cooked bacon aside.
3. Using chilled muffin batter, prepare and cook muffins. Place in a basket and cover. Set aside.
4. In a 4-cup glass measure, combine eggs and milk. Microwave the eggs according to directions, and set aside for cooking to continue.
5. Place applesauce in a glass serving bowl. Microwave to heat.
6. Serve and enjoy!

Micronote: Use microwave oven features, such as cook and hold or the temperature sensor probe, to make microwave meal planning and preparation really carefree.

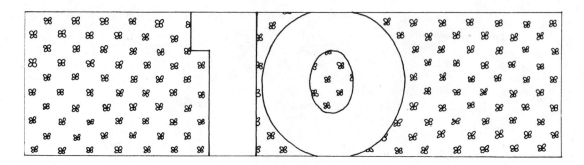

KNOW HOW TO MAKE
THE MOST OF YOUR MICROWAVE

After you study all the steps to follow when microwaving and learn foods which microwave well, you need to think about what the microwave oven can be used for in daily food preparation activities. It not only works well for total cooking of about 95% of all foods, but frequently can be used for many steps in preparing foods to be cooked conventionally.

FOOD PREPARATION PROCESSES

There are many food preparation processes which can be performed in the microwave oven. The next time you are cooking, baking, or just taking a break, remember what you can use your microwave to do:

- Soften either frozen or refrigerated butter to make creaming easier.
- Heat 1 cup of water to boiling for use in dissolving gelatin, bouillon granules, making instant coffee or spiced tea.
- Melt caramels for use in dipping apples or combining with other ingredients for a sauce.
- Soften cream cheese for use in cooking or baking.
- Remove the lid from glass jars of canned sauces or toppings and baby food and heat.
- Store any leftover coffee in the refrigerator and reheat it quickly in the microwave for a second coffee break.

CHARTS FOR MICROWAVING CONVENIENCE FOODS

The microwave also can be used to rapidly cook convenience foods for that "surprise" guest or last minute meal addition. See the following charts for suggested quick uses for the microwave oven.

CONVENIENCE FROZEN APPETIZERS

Remove hors d'oeuvres from metal container. Place in a microwave container and microwave according to the times below. Serve immediately.

Frozen Hors D'Oeuvres	Package Size	Number of Pieces	Container/Technique	Microwave Time at HIGH
Egg Rolls, any kind (bite size)	6-ounces	12 pieces	Paper towel-lined paper plate.	4 to 5 minutes
Pigs'n Blanket (cocktail franks wrapped)	5-ounces	12 pieces	Brush with Worcestershire sauce. Place on 12-inch round glass pizza plate or waxed paper-lined oven tray.	4 to 6 minutes
Assorted Puffs	10-ounces	72 pieces	Brush with Worcestershire sauce before cutting apart. Heat 24 at a time on waxed paper-lined oven tray.	3 to 4 minutes
Pizzas	7¼-ounces	15 pieces	12″ round glass pizza dish or waxed paper-lined oven tray.	3 to 4 minutes

CONVENIENCE MEATS

Item	Technique	Amount	Microwave Time at HIGH
Bacon	Arrange bacon slices between 2 sheets of paper towel.	2 slices	1½ to 1¾ minutes
		4 slices	2½ to 3½ minutes
		6 slices	3½ to 4½ minutes
Canadian Bacon, sliced	Arrange slices around outside of glass plate or pie plate. Cover with waxed paper.	1 serving	30 seconds per side
		2 servings	1 minute per side
Franks/Wieners	Place link in bun. Wrap in paper napkin.	1 serving	30 to 45 seconds
		2 servings	1 to 1½ minutes
Brown and Serve Sausage	Arrange sausage in a paper-lined glass pie plate. Cover with waxed paper.	2 links	2 to 2¼ minutes
		4 links	3½ to 4½ minutes
		8 links	6 to 6½ minutes

DEFROSTING AND REHEATING FROZEN BREADS

Item	Amount	Defrosting Time at MEDIUM	Reheating Time at HIGH
White or Whole Wheat	Whole loaf	2¼ minutes	1 minute
	Half loaf	1¼ minutes	30 seconds
Rolls	6	30 to 40 seconds	20 to 30 seconds
Coffee Cake	9-inch round	1 minute	40 to 50 seconds
Muffins or non-iced Cupcakes	6	40 to 50 seconds	30 to 40 seconds
Biscuits	6	40 to 50 seconds	30 to 40 seconds

RULES FOR CONVERTING CONVENTIONAL RECIPES TO MICROWAVE

Many of your family's favorite recipes can be easily converted to a microwave recipe. Some people think recipes have to be especially formulated to work for microwaving. However, by following some simple steps and guidelines and using some of our recipes as guides, you will be able to turn your own, often used recipes into microwave delights—and make them even more of a family favorite.

- **To establish basic microwaving times,** start with one-fourth of the conventional time. For example, if a recipe cooks conventionally in 60 minutes, 15 minutes will be a rule of thumb for microwaving time. If more time is needed, you can always add a minute or two.
- **Always undercook!** You can never uncook foods, but you can always add additional cooking minutes, if they are needed. Overcooking is the major problem for beginning microwavers and is the most common cause of failure with microwaved foods.
- **Use your eyesight** and common sense when judging doneness. If foods appear to be cooking too fast, they probably are, and the power level should be lowered. By lowering the power setting or selecting LOW power, overcooking will be less likely to occur.
- **Find a "written for microwave" recipe** similar to your conventional one and follow it as a guide for ingredients, dish size, microwaving techniques, covering, and timing.
- **Increased amounts of food being microwaved** require an increased amount of time. Remember also to decrease microwaving time if the amount of food is decreased.
- **Think microwave.** Remember the types of foods which microwave well. Moist foods and recipes high in moisture content can usually be microwaved with very little adjustment, except in cooking time.

RECIPES

The recipes in Microwave Cooking Made Easy *have all been kitchen-tested. A variety of foods which can be prepared and served at mealtimes or for special occasions have been included.*

Many of the recipes first appeared as conventional recipes in Southern Living *magazine and have been converted and tested for use in the microwave. Others are prize winning recipes selected at the Georgia Electrification Council Microwave Cook-Off contests. The Grand Prize winners from these contests are marked with a double star and the other winners are marked with a single star.*

A conventional recipe leads off in most of the following chapters to be followed by its microwave counterpart. This pair of recipes should help you in converting your own conventional recipe of the same type to a microwave recipe.

APPETIZERS AND SNACKS

If you like to entertain, or if your family enjoys hot dips and snacks, you have a real treat in store. This is one area where the microwave oven can really star.

Where possible, mix dips or spreads in safe-for-microwave dishes or containers. Pottery and ceramic bowls and containers without a metal base glaze can be used, making clean-up just as easy as cooking.

Spread toppings on crackers or toast at the last minute to prevent sogginess. Arrange small pieces or individual servings, like crackers topped with a spread, in a circle. They will heat more evenly. Most of the time these foods need to be covered with paper towel or waxed paper to hold in heat and prevent spattering.

Use a lower power for delicate foods such as a dip made with sour cream, or shellfish like shrimp or oysters, which might overcook and toughen at higher power levels. Cheese-based spreads and dips can be heated at MEDIUM, but watch carefully to prevent overcooking.

Stir dips and spreads after microwaving.

Crisp stale crackers and chips by microwaving at HIGH power 30 to 45 seconds to heat.

Wooden serving platters, bowls, skewers, and wicker baskets can all be used for heating snack-type foods because they will heat in fairly short times.

Micronote: Many appetizers can be prepared in advance and frozen. Properly wrapped in heavy-duty plastic wrap, freezer paper, or sealable freezer bags, they can be kept up to 3 months. Use MEDIUM-LOW to defrost and reheat these items.

CHILI-CHEESE DIP
(Conventional recipe)

1   (2-pound) block processed American cheese
2   medium-size onions, chopped
2   tablespoons butter or margarine
2   (15½-ounce) cans chili without beans
    Chili powder to taste
    Dash of hot sauce

Melt cheese in top of double boiler. Brown chopped onions in butter or margarine; add to cheese with other ingredients. Blend well. Serve hot.

Yield: 8 cups.

To Microwave Chili-Cheese Dip

- Cut ingredients in half.
- Delete raw onion; substitute onion powder.
- Use a 1½-quart casserole for cooking and serving.

CHILI-CHEESE DIP

Power: MEDIUM-HIGH
Microwave Time: 10 to 14 Minutes

1 (1-pound) block processed American cheese, cut in 1-inch cubes
½ teaspoon onion powder
1 tablespoon butter or margarine
1 (15½-ounce) can chili without beans
Chili powder to taste
Dash of hot sauce

Combine cheese, onion powder, butter, chili, chili powder, and hot sauce in a 1½-quart casserole. Cover with waxed paper. Microwave at MEDIUM-HIGH 10 to 14 minutes. Stir well after 5 to 7 minutes of microwaving. Let stand 3 to 4 minutes before serving.
Yield: 4 cups.

HOT CHEDDAR DIP

Power: MEDIUM-HIGH
Microwave Time: 2 to 3 Minutes

1 (11-ounce) can Cheddar cheese soup, undiluted
⅛ teaspoon ground oregano
2 tablespoons catsup
⅛ teaspoon garlic powder
Corn chips

Combine all ingredients except corn chips in a 1-quart casserole or glass bowl. Microwave, uncovered, at MEDIUM-HIGH 2 to 3 minutes. Stir 1 or 2 times during cooking. Serve hot with corn chips.
Yield: 1½ cups.

DIABLO'S DIP

Power: HIGH
Microwave Time: 3 Minutes

1 (10¾-ounce) can chili without beans
1½ tablespoons spicy brown mustard
1 tablespoon Worcestershire sauce
8 ounces Cheddar cheese, shredded
Corn chips

Combine all ingredients except corn chips in a 4-cup glass measuring cup. Microwave at HIGH 1 minute. Stir mixture. Rotate dish ¼ turn. Microwave at HIGH for 2 minutes. Stir mixture to be sure the cheese is melted and the chili is hot. Serve immediately with corn chips.
Yield: 3 cups.

MEXICAN DIP

Power: HIGH/MEDIUM-LOW
Microwave Time: 9½ to 11½ Minutes

1 (7½-ounce) can tomatoes and jalapeño peppers, drained
1 tablespoon butter or margarine
¼ cup onion, finely chopped
¼ teaspoon chili powder
¼ teaspoon cayenne (optional)
1 pound processed American cheese
Corn chips, raw vegetable dippers, or toast points

Drain tomatoes. Place butter in small bowl, and microwave at HIGH 30 seconds to melt. Add chopped onion. Microwave, uncovered, at HIGH 3 minutes or until tender. Add tomatoes and spices. Microwave, uncovered, at HIGH about 2 minutes. Place cheese in 1½-quart casserole. Microwave at MEDIUM-LOW 4 to 6 minutes. Stir occasionally and rotate casserole once. Add tomato mixture to cheese. Stir well.
Serve hot as a dip with corn chips or raw vegetables or serve on toast points.
Yield: 3 cups.

CORN DIPPERS ★

Power: HIGH
Microwave Time: 1½ to 2 Minutes
  for 12 triangles

    ½ cup warm water
    1 (6½-ounce) package commercial
         pizza mix
    ½ cup yellow cornmeal
         All-purpose flour

Pour warm water into a medium-size mixing bowl. Thoroughly blend in pizza mix.
Sprinkle pastry board with cornmeal.
Lightly flour rolling pin. Turn dough onto
the pastry board. Roll dough into a thin
circle (approximately ⅛-inch thick). Cut
dough into 2-inch triangles. Pinch lightly in
center of triangle. Place 10 to 12 triangles on
a paper towel. Microwave at HIGH 1½ to 2
minutes. Repeat with remaining triangles.
Serve warm with a dip.
  Yield: 40 triangles.

CREAMY BEEF-CHEESE DIP ★

Power: HIGH/MEDIUM
Microwave Time: 4 to 5 Minutes

    1 (8-ounce) package cream cheese
    1 (2½-ounce) jar sliced dried beef,
         finely chopped
    ¼ cup walnuts, coarsely chopped
    ¼ cup commercial sour cream
    2 tablespoons onion, finely
         chopped
    2 tablespoons green pepper, finely
         chopped
    2 tablespoons milk
    ¾ teaspoon pepper

Unwrap and place block of cream cheese in
a 1-quart glass casserole. Microwave at
HIGH 45 seconds to 1 minute, or until
cheese is softened. Add remaining ingredients and stir until well blended.
  Cover and microwave at HIGH 1½ minutes. Stir. Microwave at MEDIUM an additional 2 to 2½ minutes. Serve with melba
toast rounds, crisp toast points, rice crackers, or Corn Dippers (see above).
  Yield: 2 cups.

ONIONY CHEESE FONDUE DIP ★

Power: MEDIUM-LOW/MEDIUM
Microwave Time: 7 to 9 Minutes

    1 (10-ounce) package frozen Welsh
         Rarebit
    ½ cup commercial sour cream
    1 tablespoon dry onion soup mix
         French bread cut into 1-inch
         cubes
         Cherry tomatoes and other fresh
         vegetables

Remove rarebit from metal tray and place in
a 1½-quart casserole. Microwave at ME-
DIUM-LOW about 4 minutes or until easily
stirred.
  Add remaining ingredients and mix well.
Microwave at MEDIUM 3 to 5 minutes or
until bubbly.
  Serve hot as a dip with bread cubes,
cherry tomatoes, and other fresh vegetable
dippers.
  Yield: 2 cups.

MOCK OYSTER DIP ★

Power: HIGH/MEDIUM-HIGH
Microwave Time: 15 to 19 Minutes

    1 (10-ounce) package frozen
         chopped broccoli
    6 tablespoons butter or margarine
    1⅓ cups minced onion
    1 (10¾-ounce) can cream of
         mushroom soup, undiluted
    1 (4-ounce) can mushrooms,
         drained and minced
    1 (6-ounce) package garlic-flavored
         cheese spread, cut in pieces
    ¼ teaspoon hot pepper sauce
    ¼ teaspoon salt

Pierce broccoli package and place on paper plate. Microwave at HIGH 5 to 6 minutes. Drain well and set aside.

Microwave butter in a 2-quart casserole at HIGH 30 seconds to melt. Stir in onion. Cover with plastic wrap and microwave at HIGH 5 to 6 minutes. Stir well after 3 minutes.

Add soup, mushrooms, cheese spread, and hot sauce. Cover with plastic wrap and microwave at MEDIUM-HIGH 5 to 6 minutes or until cheese melts. Stir in cooked broccoli and salt. Mix well. Serve warm as a dip.

Yield: approximately 5 cups.

CRABMEAT SUPREME

Power: HIGH
Microwave Time: 6½ to 8 Minutes

    2   (8-ounce) packages cream cheese
    2   (6½-ounce) cans crabmeat, drained
    1   clove garlic, minced
    ½   cup mayonnaise
    2   teaspoons Dijon mustard
    ¼   cup dry white wine
    2   tablespoons powdered sugar
    ½   teaspoon salt
    ⅛   teaspoon pepper

Unwrap cheese. Place in a 3-quart casserole. Microwave at HIGH 1½ to 2 minutes or until cheese is softened. Add remaining ingredients and mix well. Chill several hours or overnight.

When ready to serve, microwave at HIGH 5 to 6 minutes. Stir after 3 minutes. Serve hot as a dip with crackers, melba toast rounds, or breadsticks.

Yield: 4 cups.

HOT CRABMEAT APPETIZER

Power: HIGH/MEDIUM
Microwave Time: 6 to 9 Minutes

    1   (8-ounce) package cream cheese
    1½ cups flaked crabmeat
    2   tablespoons finely chopped onion
    1   tablespoon milk
    1   teaspoon prepared horseradish
    ½   teaspoon salt
    ⅛   teaspoon pepper
    ⅓   cup sliced almonds
        Crackers

Unwrap cheese and place in a 1½-quart casserole. Microwave at HIGH 1 to 2 minutes or until cheese is softened. Add remaining ingredients except almonds and crackers and combine well. Spoon mixture into an 8-inch round baking dish. Microwave at MEDIUM 5 to 7 minutes or until heated through. Sprinkle top with almonds. Serve hot with crackers.

Yield: 2½ cups.

Micronote: Freshen stale snacks like pretzels and chips. Microwave at HIGH for 5 to 10 seconds. They will crisp while standing. Use a wicker basket or wooden bowl as a container for heating crackers, pretzels, and chips.

CHEESE CANAPÉS ★

Power: HIGH
Microwave Time: ½ to 1 Minute for
  12 canapés

  ⅓ cup bacon bits
  2 cups shredded sharp Cheddar
     cheese
  1 medium-size onion, minced
  3 tablespoons chili sauce
  36 melba rounds or other crackers

Mix together bacon bits, cheese, onion, and
chili sauce. Spread mixture on melba
rounds. Place 12 appetizers on a paper plate
or serving dish suitable for microwaving.
Microwave at HIGH ½ to 1 minute. Microwave remaining canapés following same
directions. Serve warm.
  Yield: 3 dozen canapés.

CANAPÉ SPREAD

Power: HIGH
Microwave Time: ½ to 1 Minute for
  12 crackers

  ½ pound sharp Cheddar cheese,
     shredded
  8 slices bacon, cooked and
     chopped
  ½ teaspoon Worcestershire sauce
  1 medium-sized onion, finely
     chopped
  1 teaspoon prepared mustard
  1 tablespoon mayonnaise
  60 crackers

Combine first 6 ingredients and mix well.
Spread on crackers. Arrange crackers on 8-
to 9-inch glass dish or paper plate. Microwave 10 to 12 at a time at HIGH for ½ to 1
minute or until cheese melts.
  Yield: 1½ cups or 60 crackers.

HOT CRABMEAT CANAPÉS

Power: MEDIUM-HIGH
Microwave Time: 2 to 2½ Minutes
  for 8 canapés

  2 tablespoons soft butter or
     margarine
  1 (3-ounce) package cream cheese
  1 (3½-ounce) can crabmeat,
     drained
  ¼ cup mayonnaise
  1 egg yolk
  1 teaspoon chopped onion
  ¼ teaspoon mustard
     Dash of salt
     Melba toast rounds or crackers

Place butter and cream cheese in medium-
size bowl. Microwave at MEDIUM-HIGH 1
minute to soften. Using fork, shred crabmeat. Combine with butter mixture and
remaining ingredients except crackers. Pile
a teaspoon of crabmeat on melba rounds or
similar crackers. Arrange 8 squares on

serving dish. Microwave at MEDIUM-HIGH 1 to 1½ minutes. Microwave remaining canapés following same directions. Serve warm.

Yield: 25 canapés.

Micronote: Hollow out cherry tomatoes. Stuff with crabmeat mixture and microwave at MEDIUM-HIGH to heat. Garnish with parsley to serve.

To serve as dip, place entire mixture in an attractive serving dish. Microwave at MEDIUM-HIGH 4 to 5 minutes. Serve with crackers.

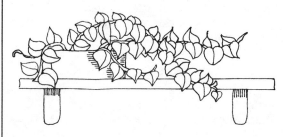

CRABMEAT BE-GONES IN BACON ★

Power: HIGH
Microwave Time: 6 to 7 Minutes
  for 10 to 12 rolls

    2   (6½-ounce) cans crabmeat,
        drained and flaked
    8   to 10 soda crackers, crushed
    2   tablespoons catsup
    ⅛   teaspoon pepper
    ¼   teaspoon salt
    ½   teaspoon Worcestershire sauce
    ¼   teaspoon lemon juice
        Dash of hot sauce
    1   egg, slightly beaten
    7   bacon strips
        Cocktail sauce (optional)

Mix together crabmeat, cracker crumbs, catsup, pepper, salt, Worcestershire sauce, lemon juice, hot sauce, and beaten egg. Shape mixture into small rolls about 1½-inches long. Cut bacon strips into thirds. Wrap bacon pieces around crabmeat rolls. Secure with a toothpick.

Place a double layer of paper towels on a paper plate or dish suitable for microwaving. Arrange about 12 rolls on the plate.

Cover with a paper towel. Microwave at HIGH 3 to 3½ minutes. Rotate plate ½ turn. Microwave at HIGH an additional 3 to 3½ minutes, or until bacon is crisp. Serve hot with cocktail sauce, if desired. Microwave remaining rolls following same directions.

Yield: 21 rolls.

FANTASTIC ANTIPASTO

Power: HIGH
Microwave Time: 7 to 9½ minutes

    ½   cup catsup
    ½   cup vegetable oil
    1   (8-ounce) can tomato sauce
    1   bay leaf
    ½   teaspoon garlic powder
    1   teaspoon salt
    ½   teaspoon pepper
    1   teaspoon chili powder
    ½   cup thinly sliced carrots
    1   (7½-ounce) can white tuna fish,
        drained
    1   (7½-ounce) can shrimp, drained
    1   (6½-ounce) package frozen
        crabmeat
    1   (6½-ounce) can mushrooms,
        drained and sliced
    1   (6½-ounce) jar stuffed green
        olives, drained
    1   (13½-ounce) jar pickled onions,
        drained
    1   cup sweet pickle cubes
    1   cup chopped cauliflower

Combine catsup, oil, tomato sauce, bay leaf, and spices in a 3-quart casserole. Stir in carrot slices. Cover with plastic wrap and microwave at HIGH 2 to 2½ minutes.

Remove bay leaf. Stir in remaining ingredients. Mix well and cover with plastic wrap. Microwave at HIGH 5 to 7 minutes, rotating dish ½ turn after 3 to 4 minutes. Let stand 2 to 3 minutes before serving. Serve hot or cold.

Yield: 4 to 5 cups.

Micronote: This also makes a good salad or main dish.

BANANA ROLL-UPS

Power: HIGH
Microwave Time: 4½ to 6 Minutes

- 4 **bananas, peeled**
- 8 **thin slices ham**
- 2 **tablespoons prepared mustard**
- 4 **tablespoons whole cranberry sauce**

Halve each banana vertically and wrap in a ham slice. Arrange in a 12- x 8-inch baking dish.

Combine mustard and cranberry sauce in a custard cup. Microwave at HIGH 30 to 45 seconds or until heated.

Spread the cranberry sauce mixture over banana rolls. Cover with waxed paper. Microwave at HIGH 4 to 5 minutes or until heated through. Let stand 2 minutes before serving.

Yield: 8 servings.

SWEET'N SOUR PEGLEGS

Power: HIGH
Microwave Time: 10 to 12 Minutes

- 12 **chicken wings (use the 1st section)**
- ⅓ **cup dry white wine**
- ½ **teaspoon seasoned salt**
- ½ **teaspoon garlic salt**
- ½ **teaspoon onion salt**
- ½ **teaspoon paprika**
- ½ **teaspoon commercial brown bouquet sauce**
- 1 **teaspoon soy sauce**
- ½ **teaspoon Worcestershire sauce**
- ½ **cup grated onion**
- 1 **teaspoon dry mustard**
- ¼ **cup catsup**
- ⅔ **cup firmly packed brown sugar**
- 2 **tablespoons cornstarch**
- 1 **(18-ounce) can pineapple tidbits with ½ cup juice**
- ½ **lemon, sliced**

Early in the day combine all ingredients in a 2-quart casserole and chill 2 to 8 hours. Just before serving, microwave at HIGH 10 to 12 minutes. Stir occasionally. Serve with party picks.

Yield: 12 peglegs.

SAUCY CHICKEN LIVERS

Power: HIGH
Microwave Time: 6 Minutes

- 12 **chicken livers**
- 1 **(5-ounce) bottle soy sauce**
- 3 **water chestnuts, cut in quarters**
- 6 **slices bacon, cut in half**
- 1 **cup firmly packed brown sugar**

Marinate chicken livers in soy sauce overnight. Insert ¼ water chestnut in each liver. Wrap with ½ slice bacon; roll in brown sugar. Let stand in soy sauce for 1 hour .

Microwave at HIGH 3 minutes. Turn each piece. Microwave at HIGH 3 minutes.

Yield: 12 chicken livers.

MINI-MEATBALLS

Power: HIGH
Microwave Time: 8 to 9 Minutes

- 1 **pound ground chuck**
- ½ **teaspoon salt**
- ¼ **teaspoon pepper**
- ¼ **teaspoon garlic salt**
- ¼ **teaspoon oregano**
- 1 **egg**
- 1 **tablespoon finely chopped onion**
- ¼ **cup dry bread crumbs**
- 1 **(8-ounce) can tomato sauce, divided**

Combine all ingredients except ½ of the tomato sauce. Shape into ½-inch meatballs. Place in a 12- x 8-inch baking dish. Spoon reserved tomato sauce over meatballs. Cover with plastic wrap. Microwave at HIGH 8 to 9 minutes. Let stand, covered, 2 to 3 minutes before serving.

Yield: 35 meatballs.

SWEET AND SOUR MEATBALLS

Power: HIGH/MEDIUM-LOW
Microwave Time: 36 to 47 Minutes

  1½   **pounds ground chuck**
  ¾   **cup quick-cooking oats,**
        uncooked
  1   **(4-ounce) can water chestnuts,**
        drained and finely chopped
  ½   **cup milk**
  1   **egg, beaten**
  1   **teaspoon soy sauce**
  1   **teaspoon onion salt**
  ½   **teaspoon garlic salt**
  1   **(8¼-ounce) can crushed**
        pineapple
  1   **cup firmly packed brown sugar**
  2   **tablespoons cornstarch**
  1   **cup beef bouillon**
  ½   **cup lemon juice**
  2   **tablespoons soy sauce**
  ⅓   **cup chopped green pepper**

Combine first 8 ingredients in a mixing bowl. Mix lightly and form into 1-inch balls. Arrange half the meatballs on a microwave roasting rack placed in a 12- x 8-inch baking dish. Cover with waxed paper.

Microwave at HIGH 5 to 7 minutes or until done. Remove cooked meatballs. Repeat the procedure to cook remaining meatballs. Pour drippings from the baking dish and return cooked meatballs to dish.

Drain pineapple and reserve juice. Combine juice, sugar, and cornstarch in a 4-cup glass measure. Gradually stir in bouillon, lemon juice, and soy sauce. Microwave at HIGH 6 to 8 minutes or until thickened, stirring once or twice. Add reserved pineapple and green pepper. Pour the thickened sauce over the meatballs. Microwave at MEDIUM-LOW 20 to 25 minutes.
    Yield: 50 to 70 meatballs.

MARINATED MUSHROOMS

Power: HIGH
Microwave Time: 8 to 9 Minutes

  ½   **cup red wine vinegar**
  ½   **cup salad oil**
  1   **teaspoon prepared mustard**
  1   **tablespoon firmly packed brown**
        sugar
  1   **teaspoon finely chopped parsley**
  1   **teaspoon salt**
  ⅛   **teaspoon pepper**
  1   **small onion, thinly sliced**
  2   **(8-ounce) cans button**
        mushrooms, drained

Combine vinegar, oil, mustard, sugar, parsley, salt, pepper, and onion slices in a 4-cup glass measure. Microwave at HIGH 4 minutes. Stir after 2 minutes.

Add mushrooms to hot mixture. Cover with plastic wrap. Microwave at HIGH 4 to 5 minutes. Stir well. Cool, covered, and chill overnight. Drain before serving.
    Yield: 2 to 3 cups of mushrooms.

STUFFED MUSHROOMS SAVANNAH

Power: HIGH
Microwave Time: 3 to 4 Minutes

 12   **large fresh mushrooms**
  3   **tablespoons butter or margarine,**
        melted
  ⅓   **cup seasoned bread crumbs**
     Dash of salt
     Dash of red pepper
  ½   **cup cooked shrimp, chopped**

Wipe mushrooms with a damp paper towel to clean. Remove stems. Dip caps in butter and place top side down in flat baking dish.

Chop stems and combine with remaining ingredients. Fill mushroom caps. Cover with waxed paper. Microwave at HIGH 3 to 4 minutes.
    Yield: 12 mushrooms.

STUFFED MUSHROOMS

Power: HIGH
Microwave Time: 6 to 7 Minutes

  8 large fresh mushrooms
  1 tablespoon butter or margarine
  1 small onion, finely chopped
  1 clove garlic, minced
  2 ounces summer sausage or
       pepperoni, finely chopped
  6 crackers, crushed
  3 tablespoons grated Parmesan
       cheese
  1 tablespoon minced parsley
  ¼ teaspoon lemon pepper
       seasoning
  ⅛ teaspoon Italian seasoning

Wipe mushrooms with a damp paper towel to clean. Remove stems. Chop finely. Combine butter, chopped mushroom stems, onion, garlic, and chopped meat in a 2-cup glass measure. Microwave at HIGH 3 minutes.

Add cracker crumbs, cheese, parsley, and seasonings. Mix well. Fill mushroom caps with mixture. Arrange in a circle on a 9-inch glass pie plate or other plate suitable for microwaving. Cover with waxed paper. Microwave at HIGH 3 to 4 minutes or until heated through.

Yield: 8 large mushrooms.

HOT BROWN SANDWICH

Power: HIGH
Microwave Time: 5 to 8½ Minutes

  4 tablespoons butter or margarine
  ⅓ cup all-purpose flour
  ¼ teaspoon salt
  ⅛ teaspoon pepper
  1 cup turkey or chicken broth
  1 cup milk
  ½ cup grated Parmesan cheese
       Sliced turkey or chicken
  6 slices bread, toasted
  6 slices tomato
  6 slices bacon, cooked
       Paprika
       Parsley

Place butter in a 4-cup glass measure. Microwave at HIGH 1 to 1½ minutes or until melted. Stir in flour, salt, pepper, turkey broth, and milk. Microwave at HIGH 2 to 3 minutes, stirring once or twice to mix well during cooking.

When thickened, stir in cheese. Microwave at HIGH 1 to 2 minutes. Cover by pressing a piece of plastic wrap directly on top of sauce. Set aside.

Wrap turkey or chicken slices in plastic wrap. Microwave at HIGH 1 to 2 minutes or until heated. Divide turkey slices among toast slices. Cover with hot cheese mixture. Top each with 1 tomato slice and 1 slice bacon. Sprinkle lightly with paprika and garnish with parsley.

Yield: 6 servings.

HOT SAUSAGE IN SOUR CREAM

Power: HIGH/MEDIUM-LOW
Microwave Time: 7 to 9 Minutes

  1 pound lean, highly seasoned
       sausage
  1 (8-ounce) jar chutney, chopped
       fine
  1 cup sherry
  1 (8-ounce) carton commercial sour
       cream

Roll sausage into bite-size balls. Place on plastic rack in 12- x 8-inch dish. Microwave at HIGH 4 to 6 minutes. Rotate dish ½ turn after 2 minutes. Transfer sausage to a chafing dish.

Combine chutney and sherry in a 4-cup glass measure. Add sour cream. Microwave at MEDIUM-LOW 3 minutes. Stir well at 1 minute intervals.

To serve, pour chutney mixture over sausage in chafing dish.

Yield: 20 to 30 sausages.

GARLIC SHRIMP

Power: HIGH
Microwave Time: 8 Minutes

- 1½ pounds shrimp, peeled and deveined
- 4 whole garlic cloves, peeled
- 5 tablespoons olive oil
- 1 tablespoon lemon juice
- ½ teaspoon tarragon
  Hot Lemon Butter

Place shrimp in a 12- x 8-inch baking dish. Add garlic, olive oil, lemon juice, and tarragon. Microwave at HIGH 4 minutes.

Turn the shrimp. Rotate the dish ¼ turn. Microwave at HIGH 4 additional minutes until the shrimp are pink. Serve hot with Hot Lemon Butter. Use toothpicks to pick up the shrimp.

Yield: 10 to 12 servings.

Hot Lemon Butter:

Power: HIGH
Microwave Time: 2 to 4 Minutes

- 1 cup butter or margarine
  Juice from 2 lemons
- ⅛ teaspoon salt

Combine all ingredients in a 2-cup glass measure. Cover with paper towel. Microwave at HIGH 2 to 4 minutes or until butter is melted. Stir well. Pour into individual dishes to serve with hot artichokes or seafood such as lobster or shrimp.

Yield: 1 cup.

Micronote: Use LOW setting on the microwave oven to soften cheese for cutting or spreading; cold, leftover icings or frostings; honey and spreads; butter or cream cheese.

BACON-WRAPPED WATER CHESTNUTS

Power: HIGH
Microwave Time: 6 to 7 Minutes

- 1 (8-ounce) can water chestnuts, drained and cut in half
- ¼ cup soy sauce
- 6 slices bacon, cut in half

Marinate water chestnuts in soy sauce 30 minutes. Place bacon on paper towels. Cover with paper towel. Microwave at HIGH 3 minutes.

Wrap each water chestnut with strip of bacon; secure with toothpick. Place on plate lined with paper towels. Microwave at HIGH 3 to 4 minutes until bacon is crisp.

Yield: 12 water chestnuts.

KABOBS POLYNESIA

Power: HIGH
Microwave Time: 2 Minutes for 6 to 8 kabobs

- 1 (8-ounce) can pineapple chunks
- 1 (8-ounce) can water chestnuts
- 6 bacon slices
  Curry powder

Drain pineapple and water chestnuts. Cut each piece in half. Cut bacon slices into thirds. Wrap pineapple and water chestnut pieces with a piece of bacon. Secure with a wooden toothpick or thread onto short bamboo skewers.

Place 6 to 8 kabobs on a paper or glass plate. Cover with waxed paper. Microwave at HIGH 2 minutes. Dust lightly with curry powder and serve. Microwave remaining kabobs following same directions.

Yield: 16 to 20 kabobs.

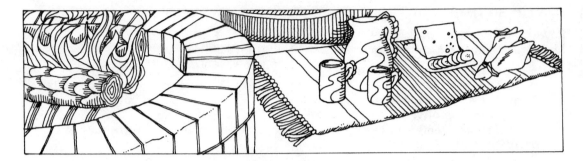

BEVERAGES

Single servings or several servings of favorite hot beverages can be microwaved in a cup, heat-proof pitcher, or a serving bowl.

Among the single serving-sized containers useful for hot beverages are disposable plastic foam cups, paper cups with handles, and cups or mugs made of glass or pottery. Avoid glued-on handles because they might come loose during the microwaving process.

When heating milk, allow room for the milk to expand, which it does rapidly as it heats. Cups should be filled only ⅔ full. For a really easy hot drink, heat milk in its waxed paper carton (without staples) until it is steamy, but not boiling. Add chocolate syrup to taste.

Use lower power settings for beverages containing alcohol because they will evaporate if heated too rapidly.

When heating 2 or 3 single servings, place the mugs or cups about 2 inches apart, either in a line or in a triangle, in the center of the oven. If preparing more than 3 servings, heat in a bowl or casserole or choose a serving pitcher which will fit into the microwave oven.

Stir beverages heated in the microwave oven thoroughly before serving to combine the heated and unheated portions.

If your microwave oven has a temperature probe, you may heat beverages to serving temperature of 190°.

Micronote: Store extra coffee in the refrigerator and reheat quickly in the microwave oven or heat milk for cocoa. Pour single servings of milk or coffee into a safe-for-microwave cup or mug, or use a heat-resistant 1-quart measure.

Follow the times on the charts below:

COFFEE

Number of Cups	Microwave Time at HIGH
1	1 to 1½ minutes
2	2 to 2½ minutes
3	3 to 4 minutes
4	4 to 5 minutes

MILK FOR COCOA

Number of Cups	Microwave Time at HIGH
1	2 minutes
2	3 minutes
3	4 minutes
4	5 minutes

SOUTHERN HOT CHOCOLATE

Power: MEDIUM/HIGH
Microwave Time: 9 to 11 Minutes

    2 (1-ounce) squares unsweetened
       chocolate
    ¼ cup sugar
    ½ cup water
    ¼ cup light molasses
    1 quart milk
    ⅛ teaspoon salt
       Whipping cream, whipped

Place chocolate in a 2-quart casserole. Microwave at MEDIUM 3 to 4 minutes. Stir in sugar to make a paste. Add water, molasses, milk, and salt. Stir to blend well.

Microwave at HIGH 6 to 7 minutes or until bubbly hot, but not boiling. Stir well at 2 minutes intervals.

Pour into mugs and serve hot, topped with whipped cream.

Yield: 6 to 8 servings.

HOT SPICY CIDER

Power: HIGH
Microwave Time: 4 to 7 Minutes

    3 cups apple cider
    3 tablespoons firmly packed
       brown sugar
    ⅛ teaspoon nutmeg
    ¼ teaspoon whole allspice
    ½ teaspoon whole cloves
    1 stick cinnamon
    2 thin orange slices, cut in half

Combine cider, brown sugar, and nutmeg in a 4-cup glass measure. Add whole allspice, cloves, and cinnamon.

Microwave at HIGH 4 to 7 minutes. Let stand 3 to 5 minutes.

To serve, strain into serving mugs. Garnish with orange slices.

Yield: 4 servings.

IRISH COFFEE

Power: HIGH
Microwave Time: 1½ Minutes

    1 (1½-ounce) jigger Irish whiskey
    1 teaspoon sugar
    2 teaspoons instant coffee granules
       Water
       Whipping cream, whipped

Combine whiskey and sugar in a mug or cup. Add coffee granules; then add water to make container ¾ full. Microwave at HIGH 1½ minutes or until mixture is hot but not boiling. Stir well.

Top with whipped cream. *Do not stir.*

Yield: 1 serving.

SPICED COFFEE

Power: HIGH/MEDIUM
Microwave Time: 13 to 17 Minutes

    4 cups extra strong coffee
    2 to 3 sticks cinnamon
    4 whole cloves
    4 whole allspice
       Whipping cream, whipped
       Ground nutmeg

Combine coffee, cinnamon sticks, cloves, and allspice in a 1½-quart casserole. Microwave at HIGH 3 to 4 minutes. Stir well. Microwave at MEDIUM 10 to 13 minutes.

To serve, strain into serving glasses. Top with whipped cream and sprinkle with nutmeg.

Yield: 6 to 8 servings.

Micronote: Warm baby bottles by loosening the cap, and microwaving at HIGH 15 seconds. Test to see if additional heating is needed. Stir or shake well to combine heated and unheated portions.

TIDEWATER TEA

Power: HIGH
Microwave Time: 12 to 15 Minutes

>   1   **quart strong tea**
>   1   **cup cherry juice**
>   3   **tablespoons lemon juice**
>   ¼   **cup orange juice**
>   4   **whole cloves**
>   1   **stick cinnamon**

Combine all ingredients in a large mixing bowl. Microwave at HIGH 12 to 15 minutes or until hot.
   Yield: 4 to 6 servings.

WASSAIL

Power: HIGH
Microwave Time: 14 to 18 Minutes

>   ½   **cup sugar**
>   1   **cup water**
>   3   **whole cloves**
>   1   **stick cinnamon**
>   1   **whole allspice**
>   ¼   **teaspoon ground ginger**
>   ¾   **cup orange juice**
>   ½   **cup lemon juice**
>   2   **cups apple juice**

Combine sugar, water, and spices in a 4-cup glass measure. Microwave at HIGH 8 to 10 minutes. Let stand at room temperature at least 1 hour.
   When ready to serve, strain the sugar-spice liquid into a 3-quart casserole or large

Micronote: Place frozen juice concentrate in a glass or plastic pitcher. Microwave at HIGH 30 to 50 seconds or until soft. Add water and stir.

mixing bowl. Stir in remaining ingredients. Microwave at HIGH 6 to 8 minutes or until hot.
   Pour into cups or mugs and serve immediately.
   Yield: 4 to 5 cups.

ORANGE WASSAIL

Power: HIGH
Microwave Time: 15 to 20 Minutes

>   ½   **cup sugar**
>   ½   **cup water**
>   6   **whole cloves**
>   1   **stick cinnamon**
>   6   **cups orange juice**
>   2   **cups cranberry juice**

Combine all ingredients in a large mixing bowl or 3-quart casserole. Stir well. Microwave at HIGH 15 to 20 minutes or until sugar is dissolved and mixture is hot. Stir well after 10 minutes.
   To serve, strain and pour into cups or mugs.
   Yield: 2 quarts.

Micronote: Heat lemons, limes, and oranges before squeezing. Microwave each at HIGH 20 to 30 seconds, and it will be easier to squeeze and will also yield more juice.

BREADS

Because microwaved breads will not have a crusty brown crust, some people think they are not appealing. But with some adjustments, such as learning to add color with toppings, quick breads can be a microwave treat.

Some of the ingredients which can be used for toppings and glazes are:
• crushed French fried onion rings or crumbled bacon
• chopped nuts and brown sugar or toasted coconut
• shredded cheese combined with seasonings or fresh herbs

Another way to add color and eye-appeal to breads, coffeecakes, and muffins is to use dark ingredients like whole wheat flour, brown sugar, molasses, and spices like cinnamon and nutmeg that add color.

Breads with leavening agents such as baking powder can be microwaved with good results, but yeast breads usually should be cooked conventionally because a thick brown crust is needed to hold their "structure." Proofing may be done in the microwave by using the LOW power level.

Many batters will hold well, stored in a tightly covered container in the refrigerator. These refrigerated batters can be used for serving as a breakfast bread or for after-school treats for youngsters.

When microwaving breads and muffins, leave them uncovered to allow for the steam to escape. They should be slightly sticky on top when removed from the oven but will continue cooking and develop a dry look upon standing.

CONTAINERS FOR MICROWAVE BREADS, COFFEECAKES, AND MUFFINS

These containers should be carefully selected to meet the "donut" shape preferred for microwaving. They may be paper, plastic, or glass.

Many donut or ring-shaped containers are now available, and more will likely become available in the future as the number of microwave oven owners increases. Plastic muffin rings, with places for 6 or 7 muffins, are available from several manufacturers. Ring molds made of plastic or glass are available in a number of different sizes.

There are some simple baking containers which you can make yourself. If you want to make your own ring-shaped container for microwaving, try one of the following ideas.
• Select an 8-inch glass or plastic baking dish and place a greased 5-ounce custard cup in the center.
• Cut paper or foam drink cups down to about 2 inches. Line with 2 paper cupcake liners.

- Arrange the filled muffin molds in a circle in the microwave oven to cook.
- Save the cups and reuse them for muffins or cupcakes.

YEAST BREADS
IN THE MICROWAVE OVEN

Because there is no layer of hot air to surround yeast breads and form a rich brown crust, yeast breads cooked in the microwave oven will have a different appearance and texture from yeast breads cooked conventionally. Some manufacturers' instruction books include recipes for specially formulated yeast breads. Our preference is for conventionally cooked yeast breads.

However, you may use the microwave oven to speed the rising process of prepared yeast doughs:

Form the yeast dough into a ball and place in a lightly greased bowl, or prepare for baking and place in a greased microwave casserole or baking dish. Cover with a damp cloth. Microwave at LOW 10 to 15 minutes or until the dough is doubled in size. Then bake conventionally.

BANANA NUT BREAD
(Conventional Recipe)

- ½ cup salad oil
- 1 cup sugar
- 2 eggs, beaten
- 3 ripe bananas, mashed
- 2 cups all-purpose flour
- ½ teaspoon baking powder
- ½ teaspoon salt
- 3 tablespoons milk
- ½ teaspoon vanilla extract
- 1¼ cups chopped nuts

Beat oil and sugar together. Add eggs and banana pulp and beat well. Add sifted dry ingredients, milk, and vanilla. Mix well and stir in nuts. Pour into greased and floured 9- x 5- x 3-inch loaf pan. Bake in preheated 350° oven for about 1 hour. Cool well and store overnight before cutting.

Yield: 1 loaf. Good with cream cheese for tea sandwiches.

To Microwave Banana Nut Bread

- Combine all ingredients as for conventional except increase baking powder and salt to 1 teaspoon each.
- Coat a greased tube-shaped pan with nut mixture before filling with the bread batter.

BANANA NUT BREAD

Power: MEDIUM-HIGH
Microwave Time: 11 to 13 Minutes

- ½ cup salad oil
- 1 cup sugar
- 2 eggs, beaten
- 3 ripe bananas, mashed
- 2 cups all-purpose flour
- 1 teaspoon baking powder
- 1 teaspoon salt
- 3 tablespoons milk
- ½ teaspoon vanilla extract
- 1¼ cups chopped nuts, divided
- 3 tablespoons firmly packed brown sugar

Beat oil and sugar together in a mixing bowl. Add eggs and banana pulp.

Combine dry ingredients. Add dry ingredients, milk, and vanilla to the egg mixture. Stir in 1 cup of nuts.

Generously butter a 10-inch microwave fluted ring mold. Combine remaining ¼ cup nuts and brown sugar. Coat the fluted ring with the nut mixture. Pour batter into the prepared mold.

Microwave at MEDIUM-HIGH 11 to 13 minutes. Let stand on counter to cool 5 minutes before removing from pan.

Top with Caramel Glaze to serve.
Yield: 1 loaf.

Caramel Glaze:

Power: HIGH
Microwave Time: 1½ to 2 Minutes

- 2 tablespoons butter
- 2 tablespoons milk
- ¼ cup firmly packed dark brown sugar
- ½ cup sifted powdered sugar

Combine butter, milk, and brown sugar in a 4-cup glass measure. Microwave at HIGH 1½ to 2 minutes or until boiling.

Stir in powdered sugar. Pour over cooled Banana Nut Bread as a glaze.

Yield: ½ cup.

APPLE SPICE BREAD

Power: HIGH
Microwave Time: 7½ to 9 Minutes

- ½ cup butter or margarine
- ¾ cup applesauce
- 2 eggs, beaten
- ¼ cup red cooking wine
- 2 cups all-purpose flour
- 1½ cups sugar
- 1½ teaspoons ground cinnamon
- 1 teaspoon soda
- ¾ teaspoon salt

Microwave butter in a 2½-quart glass mixing bowl at HIGH 30 seconds to 1 minute. Stir in applesauce, eggs, and red wine.

Sift together flour, sugar, cinnamon, soda, and salt. Blend dry ingredients into applesauce mixture.

Line a 9-inch round glass baking dish with a circle cut from a paper towel. Fill ½ full with batter. Reserve remaining batter. Microwave at HIGH 5 to 6 minutes. Rotate dish ½ turn after 3 minutes. Place baking dish directly on a counter top or wooden board. Immediately cover bread with waxed paper. Cool 15 to 20 minutes. Turn bread out of pan. Cover with baking dish.

Remaining batter may be chilled 3 to 5 days. Use extra batter to make muffins. Line each microwave muffin ring with paper liners, and fill ½ full. Microwave at HIGH 2 minutes for 7 to 8 muffins.

Yield: one 9-inch round loaf and 7 to 8 muffins.

FANCY CORNBREAD

Power: HIGH and MEDIUM
Microwave Time: 4½ to 6 Minutes for ring; 2 to 3 Minutes for 6 muffins

- 1 cup yellow cornmeal
- ½ cup all-purpose flour
- 2 tablespoons sugar
- 1 tablespoon baking powder
- ¼ teaspoon chili powder
- ½ teaspoon salt
- 2 eggs, beaten
- ¾ cup milk
- 2 tablespoons butter or margarine, melted
- 1 (12-ounce) can whole kernel corn, drained
- ½ cup finely crushed French fried onion rings

Sift and combine dry ingredients in a bowl. Stir in eggs, milk, and butter. Mix in corn. Pour into prepared microwave baking ring or muffin cups to cook.

Microwave Baking Ring Method:

Place crushed onion rings in a buttered microwave baking ring. Turn to coat sides and bottom. Reserve extra crushed onions. Pour batter into prepared ring. Top with reserved onions. Microwave at MEDIUM 4½ to 6 minutes. Rotate dish after 3 minutes. Remove ring and serve warm.

Yield: one 9-inch ring.

Muffin Ring Method:

Line a 6- or 7-cup microwave muffin ring with paper liners. Fill each cup ½ full with batter. Sprinkle crushed onion over batter. Microwave at HIGH 2 to 3 minutes. Rotate ring ½ turn after 1 minute. Remove muffins to a cooling rack. Repeat with remaining batter.

Yield: 12 to 14 muffins.

ORANGE-DATE NUT BREAD

Power: HIGH
Microwave Time: 10 to 12 Minutes

> 1 orange
> ½ cup boiling water
> 1 cup dates
> 1 cup sugar
> 1 tablespoon melted butter or
>   margarine
> 1 egg, beaten
> 2 cups all-purpose flour
> 1 teaspoon baking powder
> 1 teaspoon soda
> ½ teaspoon salt
> 1 cup chopped pecans

Squeeze juice from orange and add boiling water to make 1 cup liquid. Set aside. Cut orange rind into thin ½-inch pieces. Place cut rind and dates in blender. Cover. Process at High 10 seconds.

Combine liquid, orange rind and dates, sugar, butter, and egg. Sift flour, baking powder, soda, and salt together. Add to liquid mixture. Combine well and add nuts.

Pour into greased 9- or 10-inch microwave tube pan or casserole dish with glass in center. Microwave at HIGH 10 to 12 minutes. Rotate baking dish ½ turn at 3 minute intervals. Place directly on counter and let cool in pan 15 to 20 minutes.

Yield: 1 loaf.

QUICK BREAKFAST BARS

Power: HIGH
Microwave Time: 8 Minutes

> ½ cup butter or margarine
> ½ cup sugar
> ½ cup firmly packed light brown
>   sugar
> 1 egg
> ½ teaspoon vanilla extract
> 1½ cups quick-cooking rolled oats,
>   uncooked
> ¾ cup whole wheat flour
> ½ teaspoon soda
> ¼ teaspoon salt
> 1 cup chopped peanuts
> ½ cup seedless raisins

Cream butter, sugar, and brown sugar. Mix in egg and vanilla. Stir in oats, flour, soda, salt, peanuts, and raisins. Pat mixture into a greased 9-inch round glass baking dish. Let mixture stand 5 minutes.

Microwave at HIGH 8 minutes. Rotate dish ½ turn after 4 minutes. Cool completely before icing. Top with Peanut Butter Icing.

Yield: 6 to 8 servings.

Peanut Butter Icing:

Power: HIGH
Microwave Time: 1½ to 2 Minutes

> 2 tablespoons peanut butter
> 2 tablespoons milk
> ½ cup powdered sugar
> ½ teaspoon vanilla extract

Combine peanut butter, milk, and sugar in a 2-cup glass measure. Microwave at HIGH 1½ to 2 minutes. Stir in vanilla. Drizzle over cooked bar mixture. Cool completely before cutting.

BRAN MUFFINS

Power: HIGH/MEDIUM-HIGH
Microwave Time: See below

> ½ cup dark molasses
> 1 cup buttermilk
> 1¾ cups bran cereal
> ½ cup butter or margarine, cut in
>   pieces
> ¾ cup firmly packed brown sugar
> 1 egg, beaten
> 1½ cups all-purpose flour
> 2 teaspoons baking powder
> ¼ teaspoon salt
> ½ cup chopped nuts or dates

Combine molasses and buttermilk in a medium bowl. Microwave at HIGH 2 to 3 minutes. Add cereal and butter. Stir and let stand until butter is softened.

Mix in sugar and egg. Combine flour,

baking powder, and salt and add to the cereal mixture. Stir in nuts.

Fill paper-lined microwave muffin rings ½ full. Microwave at MEDIUM-HIGH according to the following times. Rotate ring or redistribute individual cooking utensils once during cooking.

Muffins	Microwave Time
1 to 2	1 to 2 minutes
3 to 4	1½ to 2½ minutes
5 to 6	2½ to 3 minutes

Yield: 24 to 30 muffins.

Micronote: This batter stores well, covered and chilled, up to 4 weeks. Use as needed. Allow a few seconds more for cooking chilled batter. *Do not stir* before dipping.

BREAKFAST MUFFINS

Power: HIGH
Microwave Time: 3 to 5 Minutes for 6 to 7 muffins

    2 cups all-purpose flour
    ¼ cup sugar
    1 tablespoon baking powder
    ½ teaspoon ground ginger
    ½ teaspoon salt
    1 egg, well beaten
    ¼ cup salad oil
    ½ cup milk
    ¼ cup dark molasses

Sift together flour, sugar, baking powder, ginger, and salt in a mixing bowl. Combine the egg, salad oil, milk, and molasses. Add all at once to the dry ingredients. Stir just to mix.

Fill paper-lined microwave muffin ring ½ full with batter. Microwave 6 to 7 muffins 3 to 5 minutes at HIGH. Redistribute or rotate ½ turn after 3½ to 4 minutes. Repeat with remaining batter. Serve warm.

Yield: 18 muffins.

CRUNCHY ORANGE MUFFINS

Power: HIGH
Microwave Time: 2½ to 3 Minutes for 6 muffins

    2 cups all-purpose flour
    ⅓ cup sugar
    1 teaspoon baking powder
    ½ teaspoon soda
    ½ teaspoon salt
    1 cup crunchy nutlike cereal
    ½ cup seedless raisins
    2 eggs, beaten
    1 cup orange juice
    1 tablespoon grated orange rind
    ⅓ cup salad oil
    ½ cup orange marmalade

Sift flour, sugar, baking powder, soda, and salt into a mixing bowl. Stir in cereal and raisins.

Combine eggs, orange juice, orange rind, and salad oil. Add liquids all at once to dry ingredients. Stir just until all ingredients are moistened.

Fill paper-lined microwave muffin cups ½ full with batter. Microwave muffins 6 at a time at HIGH 2½ to 3 minutes. Repeat with additional batter.

Spread orange marmalade on muffins. Serve warm.

Yield: 15 to 18 muffins.

CROUTONS

Power: HIGH
Microwave Time: 6 to 8 minutes

    4 cups cubed bread
    1 tablespoon garlic herb seasoning

Combine bread cubes and seasoning in a 12- x 8-inch baking dish. Toss well.

Microwave at HIGH 6 to 8 minutes. Stir well at 2 minute intervals. Cool thoroughly, and store in a tightly covered container.

Yield: 4 cups croutons.

CARAMEL BISCUIT RING

Power: HIGH
Microwave Time: 3 to 3½ Minutes

- ½ cup caramel ice cream topping
- ¼ cup chopped nuts
- ⅓ cup butter or margarine
- 1 (10-ounce) package refrigerated biscuits

Pour caramel topping in bottom of a 9-inch round glass or microwave plastic cake pan. Sprinkle nuts over topping.

Place butter in a custard cup. Microwave at HIGH 30 seconds to melt. Dip biscuits in melted butter to coat all sides. Arrange biscuits in a ring against sides of pan holding caramel topping.

Cover with waxed paper. Microwave at HIGH 2½ to 3 minutes or until biscuits are not doughy on top. Turn upside down on a serving plate. Let stand for sauce to drain down over biscuits. Serve immediately.

Yield: 10 servings.

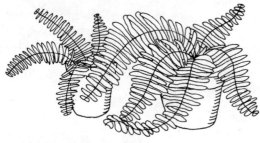

PEANUT TEA RING

Power: HIGH/MEDIUM-HIGH
Microwave Time: 4½ to 6½ Minutes

- ¼ cup butter or margarine
- 1 (10-ounce) package refrigerated biscuits
- 1 cup chopped peanuts
- ½ cup powdered sugar
- 1 tablespoon water

Place butter in small bowl. Microwave at HIGH 30 seconds to melt. Separate biscuits and dip both sides in melted butter, then in peanuts to coat well. Arrange biscuits in overlapping circle around the inside edge of a buttered 9-inch glass pie plate.

Microwave at MEDIUM-HIGH 4 to 6 minutes. Rotate dish ½ turn after 3 minutes of cooking.

To serve, invert onto a serving plate. Let stand, covered with baking dish, to allow sauce to drizzle over biscuits.

Combine sugar and water and drizzle over the hot ring. Serve warm.

Yield: 10 servings.

OATMEAL SCONES

Power: HIGH
Microwave Time: 5 to 6 Minutes for
  8 to 10 wedges

- 1½ cups all-purpose flour
- ¼ cup firmly packed brown sugar
- 1 tablespoon baking powder
- ¾ teaspoon salt
- ¾ cup butter or margarine
- 1½ cups regular oats, uncooked
- ⅓ cup chopped nuts
- ⅓ cup milk
- ½ cup butter
- ¼ cup honey

Combine flour, brown sugar, baking powder, salt, ¾ cup butter, oats, nuts, and milk. Stir to blend well.

Divide batter in half. Place each half on a microwave baking tray and flatten into a 9-inch circle. Cut each circle into 8 to 10 wedges. Microwave at HIGH 3 minutes. Rotate tray ½ turn. Microwave at HIGH 2 to 3 minutes.

Combine ½ cup butter and honey. Brush on scones.

Yield: 16 to 20 wedges.

For a delightful breakfast or brunch serve Scrambled Eggs (p.99) with bacon and freshly baked bread or muffins.

CAKES AND FROSTINGS

Cakes fall into the same category as breads when people try to microwave them. Because they will not develop a crusty brown surface, microwaved cakes will be completely different in appearance from conventionally cooked cakes. They will rise higher, be lighter in texture, and have a finer grain than conventionally cooked cakes.

One of the advantages of microwaved cakes is the fact they can be mixed and cooked in less than 15 minutes. A single layer will microwave at HIGH power in 6 to 8 minutes and two layers can be cooked in a flat shallow dish or a fluted tube pan in 12 to 15 minutes.

Choosing a rich, heavy batter will ensure better results and chocolate or spice cake batter will be attractive and appealing.

PREPARING CAKE PANS

Whether you choose flat, round containers for microwaving cakes or one of the newer fluted, plastic tube-shaped pans,

Desserts, always a favorite, are bound to become even more popular when microwaved. Try Sweet Potato Cake with Coconut Filling (p.62), Ginger Mincemeat Bars (p.82), or Apricot-Almond Bars (p.79).

some simple preparation techniques will help assure good results when baking.

Layer cake dishes, either glass or plastic, should be lined with a paper towel circle, cut to fit the bottom of the pan. This absorbs some of the moisture at the bottom of the pan and makes the cooked layer easy to remove from the pan. Flat, shallow containers, 12- x 8-inch and 13- x 9-inch, can be lined with a single sheet of paper towel, which should come up the sides of the dish. The cake batter clings to the towel as the cake rises during microwaving and can be removed easily from the pan after cooling.

A lightly greased pan can be coated with chopped nuts, coconut, or cookie crumbs to make a coating over the cakes when they are turned out. Do not flour pans. Use shortening, butter, or margarine to grease pan. This technique works very well for the fluted tube pan.

Single cake layers or cakes baked in a rectangular-shaped dish may microwave better if elevated. To elevate, place the baking dish on a glass pie plate turned upside down.

HOW MUCH CAKE BATTER TO MICROWAVE

Because cakes rise higher when microwaved, many recipes will make too much batter for microwave layers. For these recipes you may choose to do one of the following:

- Use deeper cake pans designed just for microwave ovens because they will take the extra batter.
- Make two regular 8-inch layers and use the extra batter for cupcakes.
- After cooking one layer, freeze the remaining layer for use as a freshly baked cake for another meal.

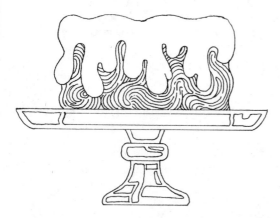

TYPE BATTERS TO MICROWAVE

Rich, heavy batters are the best choice for microwave cakes. If using a mix, choose one of the pudding-added varieties, which microwave with exceptional quality and remain moist and light. These mixes are formulated to be exactly two layers and can be cooked in two layers or in a fluted tube pan, either plastic or glass.

To prevent dryness, cover cooked cake layers tightly, if they are not to be eaten immediately. Use plastic wrap or a covered cake container.

FREEZING CAKE BATTER

Cake batter can be frozen. Pour the batter into a prepared glass or microwave plastic cake dish. Package tightly with plastic wrap. Seal, label, and freeze.

When ready to serve, microwave, covered with plastic wrap, at LOW 4 to 5 minutes. Rotate dish ¼ turn at 1 minute

intervals. Remove plastic wrap and microwave at HIGH 5 to 6 minutes.

OTHER MICROWAVE BAKING TIPS

Use the microwave oven to soften butter or margarine which has been frozen or refrigerated.

Use the microwave oven to melt chocolate to be used in baking. It can be left in the paper wrap, placed in a paper bowl or a custard cup, and microwaved uncovered at MEDIUM.

- Six ounces of chocolate morsels will melt in about 2 minutes. They will be shiny and still chip-shaped. Stir to combine.
- One-ounce chocolate squares will melt in about 1½ to 2 minutes.
- Remove wrapper from cream cheese and soften at MEDIUM or LOW power.
- Spread seeds or chopped nuts in a glass pie plate. Use HIGH or MEDIUM-HIGH to toast before adding them to other ingredients.

FROSTING

When you have learned the techniques to follow for cakes, you will appreciate the ease with which frostings can be microwaved. Very few changes will need to be made in your conventionally prepared frostings.

Choose a large glass bowl or a 1-quart glass measure to allow for the liquid to expand during cooking. Usually HIGH power can be used for frostings. Extra frosting can be refrigerated and reheated in the microwave oven when ready to use.

Because of the high sugar content, cooked frosting mixtures will become very hot. Use containers with handles, if possible, and hold the bowl with a dry pot-holder.

The following recipe for Golden Butter Frosting makes a good all-purpose frosting for almost any cake.

GOLDEN BUTTER FROSTING

Power: HIGH
Microwave Time: 3 to 4 Minutes

    ¾   cup butter
    4   cups sifted powdered sugar
    1   teaspoon vanilla extract
    3   to 4 tablespoons milk

Microwave butter in a 2-quart casserole at HIGH 3 to 4 minutes or until golden brown. Gradually beat in sugar, vanilla, and enough milk to make of spreading consistency.
    Yield: frosting for two 8- or 9-inch layers.

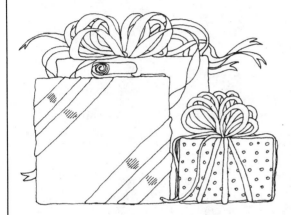

SWEET POTATO CAKE
(Conventional Recipe)

    1½   cups salad oil
    2   cups sugar
    4   eggs, separated
    4   tablespoons hot water
    2½   cups all-purpose flour
    1   tablespoon baking powder
    ¼   teaspoon salt
    1   teaspoon ground cinnamon
    1   teaspoon ground nutmeg
    1½   cups grated raw sweet potato
    1   cup chopped pecans
    1   teaspoon vanilla extract
         Coconut Filling

Combine oil and sugar in a large mixer bowl; beat until smooth. Add egg yolks;

beat well. Stir in hot water. Combine dry ingredients; blend into sugar mixture. Stir in grated potato, pecans, and vanilla, blending thoroughly. Beat egg whites until stiff, fold into batter.
    Spoon mixture into three greased 8-inch cakepans. Bake at 350° for 25 to 30 minutes. Remove from pans; cool on wire racks. Spread Coconut Filling between layers and on top of cake.
    Yield: three 8-inch layers.

Coconut Filling:

    1   (13-ounce) can evaporated milk
    1   cup sugar
    ½   cup butter or margarine
    3   tablespoons all-purpose flour
    1   teaspoon vanilla extract
    1   (3½-ounce) can or 1⅓ cups
        flaked coconut

Combine milk, sugar, butter, flour, and vanilla in a saucepan. Cook, stirring constantly, over medium heat until thickened, about 12 minutes. Remove from heat; stir in coconut. Beat until thickened and cooled.
    Yield: enough to fill and top one 3- layer cake.

To Microwave Sweet Potato Cake

- Heat water to boil. Set aside.
- Combine oil and sugar.
- Add hot water and eggs.
- Stir combined dry ingredients into sugar mixture.
- Add remaining ingredients.
- Microwave in a 9-inch plastic cake pan. (This deeper, larger pan allows for the extra volume achieved when microwaving cakes.)

To Microwave Coconut Filling

- Microwave butter in a 4-cup glass measure.
- Add milk, sugar, and other ingredients.
- Microwave about 6 minutes or until thickened.
- Cool before spreading over Sweet Potato Cake Layers.

SWEET POTATO CAKE

Power: HIGH
Microwave Time: 13 to 15 Minutes

> 3 tablespoons water
> 1½ cups salad oil
> 2 cups sugar
> 4 eggs
> 2½ cups all-purpose flour
> 1 tablespoon baking powder
> ¾ teaspoon salt
> 1 teaspoon ground cinnamon
> 1 teaspoon ground nutmeg
> 1½ cups grated raw sweet potato
> 1 cup chopped pecans
> 1 teaspoon vanilla extract
>   Coconut Filling

Microwave water in 1-cup glass measure at HIGH 1 minute.

Mix oil and sugar until smooth. Add hot water and eggs. Beat well.

Combine flour, baking powder, salt, cinnamon, and nutmeg. Stir dry ingredients into sugar mixture. Add potato, pecans, and vanilla. Blend well. Microwave in two 9-inch round microwave plastic dishes at HIGH 6 to 7 minutes per layer. Let stand directly on counter 5 to 10 minutes before removing from pan. Cool. Fill and top layers with Coconut Filling.

Yield: two 9-inch round layers.

Coconut Filling:

Power: HIGH
Microwave Time: 6 to 7 Minutes

> ½ cup butter or margarine
> 1 (13-ounce) can evaporated milk
> 1 cup sugar
> 3 tablespoons all-purpose flour
> 1 teaspoon vanilla extract
> 1⅓ cups flaked coconut
> ½ cup chopped pecans

Microwave butter in a 1½-quart casserole at HIGH 1 minute. Stir in milk, sugar, flour, and vanilla. Microwave at HIGH 6 minutes. Stir after 3 minutes. Stir in coconut and pecans. Cool filling completely before using.

Yield: topping for two 9-inch layers.

FRESH APPLE CAKE

Power: HIGH
Microwave Time: 10 to 12½ Minutes

> 1 cup butter or margarine, divided
> 1 cup sugar
> 1 egg
> 3 cups pared, chopped apple
> 1 cup all-purpose flour
> 2 teaspoons soda
> ¼ teaspoon salt
> 1 teaspoon ground cinnamon
> 1 teaspoon ground nutmeg
> ¾ cup finely chopped pecans
> 1 cup firmly packed light brown sugar
> ¼ cup milk

Microwave ½ cup butter in a 2-quart glass casserole at HIGH 30 seconds. Cream sugar and softened butter. Beat in egg and apple.

Sift together flour, soda, salt, cinnamon, and nutmeg. Add nuts to dry ingredients. Mix dry ingredients and apple mixture.

Cover the bottom of a 9-inch round microwave baking pan with waxed paper or paper towel. Spread batter in baking pan. Microwave at HIGH 10 minutes. Rotate dish ½ turn after 5 minutes. Let cake stand 5 minutes.

Mix brown sugar, remaining ½ cup butter, and milk in a 2-cup glass measure. Microwave at HIGH 2 minutes. Stir after 1 minute. Spread over cake.

Yield: 6 to 8 servings.

APPLE NUT CAKE

Power: HIGH
Microwave Time: 14 to 15 Minutes

    3   eggs
  1½   cups sugar
    ¾   cup salad oil
    2   cups all-purpose flour
    ½   teaspoon salt
    1   tablespoon ground cinnamon
    ½   teaspoon ground nutmeg
    ½   cup chopped nuts
    5   medium-size apples, cored,
          peeled, and thinly sliced

Cream eggs and sugar. Add oil and mix well.

Sift together flour, salt, cinnamon, and nutmeg. Mix dry ingredients with sugar mixture. Stir in nuts and apples.

Pour cake batter into a tube pan suitable for microwave. Microwave at HIGH 14 to 15 minutes. Rotate dish ½ turn after 7 minutes. Cool in pan.

Yield: 8 to 10 servings.

APPLE-BRAN SPICE CAKE

Power: HIGH/MEDIUM-HIGH
Microwave Time: 15 to 16 Minutes

    ½   cup butter or margarine
  1½   cups firmly packed dark brown
          sugar
    2   eggs
    1   teaspoon vanilla extract
    1   teaspoon black walnut extract
    2   cups all-purpose flour
    ¾   teaspoon soda
    ½   teaspoon baking powder
    1   teaspoon ground cinnamon
    1   teaspoon ground ginger
    ½   cup milk
    2   cups chopped, pared apples
    1   cup bran flakes cereal
    1   cup chopped, pitted,
          ready-to-eat prunes

Microwave butter in a 2-cup glass measure at HIGH 1 minute.

Combine brown sugar and melted butter. Beat in eggs, vanilla, and black walnut extract.

Sift together flour, soda, baking powder, cinnamon, and ginger. Alternately stir dry ingredients and milk into egg mixture. Blend in apples, cereal, and prunes.

Pour cake batter into a microwave plastic fluted tube pan. Microwave at MEDIUM-HIGH 14 minutes. Rotate pan ¼ turn at 4 minute intervals.

Cover cake with waxed paper. Cool on wire rack for 10 minutes.

Yield: 10 to 12 servings.

Micronote: Soften hard sugar, either white or brown, by adding an apple slice to the sugar in a safe-for-microwave casserole. Cover with plastic wrap and microwave at HIGH 15 to 30 seconds, or more if needed.

APRICOT SPICE CAKE

Power: HIGH
Microwave Time: 8 Minutes

> 1 (17½- to 18½-ounce) package
>   spice cake mix
> 1½ teaspoons apple pie spice
> 1 (7¾-ounce) jar junior baby food
>   apricots
> ½ cup water
> 2 eggs
> ¼ cup salad oil
> ¾ cup chopped pecans
>   Powdered Sugar Glaze

Combine all ingredients except Powdered Sugar Glaze in a 2-quart mixer bowl. Beat mixture until well blended. Pour batter into ungreased 10-inch microwave tube cake pan. Let stand 10 minutes.

Microwave at HIGH 8 minutes. Rotate dish at 2 minute intervals. Test cake for doneness.

Let cake stand 10 minutes on a heat-proof surface. Invert cake on a serving plate. Cool completely. Glaze with Powdered Sugar Glaze.

Yield: one 10-inch cake.

Powdered Sugar Glaze:

Power: HIGH
Microwave Time: 1 to 1½ Minutes

> 1 (1-pound) box powdered sugar
> ¼ cup milk
> 1 teaspoon vanilla extract
> ¼ cup butter or margarine

Combine sugar, milk, and vanilla in a 1½-quart glass casserole. Add butter. Microwave at HIGH 1 to 1½ minutes. Beat mixture until smooth. Pour over cooled cake.

CRANBERRY-CARROT CAKE

Power: HIGH/MEDIUM
Microwave Time: 14 Minutes

> 1 cup grated carrots
> 1 tablespoon water
> 3 cups all-purpose flour
> 2 teaspoons baking powder
> ½ teaspoon soda
> ½ teaspoon ground cinnamon
> ½ teaspoon ground nutmeg
> ½ teaspoon ground cloves
> 1 teaspoon salt
> 1 cup whole cranberry sauce
> 1 cup sugar
> 1 cup firmly packed brown sugar
> 1 cup salad oil
> 4 eggs, well beaten
> 1 teaspoon lemon extract
> ½ cup chopped nuts

Microwave carrots and water in a 1-cup glass measure covered with plastic wrap at HIGH 2 minutes.

Sift flour, baking powder, soda, cinnamon, nutmeg, cloves, and salt into a mixer bowl. Add carrots, cranberry sauce, sugars, salad oil, eggs, lemon extract, and nuts. Beat until well blended.

Pour cake batter into a 10-inch tube pan suitable for microwave. Let batter stand 5 to 10 minutes. Microwave at HIGH 5 minutes. Rotate pan ½ turn. Microwave at MEDIUM 7 minutes. Let stand directly on counter 5 to 10 minutes before removing from pan.

Yield: 8 to 10 servings.

Micronote: Need a quick frosting for cakes or cupcakes? Place mint chocolate patties (16 will be just about right) over a layer cake, or top cupcakes with one patty. The layer cake patties will melt in 2 minutes at HIGH and one patty on a cupcake will take 10 to 15 seconds.

CARROT-ALMOND CAKE

Power: HIGH
Microwave Time: 6 to 9 Minutes

    3 to 4 medium-size carrots, peeled
       and grated
 1⅔ cups whole almonds, with
       skins, ground
 1¼ cups dry bread crumbs,
       unseasoned
    1 teaspoon ground cinnamon
    6 eggs
 1¼ cups sugar
    2 tablespoons lemon juice
       Confectioner's Glaze

Grease a 9- x 2-inch round or a 10- x 6-inch baking dish. Line the bottom with parchment paper.

Place carrots and almonds in a large bowl; thoroughly blend in bread crumbs and cinnamon. Combine eggs and sugar in a large mixer bowl. Beat until lemon colored. Add lemon juice. Pour over the carrot mixture and stir thoroughly.

Pour into the prepared dish. Microwave at HIGH 6 to 9 minutes, rotating dish ½ turn during cooking. Let stand directly on counter 5 to 10 minutes before removing from pan. Turn out on a cake rack; cool. Wrap in plastic or foil and chill to mellow before glazing with Confectioner's Glaze.

Yield: one 9-inch or one 10- x 6-inch cake.

Confectioner's Glaze:

    2 cups sifted powdered sugar
    2 teaspoons lemon juice
    3 to 4 tablespoons milk

Combine all ingredients and mix until smooth. Spread over top of cooled Carrot Almond Cake.

Micronote: To make shelling nuts easier, microwave them before cracking. Combine pecans or walnuts and water in a casserole. For 2 cups of nuts, use 1 cup of water and microwave at HIGH 1½ to 2 minutes.

GRANOLA CARROT CAKE ★

Power: HIGH
Microwave Time: 7½ to 8½ Minutes

 ½ cup butter or margarine
 ¾ cup firmly packed brown sugar
    2 eggs
    2 cups grated carrots
 ¾ cup all-purpose flour
 ½ teaspoon soda
 ½ teaspoon baking powder
 ½ teaspoon salt
 ½ teaspoon ground cinnamon
 ½ teaspoon ground nutmeg
    1 cup granola cereal
       Cream Cheese Frosting

Microwave butter in a 2½-quart glass casserole at HIGH 30 seconds. Blend in brown sugar. Beat in eggs. Stir in carrots, flour, soda, baking powder, salt, cinnamon, nutmeg, and granola cereal.

Grease the bottom only of an 8-inch round glass baking dish. Pour in cake batter. Microwave at HIGH 7 to 8 minutes. Rotate dish at 3 minute intervals. Cool thoroughly before frosting with Cream Cheese Frosting.

Yield: 6 to 8 servings.

Cream Cheese Frosting:

Power: HIGH
Microwave Time: ½ to 1 Minute

    2 tablespoons butter or margarine
    1 (3-ounce) package cream cheese
    2 cups powdered sugar
 ½ teaspoon vanilla extract

Microwave butter and cream cheese in a 2-quart glass mixer bowl at HIGH ½ to 1 minute. Beat in sugar and vanilla. Mixture should be spreading consistency.

Yield: frosting for one 8-inch layer.

CHERRY-BROWNIE PUDDING CAKE *

Power: HIGH
Microwave Time: 13½ to 16 Minutes

    2 (1-ounce) squares unsweetened
         chocolate
    1 cup sugar
    6 tablespoons butter or margarine
    2 eggs, separated
    ½ teaspoon peppermint extract
    ¼ cup milk
    1 cup all-purpose flour
    ½ teaspoon soda
    ¼ teaspoon salt
    ⅓ cup chopped pecans
    1 (22-ounce) can cherry pie filling
    2 tablespoons lemon juice
         Whipped cream topping, and
           crushed peppermint candy or
           chocolate shavings

Microwave chocolate squares in a small glass dish at HIGH 1½ to 2 minutes.

Cream sugar and butter until light and fluffy. Beat in egg yolks and peppermint extract. Stir in melted chocolate and milk.

Sift together flour, soda, and salt. Stir into chocolate mixture.

Beat egg whites until stiff. Fold egg whites and pecans into the chocolate mixture.

Combine cherry pie filling and lemon juice in a 3-quart baking dish. Spread chocolate batter mixture over cherry pie filling. Microwave at HIGH 12 to 14 minutes. Rotate dish ¼ turn at 3 to 4 minute intervals.

To serve, top with whipped cream and crushed peppermint or chocolate shavings.

Yield: 8 to 10 servings.

Micronote: To reheat individual portions of frosted or unfrosted cake, place each piece on a paper or glass plate. Cover with waxed paper. Microwave at HIGH 10 to 15 seconds or until heated through.

CHOCOLATE-COVERED CHERRY ROLL

Power: HIGH
Microwave Time: 3 to 4 Minutes

    4 eggs
    ¾ cup sugar
    ¾ cup all-purpose flour
    ¾ teaspoon baking powder
    1 teaspoon vanilla extract
    ¼ cup powdered sugar, divided
    ½ (22-ounce) can cherry pie filling
         Cocoa Fudge Frosting

Beat eggs until light colored and thick. Add sugar, flour, baking powder, and vanilla. Beat until well blended. Pour batter into a 12- x 8-inch baking dish lined with greased waxed paper. Microwave at HIGH 3 to 4 minutes. Rotate the dish ¼ turn at 1 minute intervals.

Turn the cake out onto a paper towel, sprinkled with half of the powered sugar. Roll cake up from the long edge. Let stand 1 to 2 minutes. Unroll and remove waxed paper. Sprinkle balance of sugar on cake. Reroll and let stand until cooled slightly.

To fill, unroll and spread with pie filling. Roll and spread with Cocoa Fudge Frosting.

Yield: 6 to 8 servings.

Cocoa Fudge Frosting:

Power: HIGH
Microwave Time: 1½ to 2½ Minutes

    ¼ cup butter or margarine
    1 cup sugar
    ⅓ cup cocoa
    2 to 3 tablespoons milk
    ¼ teaspoon salt
    1 teaspoon vanilla extract

Microwave butter in a 4-cup glass measure at HIGH 30 seconds. Stir in sugar, cocoa, milk, salt, and vanilla. Microwave at HIGH 1 to 2 minutes. Beat until creamy enough to spread.

CHOCOLATE CAKE

Power: HIGH
Microwave Time: 2 Minutes plus 6
  to 7 Minutes for 1 layer

⅔ cup cocoa
1⅓ cups water
1¾ cups all-purpose flour
¾ teaspoon soda
¼ teaspoon salt
¼ teaspoon baking powder
⅔ cup butter or margarine,
     softened
1⅔ cups sugar
2 eggs
   Fudge Frosting

Measure cocoa and place in a medium glass bowl. Slowly stir in water. Microwave at HIGH 2 minutes. Set aside to cool slightly.

Combine flour, soda, salt, and baking powder.

Cream butter and sugar until light and fluffy. Add eggs and beat well. Alternately add the cocoa mixture and flour mixture to the creamed mixture. Beat well after each addition.

Divide the batter between two 9-inch glass cake dishes lined with a paper towel circle. Let batter stand 5 to 6 minutes. Microwave layers, one at a time, at HIGH 6 to 7 minutes. Let stand directly on counter to cool. When cooled, wrap or cover tightly until ready to frost with Fudge Frosting or other preferred frosting.

Yield: one 9-inch layer cake.

Fudge Frosting:

Power: HIGH
Microwave Time: 2 to 3 Minutes

1 (6-ounce) package semisweet
     chocolate morsels
½ cup half-and-half
1 cup butter or margarine
2½ cups powdered sugar
½ teaspoon vanilla extract
⅛ teaspoon salt

Combine chocolate morsels, half-and-half, and butter in a 4-cup glass measure. Microwave at HIGH 2 to 3 minutes. Stir to combine well.

Place sugar in a mixing bowl. Slowly stir in the chocolate mixture. Add vanilla and salt. Place the bowl containing frosting in a larger bowl containing ice. Beat the mixture with a whisk until it holds its shape.

Spread on cooled chocolate or other cake layers.

Yield: frosting and filling for two 9-inch layers.

CHOCOLATE FUDGE
CAKE DELUXE

Power: HIGH
Microwave Time: 9 to 10 Minutes

½ cup plus 1 tablespoon salad oil
2 cups applesauce
½ cup seedless raisins
½ cup chopped nuts
2 cups all-purpose flour
½ cup cocoa
1 cup plus 1 tablespoon sugar
1½ tablespoons cornstarch
2 teaspoons soda
1 teaspoon ground cinnamon
½ teaspoon ground nutmeg
½ teaspoon salt
¼ teaspoon ground cloves
   Toppings: powdered sugar, ice
     cream, or whipped topping

Stir together oil, applesauce, raisins, and nuts.

Sift together flour, cocoa, sugar, cornstarch, soda, cinnamon, nutmeg, salt, and cloves. Blend dry ingredients quickly into applesauce mixture.

Microwave cake batter in lightly greased 12- x 8-inch glass baking dish at HIGH 9 to 10 minutes. Rotate dish ¼ turn at 3 minute intervals. Let cake stand 5 minutes before serving.

Serve warm with a topping.

Yield: 8 to 10 servings.

SELF-ICED CHOCOLATE CAKE

Power: HIGH
Microwave Time: 14 Minutes

  1 (17- to 18-ounce) package
      chocolate cake mix
  1 (3-ounce) package instant
      chocolate pudding
  1½ cups milk
  2 eggs
  ½ cup chopped pecans
  1 (12-ounce) package semisweet
      chocolate morsels

Blend cake mix, pudding, milk, eggs, pecans, and chocolate morsels. Pour mixture into greased 10-inch microwave tube pan. Microwave at HIGH 14 minutes. Rotate pan ¼ turn at 3 minute intervals. Allow cake to stand 5 minutes.

Invert cake onto serving platter. The chocolate morsels may be on the top and can be spread as an icing, if desired.

Yield: 8 to 10 servings.

FUDGE SURPRISE CAKE

Power: HIGH
Microwave Time: 14 to 16 Minutes

  28 vanilla caramels
  1 (15-ounce) can sweetened
      condensed milk
  2 tablespoons butter or margarine,
      divided
  1 (17- to 18-ounce) package fudge
      cake mix
  1 cup water
  3 eggs
  1 cup finely chopped pecans

Combine caramels, condensed milk, and 1 tablespoon butter in a 2½-quart glass casserole. Microwave at HIGH 4 minutes. Stir after 2 minutes.

Combine cake mix, water, eggs, and remaining 1 tablespoon of butter. Beat with mixer according to cake package directions.

Line a 13- x 9-inch glass baking dish with a paper towel. Do not trim the paper towel.

Spread one-half the cake batter over the paper towel in the pan. Top with caramel mixture. Sprinkle caramel mixture with pecans. Spread remaining batter over pecan layer.

Microwave cake at HIGH 10 to 12 minutes. Rotate dish at 4 minute intervals. Allow cake to stand 10 to 12 minutes.

Invert cake onto serving platter. Pull off paper towel. Cut in squares to serve.

Yield: 12 to 16 servings.

COCOA COLA CAKE

Power: HIGH
Microwave Time: 12 to 14½ Minutes

  1 cup all-purpose flour
  1 cup sugar
  ½ cup butter or margarine
  2 tablespoons cocoa
  ½ cup cola beverage
  ¼ cup buttermilk
  1 beaten egg
  ½ teaspoon soda
  ½ teaspoon vanilla extract
  2 cups miniature marshmallows
      Chocolate Cola Icing

Combine flour and sugar in a 2½-quart bowl; set aside. Combine butter, cocoa, and cola beverage in a 2-cup glass measure. Microwave at HIGH 2 to 2½ minutes. Stir cola mixture into flour and sugar. Add buttermilk, egg, soda, vanilla, and marshmallows; beat well. Pour mixture into a greased 13- x 9-inch baking dish. Distribute marshmallows evenly in batter. Microwave at HIGH 10 to 12 minutes. Rotate dish ¼ turn at 2 minute intervals. Frost cake while hot with Chocolate Cola Frosting.

Yield: 16 servings.

Chocolate Cola Frosting:

Power: HIGH
Microwave Time: 2 to 2½ Minutes

  ½ cup butter or margarine
  3 tablespoons cocoa
  ⅓ cup cola beverage
  1 (1-pound) box powdered sugar
  1 cup chopped, toasted peanuts

Combine butter, cocoa, and cola beverage in a 4-cup glass measure. Microwave at HIGH 2 to 2½ minutes. Stir in sugar and nuts. Spread over hot cake.
 Yield: 2½ cups.

MISSISSIPPI MUD CAKE

Power: HIGH
Microwave Time: 12 to 13 Minutes

     1 **cup butter or margarine**
     ½ **cup cocoa**
     2 **cups sugar**
     4 **eggs**
    1½ **cups all-purpose flour**
     ¼ **teaspoon salt**
     2 **teaspoons vanilla extract**
    1½ **cups chopped nuts**
     1 **cup miniature marshmallows**
        Fudge Icing

Microwave butter and cocoa in a 2½-quart glass casserole at HIGH 2 minutes. Stir in sugar. Add eggs and beat well. Blend in flour, salt, vanilla, and nuts.
 Pour batter into a 12- x 8-inch glass baking dish. Microwave at HIGH 10 to 11 minutes. Rotate dish ½ turn after 5 minutes. Leave cake in pan.
 Spread miniature marshmallows over warm cake. Top with Fudge Icing.
 Yield: 8 to 10 servings.

Fudge Icing:

Power: HIGH
Microwave Time: 2 Minutes

     ½ **cup butter or margarine**
     ⅓ **cup milk**
     ¼ **cup cocoa**
     1 **(1-pound) box powdered sugar**
        Dash of salt
     1 **teaspoon vanilla extract**

Microwave butter, milk, and cocoa in a 2-quart glass casserole at HIGH 2 minutes. Stir in sugar, salt, and vanilla. Spread while warm.
 Yield: frosting for one 12- x 8-inch cake.

EASY GINGERBREAD

Power: HIGH
Microwave Time: 6 to 7 Minutes

     1 **(14-ounce) package gingerbread mix**

Prepare mix, according to package directions, directly in an 8-inch square glass dish. Place dish on top of inverted pie plate. Microwave at HIGH 3 minutes. Rotate dish ½ turn. Microwave at HIGH remaining 3 to 4 minutes. Place directly on counter to cool.
 Serve warm with whipped cream, applesauce, or Hot Lemon Sauce.
 Yield: 9 to 12 servings.

Hot Lemon Sauce:

Power: HIGH
Microwave Time: 6 to 7 Minutes

     1 **cup sugar**
     2 **tablespoons cornstarch**
     ½ **cup water**
     ½ **cup butter or margarine**
     ¼ **cup lemon juice**

Combine all ingredients in a 4-cup glass measure or a medium-size glass bowl. Microwave 6 to 7 minutes at HIGH until mixture boils and thickens. Stir occasionally during last 3 minutes.
 Yield: 1½ cups.

APPLESAUCE GINGERBREAD

Power: HIGH
Microwave Time: 7 to 9 Minutes

     1 **(14-ounce) package gingerbread mix**
     1 **cup applesauce**
     ⅓ **cup water**

Combine gingerbread mix, applesauce, and water in a bowl. Pour batter into a 10- x 6-inch baking dish lined with paper towels.
 Cover with waxed paper. Microwave at HIGH 7 to 9 minutes or until firm. Let stand directly on counter to cool 3 to 5 minutes before removing from baking dish.
 Yield: 8 to 10 servings.

OATMEAL CAKE

Power: HIGH
Microwave Time: see below

    1½ cups water
    1   cup quick-cooking oats,
          uncooked
    1½ cups all-purpose flour
    1   teaspoon soda
    ½   teaspoon salt
    ½   teaspoon ground cinnamon
    ½   teaspoon ground nutmeg
    ½   cup shortening
    1   cup firmly packed brown sugar
    1   cup sugar
    2   eggs
    1   teaspoon vanilla extract

Measure water into a 4-cup glass measure. Microwave at HIGH 3 to 4 minutes, or until boiling. Stir in oats. Set aside to cool slightly.

Sift together flour, soda, salt, cinnamon, and nutmeg. Set aside.

Cream shortening and sugars in a mixer bowl. Add eggs, oats, and vanilla. Stir in dry ingredients; mix well.

Divide batter between one greased 12- x 8-inch baking dish and either one greased 8-inch round baking dish or 6 paper-lined microwave muffin cups.

Microwave at HIGH according to the following times:

Amount	Microwave Time
12- x 8-inch	8 to 10 minutes
8-inch	6 to 7 minutes
6 muffins	3 to 5 minutes

Yield: one 12- x 8-inch cake plus one 8-inch round cake or 6 muffins.

HAWAIIAN FRUIT CAKE

Power: HIGH
Microwave Time: 12½ to 15½ Minutes

    ½   cup butter or margarine
    1   (17- to 18-ounce) package yellow
          cake mix
    ¾   cup milk
    3   eggs
    1   cup canned peaches, drained
    1   pint whipping cream
    1   (20-ounce) can crushed
          pineapple, drained
    1   (3¾-ounce) package instant
          vanilla pudding mix
    1   (11-ounce) can mandarin
          oranges, drained

Line the bottom of three 9-inch round glass baking pans with waxed paper. Grease lightly.

Microwave butter in a 1-cup glass measure at HIGH 30 seconds. Beat together softened butter, cake mix, milk, eggs, and peaches about 3 minutes. Pour batter into cake pans.

Microwave each layer at HIGH 4 to 5 minutes. Rotate dish ½ turn at 1 minute intervals. Cool layers completely before frosting.

Whip cream until stiff. Fold in crushed pineapple and instant pudding mix. Spread filling between cake layers and on top. Arrange orange slices on top of cake. Chill cake before serving.

Yield: 12 to 16 servings.

SURPRISE CAKE

Power: HIGH
Microwave Time: 10½ Minutes

    ¾   cup butter or margarine
    1   (17½- to 18½-ounce) package
          yellow cake mix
    1   (22-ounce) can cherry pie filling
    1   (15-ounce) can fruit cocktail,
          drained
    1   cup chopped pecans
    1   cup shredded coconut

Microwave butter in a 2-cup glass measure at HIGH 30 seconds. Combine cake mix and softened butter. Add pie filling, fruit cocktail, pecans, and coconut. Mix well.

Pour batter into a well-greased 10-inch microwave tube pan. Let mixture stand 10 minutes before baking.

Microwave at HIGH 10 minutes. Rotate dish ½ turn after 5 minutes. Let cake stand directly on counter 5 to 8 minutes before serving.

Yield: 8 to 10 servings.

RAISIN PUDDING CAKE WITH CARAMEL SAUCE

Power: HIGH/MEDIUM
Microwave Time: 15 to 17 Minutes

- 1 cup all-purpose flour
- ¾ cup sugar
- 2 teaspoons baking powder
- ¼ teaspoon salt
- 1 teaspoon ground cinnamon
- ½ cup milk
- 1 cup seedless raisins
- ½ cup chopped nuts
- 1 cup water
- 1 teaspoon butter or margarine
- ¾ cup firmly packed brown sugar

Sift together flour, sugar, baking powder, salt, and cinnamon into a mixer bowl. Add milk, raisins, and nuts. Mix lightly to combine ingredients. Spread batter into a lightly greased 2-quart glass casserole.

Microwave water in a 2-cup glass measure at HIGH 2 minutes. Add butter and brown sugar. Stir mixture to dissolve sugar and butter. Pour over cake batter. Do not stir.

Microwave at MEDIUM 13 to 15 minutes. Rotate dish ¼ turn at 3 minute intervals. Let cake stand 5 minutes before serving.

Yield: 6 to 8 servings.

UPSIDE-DOWN CHRISTMAS WREATH CAKE ★

Power: HIGH
Microwave Time: 12½ to 16 Minutes

- ½ cup butter or margarine, divided
- ½ cup firmly packed light brown sugar
- 2 tablespoons light corn syrup
- 3 to 4 pear halves, drained and sliced
- ½ cup halved maraschino cherries
- ½ cup halved green maraschino cherries
- ⅓ cup chopped pecans
- 1 cup all-purpose flour
- ¼ cup cocoa
- ¼ teaspoon salt
- ¼ teaspoon soda
- ¾ cup sugar
- 1 teaspoon vanilla extract
- 1 egg
- ¼ cup buttermilk

Microwave ¼ cup butter in a 10-inch round glass dish at HIGH ½ to 1 minute. Add brown sugar and corn syrup; stir well. Spread mixture evenly in pan. Arrange pear slices, rounded side down, in a spoke design over brown sugar mixture. Alternately add red and green maraschino cherry halves around edge of pears. Place a few cherry halves in the center. Sprinkle pears and cherries with pecans. Set aside.

Sift together flour, cocoa, salt, and soda.

Cream remaining ¼ cup butter, sugar, and vanilla until light and fluffy. Beat in egg. Alternately add flour mixture and buttermilk. Beat well after each addition.

Pour batter carefully over topping. Let stand 15 minutes.

Microwave at HIGH 12 to 15 minutes. Rotate the dish ¼ turn at 3 to 4 minute intervals.

Invert onto serving plate. Let stand at least 3 minutes. Serve warm.

Yield: 8 to 10 servings.

PEACH UPSIDE-DOWN CAKE

Power: HIGH
Microwave Time: 9½ to 12½ Minutes

> ¼ **cup butter or margarine**
> ½ **cup firmly packed brown sugar**
> 1½ **cups sliced peaches, drained**
> 6 **maraschino cherries, halved**
> 1 **(8½- to 9-ounce) package yellow cake mix**

Microwave butter in an 8-inch round glass baking dish at HIGH 30 seconds. Spread softened butter to cover the bottom of the baking dish. Sprinkle brown sugar over softened butter. Arrange peaches and cherries on brown sugar.

Prepare cake mix according to package directions. Remove ¼ cup of cake batter. Reserve for cupcakes.

Spread remaining cake batter over peaches and cherries. Microwave at HIGH 9 to 12 minutes. Rotate dish ½ turn after 4 minutes. Let cake stand 5 to 10 minutes. Invert cake onto serving platter.

Yield: 6 to 8 servings.

PINEAPPLE UPSIDE-DOWN CAKE

Power: HIGH
Microwave Time: 5 to 7 Minutes

> 2 **tablespoons butter**
> ½ **cup firmly packed dark brown sugar**
> 1 **(8-ounce) can sliced pineapple**
> ¼ **cup chopped nuts**
> 1 **(8½- to 9-ounce) package yellow cake mix**

Place butter in an 8-inch round glass baking dish. Microwave at HIGH 30 seconds to melt. Stir in brown sugar and spread evenly in dish. Drain pineapple, reserving juice. Arrange pineapple slices over sugar-butter mixture. Sprinkle chopped nuts over pineapple slices.

Prepare cake mix according to package directions, using the pineapple juice for the liquid. Pour batter over the pineapple slices.

Microwave at HIGH 5 to 7 minutes. Rotate dish ¼ turn after 3 minutes of microwaving. Place cake directly on counter and let stand 5 minutes before removing from baking dish.

Yield: one 8-inch cake.

SUMMER COOLER

Power: HIGH
Microwave Time: 10½ to 12 Minutes

> 1 **(8- to 9-ounce) package yellow cake mix**
> 3 **cups water, divided**
> 1 **(6-ounce) package strawberry-flavored gelatin**
> 1 **(10-ounce) package frozen sliced strawberries**
> 1 **(9-ounce) carton non-dairy whipped topping**

Prepare cake batter according to package directions. Pour batter into lightly greased 10-inch microwave tube pan. Microwave at HIGH 6 to 7 minutes. Rotate pan ½ turn after 3 minutes. Cool cake. Remove from pan. Crumble cake into bite-size pieces.

Microwave 1 cup water in a 4-cup measure at HIGH 2 to 2½ minutes. Add gelatin; stir until dissolved. Add remaining 2 cups of water. Chill until slightly thickened.

Microwave strawberries in a 2½-quart glass casserole at HIGH 2½ minutes. Break fruit apart after 1¼ minutes. Stir strawberries into thickened gelatin.

Spread one-half of the cake pieces in the bottom of a tube cake pan. Pour one-half gelatin mixture over cake pieces. Spread remaining cake pieces over gelatin layer. Top with remaining gelatin mixture. Chill until firm.

Unmold Cooler onto a serving platter. Frost with whipped topping. Serve chilled.

Yield: 6 to 8 servings.

CANDIES

For good results follow these techniques when microwaving candies:

- Use a large casserole or heat-proof glass bowl. It should be large enough to allow for the candy mixture to expand when boiling.
- Keep hot pads and pot holders handy for removing or handling the bowl.
- Candy and sugar mixtures become extremely hot when microwaved and must be handled carefully.
- When testing the candy mixture, use a good quality candy thermometer, if possible. If you don't have a thermometer, use the cold water technique. Remember that cooking continues after the mixture is removed from the oven. Allow for this cooking. *Do not overcook.*
- When testing for doneness, use temperatures on the chart given below. When using a thermometer, allow 1 or 2 minutes for the temperature to rise and stabilize.

Water Test	Thermometer
Thread stage	230° to 234°
Soft ball stage	234° to 240°
Firm ball stage	242° to 248°
Hard ball stage	250° to 268°
Soft crack stage	270° to 290°
Hard crack stage	300° to 310°

- Remove the candy thermometer before returning the mixture to the oven if more cooking is required.
- Use wooden spoons for stirring. They may be left in the bowl or casserole but, generally, it is easier to remove the bowl from the oven if the spoon is not left in it.
- Stir candies according to the recipe instructions. As a rule, stirring only once or twice during microwaving is all that is necessary.
- Candy which is to be beaten should be allowed to cool first. Usually 110° to 120° is a good temperature at which to start beating candy mixtures.

REAL CHOCOLATE FUDGE
(Conventional Recipe)

2 cups sugar
¼ cup cocoa
¼ cup light corn syrup
1 cup milk
3 tablespoons butter
1 teaspoon vanilla extract

Mix sugar and cocoa. Add corn syrup and milk. Set over heat and stir until all sugar is dissolved. As mixture begins to boil, wipe sides of pan with wet cloth to remove any undissolved sugar. Let boil hard until it reaches a soft ball stage (240°). Add butter, but do not stir. Let cool, add vanilla, and beat until candy is stiff. Stir in pecans and pour onto a greased 8- or 9-inch platter.
Yield: 1 pound fudge.

To Microwave Chocolate Fudge

- Combine all ingredients in a large heat-resistant glass mixing bowl or casserole.
- Cut down on the amount of milk.
- Cover with waxed paper.
- Microwave to soft ball stage; then cool and beat as for conventional recipe.
- Pour into a greased flat dish or pie plate.

REAL CHOCOLATE FUDGE

Power: HIGH/MEDIUM-HIGH
Microwave Time: 18 to 24 Minutes

2 cups sugar
¼ cup cocoa
¼ cup white corn syrup
⅔ cup milk
3 tablespoons butter
1 teaspoon vanilla extract
1 cup chopped pecans

Combine sugar and cocoa in a large mixing bowl. Add corn syrup and milk. Cover with waxed paper. Microwave at HIGH 5 to 7 minutes. Mixture should be hot and bubbly. Stir well.
Microwave, uncovered, at MEDIUM-HIGH 13 to 17 minutes or until mixture

reaches soft ball stage (235°). Add butter, but do not stir. Let cool, add vanilla, and beat until candy is stiff. Stir in pecans and pour onto a greased 8- or 9-inch platter or pie plate.
Yield: 1 pound fudge.

DOUBLE FUDGE

Chocolate Layer:

Power: HIGH/MEDIUM-HIGH
Microwave Time: 10 to 14½ Minutes

2 cups sugar
⅔ cup half-and-half
¼ cup light corn syrup
1 (1-ounce) square unsweetened chocolate
¼ cup butter or margarine
2 teaspoons vanilla extract

Combine sugar, half-and-half, corn syrup, and chocolate in a deep 4- to 5-quart casserole; mix well. Cover with waxed paper, and microwave at HIGH for 3½ to 5 minutes or until bubbly. Stir well.
Cover and microwave at MEDIUM HIGH for 6½ to 9½ minutes or until mixture reaches soft ball stage (235°). Add butter and vanilla; do not stir. Let mixture cool to lukewarm; then beat until thick and creamy.
Pour candy into a buttered 9-inch square pan, spreading with a spatula to form an even layer. Top with Peanut Butter Layer.

Peanut Butter Layer:

Power: HIGH
Microwave Time: 5 to 8 Minutes

1 cup sugar
1 cup firmly packed light brown sugar
½ cup half-and-half
2 tablespoons light corn syrup
¼ cup butter or margarine
½ cup crunchy peanut butter
½ cup marshmallow creme
2 teaspoons vanilla extract

Combine sugar, half-and-half, and corn syrup in a deep 4- to 5-quart casserole; mix well. Add butter; cover with waxed paper. Microwave at HIGH for 5 to 8 minutes or until mixture reaches soft ball stage (235°), stirring twice. Add peanut butter, marshmallow creme, and vanilla; stir until smooth. Pour over chocolate layer. Chill and cut into squares. Store candy in refrigerator. Yield: about 2¾ pounds.

BUTTERSCOTCH FUDGE

Power: HIGH
Microwave Time: 2½ to 4 Minutes

- ½ cup butter
- 1 cup firmly packed brown sugar
- ¼ cup milk
- ½ teaspoon vanilla extract
- 1 (1-pound) box powdered sugar
- ½ cup chopped nuts

Microwave butter to melt at HIGH 30 to 45 seconds in a 2-quart casserole. Add brown sugar and milk. Microwave at HIGH 2 to 3 minutes.

Add vanilla. Gradually stir in sugar and nuts.

Press mixture into a buttered 8-inch cake pan. Cool completely.

Cut into squares to serve.
Yield: 5 dozen squares.

MARSHMALLOW FUDGE

Power: HIGH
Microwave Time: 8 to 10 Minutes

- 3 cups sugar
- ½ cup butter or margarine
- ⅔ cup evaporated milk
- 1 (12-ounce) package semisweet chocolate morsels
- 1 (7½-ounce) jar marshmallow creme
- 1 cup chopped pecans
- 1 teaspoon vanilla extract

Combine sugar, butter, and evaporated milk in a 3-quart casserole. Microwave, uncovered, at HIGH 5 to 7 minutes or until mixture comes to a boil. Stir well once or twice. Microwave at HIGH 3 minutes after boiling begins.

Stir in chocolate morsels, marshmallow creme, pecans, and vanilla. Pour mixture into a buttered 13- x 9-inch pan. Cool; then chill several hours until set. Cut into squares.

Yield: 8 dozen squares.

PEANUT FUDGE

Power: HIGH
Microwave Time: 11 to 13 Minutes

- 2 cups sugar
- 2 cups firmly packed brown sugar
- 1 cup evaporated milk
- ½ cup butter or margarine
- 1 cup peanut butter
- 1 (7-ounce) jar marshmallow creme
- 2 teaspoons vanilla extract
- 1 cup chopped pecans

Combine first 4 ingredients in 2½-quart casserole dish. Microwave at HIGH 11 to 13 minutes. Stir well at 4 minute intervals.

Add remaining ingredients and stir until melted. Pour into buttered 13- x 9-inch dish. Chill at least 2 hours. Cut into 1-inch squares to serve.

Yield: 9 dozen 1-inch squares.

BUTTERY BRITTLE

Power: HIGH
Microwave Time: 9 to 10 Minutes

> 1 **cup sugar**
> ½ **cup light corn syrup**
> 1 **cup roasted cashews**
> 1 **teaspoon vanilla extract**
> 1½ **teaspoons butter**
> 1 **teaspoon soda**

Combine sugar and corn syrup in a 4-cup glass measure. Microwave at HIGH 4 minutes. Stir in cashews and microwave at HIGH 3 to 4 minutes. Add vanilla and butter. Microwave at HIGH 2 minutes. Quickly stir in soda and mix well. (Work fast because brittle hardens immediately.) Turn out onto a greased cookie sheet. Spread to desired thickness.
Yield: ¾ pound.
Micronote: Roasted peanuts can be substituted for cashews.

PEANUT BRITTLE

Power: HIGH
Microwave Time: 9 to 12 Minutes

> 1 **cup sugar**
> ½ **cup light corn syrup**
> 1 **cup raw peanuts**
> ¼ **teaspoon salt**
> 1 **tablespoon butter**
> 1 **teaspoon vanilla extract**
> 1 **teaspoon soda**

Combine sugar, corn syrup, peanuts, and salt in a 2-quart casserole. Stir well. Microwave at HIGH 8 to 9 minutes. Mixture will be light brown in color.
   Add butter and vanilla. Blend thoroughly. Microwave at HIGH 1 to 3 minutes or until mixture reaches the hard crack stage (300°). Stir in soda quickly. Pour onto greased slab or cookie sheet. Let cool at least 1 hour. Break into small pieces. Store in airtight container.
Yield: 1 pound.
Micronote: Roasted salted peanuts may be used and added as the last ingredient. Omit salt if peanuts are salted.

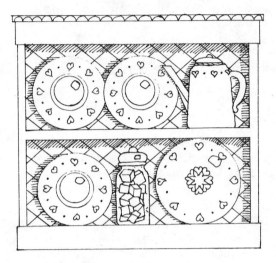

MOCHA PEANUT CLUSTERS

Power: MEDIUM/HIGH
Microwave Time: 3 Minutes

> 1 **cup semisweet chocolate morsels**
> ⅓ **cup butter or margarine**
> 16 **large marshmallows**
> 1 **tablespoon instant coffee granules**
> 2 **cups salted peanuts**

Place chocolate morsels in a 2-quart casserole. Microwave at MEDIUM 1½ minutes to melt. Add butter and marshmallows. Microwave at HIGH 1½ minutes.
   Stir until creamy; then add instant coffee granules. Stir in peanuts. Drop by teaspoonfuls onto waxed paper. Chill until set. Store in refrigerator.
Yield: 24 pieces.

NUTTY MARSHMALLOW LOG

Power: HIGH
Microwave Time: 1½ to 2 Minutes

  1 (16-ounce) package large
     marshmallows
  ¼ cup peanut butter
  2 cups coarsely chopped peanuts
  1 cup sifted powdered sugar

Microwave marshmallows and peanut butter in a large glass bowl at HIGH 1½ to 2 minutes.

Combine peanuts and powdered sugar, reserving ½ cup mixture. Stir remaining mixture into softened marshmallows and peanut butter.

Spread reserved peanut and sugar mixture onto a sheet of waxed paper and pour marshmallow mixture on top. Shape marshmallow mixture, coated with peanut-sugar mixture, into a long roll about 2 inches in diameter. Coat with remaining peanut-sugar mixture. Cool at least an hour.

Cut into ¼- to ½-inch slices.
Yield: About 50 slices.

CRISPY CONFECTIONS

Power: HIGH
Microwave Time: 1 to 2 Minutes

  1 (14-ounce) bag caramels
  3 tablespoons water
  2 cups crisp rice cereal
  2 cups corn flakes
  1 (4-ounce) package shredded
     coconut

Combine caramels and water in a 4-cup glass measure. Microwave at HIGH 1 to 2 minutes. Stir well to combine.

Combine the cereals and coconut in a large bowl; pour caramel mixture on top. Toss until well coated. Drop by teaspoonfuls onto waxed paper.
Yield: 4 dozen pieces.

FAVORITE PRALINES

Power: HIGH
Microwave Time: 9 to 12 Minutes

  2 cups firmly packed light brown
     sugar
  ¾ cup half-and-half
  3 tablespoons butter
  1½ cups chopped pecans
  ⅛ teaspoon ground cinnamon
  ⅛ teaspoon salt

Combine sugar, half-and-half, and butter in a large mixing bowl. Microwave at HIGH 9 to 12 minutes or until a small quantity dropped in cold water forms a soft ball (235°).

Add the chopped pecans, cinnamon, and salt. Cool until lukewarm. Beat until creamy smooth. Drop by teaspoonfuls onto waxed paper.
Yield: 20 to 24 pralines.

RAISIN SNACKS

Power: HIGH
Microwave Time: 2 to 3 Minutes

  ⅓ cup butter or margarine
  4 cups miniature marshmallows
  5 cups crisp rice or wheat cereal
  1½ cups seedless raisins or currants
  1 cup roasted peanuts

Combine butter and marshmallows in a large mixing bowl. Cover with waxed paper. Microwave at HIGH 2 to 3 minutes.

Add cereal, raisins, and peanuts. Stir to combine and coat all ingredients well. Press into greased 13- x 9-inch pan. Cool; cut into squares.
Yield: 4 dozen squares.

COOKIES

Shape in cookies is very critical to good results and efficient use of the microwave oven. The best cookies to microwave are bar-shaped ones, because they can be cooked in a layer or in a ring-shaped container and cut into bars or wedges to serve.

In cookies, as in cakes, color and eye appeal can be added by using brown sugar, cinnamon, or chocolate to flavor batter. Toppings of nuts and brown sugar will add color at the end of baking. Or, glaze with a browned butter filling.

Very large cookie recipes, dropped, rolled, and sliced cookies should be cooked conventionally. However, remember to use the microwave to melt, heat, or soften ingredients which will be used in mixing.

COOKIE MAKING TIPS

Microwave cookie doughs and batters uncovered to allow the steam and excess moisture to escape. Test for doneness by inserting a toothpick in the center of the dough. Any moist spots on the top of cookies will evaporate as cooking continues after the batter is removed from the oven.

CONTAINERS

Round glass or plastic dishes, or ring-shaped shallow molds all make good cooking containers for cookies. Grease but do not flour containers for cookies. You may use either butter, vegetable shortening, or spray.

APPLE-NUT SQUARES
(Conventional Recipe)

     2 cups sugar
     ¾ cup salad oil
     3 eggs
     1 teaspoon soda
     3 cups all-purpose flour
     3 cups pared, chopped apple
     2 teaspoons vanilla extract
     1 cup chopped nuts
        Topping

Combine sugar, salad oil, eggs, soda, flour, apple, vanilla, and nuts; blend well. Spread evenly in a greased 13- x 9- x 2-inch pan. Bake at 325° for 1 hour. Spread topping evenly over top. Cool and cut into squares.

  Topping:

     ½ cup butter
     1 cup firmly packed light brown
        sugar
     ¼ cup evaporated milk

Combine all ingredients in a small saucepan. Place over low heat, and bring to a boil; cook 2 minutes.
Yield: 36 squares.

To Microwave Apple-Nut Squares

- Mix ingredients as for the conventional recipe.
- Pour into a paper towel-lined baking dish.
- Combine topping ingredients in a 1-quart glass measure. Microwave at HIGH and pour over the Apple-Nut layer.
- Top with nuts for color and eye appeal.

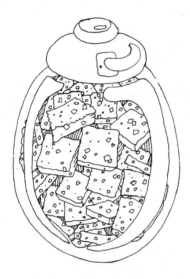

APPLE-NUT SQUARES

Power: HIGH
Microwave Time: 20 to 23 Minutes

   2   cups sugar
   ¾   cup salad oil
   3   eggs
   1   teaspoon soda
   3   cups all-purpose flour
   3   cups pared, chopped apple
   2   teaspoons vanilla extract
   ¼   cup chopped pecans

Combine sugar, oil, eggs, soda, flour, apple, and vanilla. Mix well. Spread mixture in a 13- x 9-inch glass baking dish lined with paper towels. Microwave at HIGH 16 to 18 minutes. Rotate dish ½ turn after 8 minutes. Remove from oven when done.

Topping:

   ½   cup butter or margarine
   1   cup firmly packed light brown sugar
   ¼   cup evaporated milk
   ¼   cup chopped nuts

Combine butter, light brown sugar, and evaporated milk in a 4-cup glass measure. Microwave at HIGH 4 to 5 minutes. Stir mixture at 1 minute intervals. Spread topping over apple bars. Sprinkle with nuts. Cool. Cut into squares.
   Yield: 36 squares.

APRICOT-ALMOND BARS

Power: HIGH
Microwave Time: 6 to 8 Minutes

   ¾   cup butter or margarine
   ½   cup sifted powdered sugar
   ¾   teaspoon almond extract, divided
   1   tablespoon lemon juice
   1¾ cups all-purpose flour
   ¾   cup finely chopped almonds, divided
   ¼   teaspoon salt
   1   (12-ounce) jar apricot preserves

Cream together butter, powdered sugar, ¼ teaspoon almond extract, and lemon juice. Combine flour, ½ cup chopped almonds, and salt. Stir dry ingredients into creamed mixture until crumbly. Reserve 1 cup crumb mixture for the topping.
   Pat remaining crumb mixture into an ungreased 13- x 9-inch glass baking dish.
   Combine apricot preserves and ½ teaspoon almond extract. Spread over crumb layer in the pan. Top apricot preserves layer with reserved crumb topping. Sprinkle with remaining almonds. Microwave at HIGH 6 to 8 minutes. Rotate dish ½ turn at 3 minute intervals. Let bars stand 3 to 5 minutes before cutting.
   Yield: 32 bars.

BROWNIES

Power: HIGH
Microwave Time: 6 to 7 Minutes

    1   cup sugar
    ⅔   cup butter or margarine
    2   eggs
    ½   teaspoon vanilla extract
    ½   cup cocoa
    1   cup all-purpose flour
    ½   teaspoon baking powder
        Dash of salt
    1   cup chopped nuts

Cream together sugar and butter. Add eggs and vanilla. Mix well. Combine cocoa, flour, baking powder, and salt. Blend dry ingredients into sugar mixture. Stir in nuts.

Spread mixture in an 8-inch glass baking dish. Microwave at HIGH 6 to 7 minutes. Cool. Cut into squares.

Yield: 16 squares.

CHOCOLATE CHIP BARS

Power: HIGH
Microwave Time: 5 to 7 Minutes

    ½   cup butter or margarine
    ¾   cup firmly packed brown sugar
    1   egg
    1   tablespoon milk
    1   teaspoon vanilla extract
    1   cup all-purpose flour
    ½   teaspoon baking powder
    ⅛   teaspoon salt
    ⅛   teaspoon soda
    1   (6-ounce) package semisweet
        chocolate morsels, divided

Cream butter and brown sugar together until light and fluffy in a small mixer bowl. Add egg, milk, and vanilla. Beat well.

Combine flour, baking powder, salt, and soda. Add to the sugar mixture. Stir in ½ cup chocolate morsels. Pour the batter into a greased 8-inch square baking dish. Sprinkle with remaining chocolate morsels.

Microwave at HIGH 3 minutes. Rotate dish ¼ turn. Microwave at HIGH 2 to 4 minutes, rotating ½ turn after 2 minutes. Let stand directly on the counter to cool before cutting into bars.

Yield: 25 bars.

CHOCOLATE-MINT BARS

Power: MEDIUM/HIGH
Microwave Time: 9 to 11 Minutes

    2   (1-ounce) squares unsweetened
        chocolate
    ½   cup butter or margarine
    1   cup sugar
    2   eggs, beaten
    ¼   teaspoon peppermint extract
    ½   cup all-purpose flour
    ⅛   teaspoon salt
    2   tablespoons butter
    1¼ cups powdered sugar
    ½   to 1 tablespoon milk
    1½ squares unsweetened chocolate
    1½ tablespoons butter

Combine 2 squares chocolate and ½ cup butter in a 1½-quart casserole. Microwave at MEDIUM 2 to 3 minutes. Stir to blend well. Add sugar, eggs, and peppermint extract. Blend well. Mix in flour and salt. Spread batter in greased 8-inch square baking dish. Microwave at HIGH 5 to 6 minutes. Cool.

For second layer, combine 2 tablespoons butter, powdered sugar, and milk in a small bowl. Beat until smooth. Spread icing over cooled bars. Chill thoroughly.

Combine remaining chocolate and 1½ tablespoons butter in a 1-cup glass measure. Microwave at MEDIUM 2 minutes. Stir to blend and drizzle over the cooled bars. Chill. Cut into bars to serve.

Yield: 25 bars.

CREME-FILLED CHOCOLATE COOKIES

Power: HIGH
Microwave Time: 1½ Minutes for 2
  single cookies; 3½ to 4 Minutes for
  12 single cookies

  ¾ **cup butter or margarine**
  ¾ **cup sugar**
  1 **egg**
  1¾ **cups all-purpose flour**
  ½ **teaspoon salt**
  1 **teaspoon baking powder**
  2 **tablespoons cocoa**
  ½ **teaspoon vanilla extract**
     Sugar
     Vanilla Creme Icing

Microwave butter in a 2½-quart glass mixing bowl at HIGH 30 seconds. Blend in sugar and egg. Add flour, salt, baking powder, cocoa, and vanilla. Chill, if necessary, for easier handling.

Shape dough into twenty-four 1-inch balls. Place 1 inch apart on waxed paper. Flatten each ball with bottom of a glass dipped in sugar.

Microwave 2 cookies, uncovered, at HIGH 1 minute. Microwave 12 cookies at HIGH 3 to 3½ minutes. Cool completely. Fill between two cookies with Vanilla Creme Icing.

Yield: 12 cookie sandwiches.

Vanilla Creme Icing:

Power: HIGH
Microwave Time: 3 to 5 Minutes

  1 **cup milk**
  5 **tablespoons all-purpose flour**
  ½ **cup butter or margarine**
  1 **cup sugar**
  ½ **cup shortening**
  1 **teaspoon vanilla extract**
     Dash of salt

Combine milk and flour in a 4-cup glass measure. Microwave at HIGH 3 to 5 minutes. Stir at 1 minute intervals. Cool.

Add butter, sugar, shortening, vanilla, and salt. Beat until fluffy.

Use as filling between two chocolate cookies.

Yield: filling for 12 cookie sandwiches or icing for 12 cupcakes.

WARM COFFEE BARS

Power: HIGH/LOW
Microwave Time: 11 to 14 Minutes

  ½ **cup water**
  ½ **teaspoon instant coffee granules**
  1½ **cups all-purpose flour**
  ½ **teaspoon soda**
  ½ **teaspoon salt**
  1 **cup firmly packed dark brown
     sugar**
  1 **egg**
  ½ **cup salad oil**
  1 **teaspoon vanilla extract**
  ½ **cup chopped pecans**
  1 **(6-ounce) package semisweet
     chocolate morsels**

Microwave water and coffee in a 1-cup glass measure at HIGH 1 to 2 minutes.

Combine coffee, flour, soda, salt, brown sugar, egg, oil, and vanilla. Spread batter in a greased 12- x 8-inch glass baking dish. Sprinkle nuts and chocolate morsels over mixture. Microwave at LOW 7 to 8 minutes. Rotate dish ½ turn. Microwave at HIGH 3 to 4 minutes. Cool. Cut into bars.

Yield: 24 bars.

GINGER-MINCEMEAT BARS

Power: MEDIUM
Microwave Time: 14 Minutes

> 1 (14-ounce) package gingerbread
>   mix
> 1 cup prepared mincemeat
> ¼ cup water
> 1 can ready-to-spread lemon
>   frosting

Combine gingerbread mix, mincemeat, and water. Beat until smooth. Spread mixture in a greased 12- x 8-inch glass baking dish.

Microwave at MEDIUM 14 minutes. Rotate dish ½ turn at 5 minute intervals. Let gingerbread stand 5 minutes.

Cool completely before icing with lemon frosting.

Yield: 24 bars.

GRAHAM CRACKER BARS

Power: HIGH
Microwave Time: 6 to 7 Minutes

> 2 cups finely crushed graham
>   cracker crumbs
> ⅔ cup sugar
> 3 tablespoons butter or margarine
> ½ cup semisweet chocolate morsels
> ¼ cup chopped nuts
> ⅔ cup evaporated milk
> 1 teaspoon vanilla extract

Mix graham cracker crumbs and sugar. Cut in butter. Stir in chocolate morsels and nuts. Mix in milk and vanilla.

Spread mixture in an 8-inch greased microwave tube pan. Microwave at HIGH 6 to 7 minutes. Rotate dish ¼ turn at 2 minute intervals. Cool. Cut into wedge-shape bars.

Yield: 24 bars.

LEMON BARS

Power: HIGH
Microwave Time: 9 to 12 Minutes

> ½ cup butter
> ¼ cup powdered sugar
> 1 cup all-purpose flour plus 2
>   tablespoons, divided
> 3 eggs, beaten
> ¼ teaspoon salt
> 1 cup sugar
> ¼ cup lemon juice
> 1 tablespoon grated lemon rind
> ½ teaspoon baking powder
>   Powdered sugar

Cream butter and powdered sugar. Add 1 cup flour. Pat dough ⅛ inch thick into a 12- x 8-inch baking dish. Microwave at HIGH 3 to 4 minutes. Rotate dish ½ turn after 2 minutes. Cool.

Mix beaten eggs, salt, sugar, lemon juice, lemon rind, 2 tablespoons flour, and baking powder. Pour mixture over crust. Microwave at HIGH 6 to 8 minutes. Rotate dish ¼ turn at 2 minute intervals.

Garnish with powdered sugar. Cut into bars. Serve warm.

Yield: 16 bars.

CRUNCH SQUARES

Power: HIGH
Microwave Time: 1½ Minutes

> ¼ cup butter or margarine
> 3 cups miniature marshmallows
> 5 cups honey graham cereal
> 1 cup roasted peanuts

Microwave butter in a 2½-quart glass casserole at HIGH 30 seconds. Add marshmallows. Microwave at HIGH 1 minute. Stir mixture to blend marshmallows. Add cereal and peanuts.

Press mixture into a 9-inch square pan. Chill for twenty minutes. Cut in squares.

Yield: 25 squares.

THREE-LAYER BARS

Power: HIGH/MEDIUM-HIGH
Microwave Time: 11 to 12 Minutes

  ½   **cup butter or margarine**
  1   **cup plus 2 tablespoons**
        all-purpose flour, divided
  ½   **to 1 egg white, unbeaten**
  1½ **cups firmly packed brown sugar**
  2   **eggs, beaten**
  ¼   **teaspoon baking powder**
  ½   **teaspoon salt**
  1   **cup chopped nuts**
  ½   **cup flaked coconut**
  1   **teaspoon vanilla extract**
        Orange Lemon Icing

Combine butter and 1 cup flour. Work until smooth. Add only enough egg white to make the mixture hold together. Pat into a thin layer in the bottom of a 12- x 8-inch baking dish.

Press waxed paper directly on the mixture to cover; then place a smaller oblong baking dish on the waxed paper. Microwave at HIGH 3 minutes.

Remove smaller dish and waxed paper. Rotate the dish ½ turn. Microwave at HIGH 3 minutes.

Combine brown sugar, eggs, 2 tablespoons flour, baking powder, and salt. Add nuts, coconut, and vanilla. Spread evenly over the crust layer. Microwave at MEDIUM-HIGH 5 to 6 minutes. Rotate dish ½ turn after 3 minutes. Let stand directly on the counter to cool. Spread with Orange Lemon Icing when completely cooled.
Yield: 36 to 48 bars.

Orange Lemon Icing:

Power: HIGH
Microwave Time: 30 seconds

  2   **tablespoons butter or margarine**
  1½ **cups powdered sugar**
  2   **tablespoons orange juice**
  1   **teaspoon lemon juice**

Place butter in small mixing bowl. Microwave at HIGH 30 seconds to melt. Add powdered sugar, orange juice, and lemon juice. Stir until smooth. Spread over cooled cake or bar cookies.
Yield: icing for one 12- x 8-inch layer.

PEANUT BUTTER BARS

Power: HIGH/MEDIUM
Microwave Time: 5½ to 7½ Minutes

  ½   **cup butter or margarine**
  1   **cup firmly packed brown sugar**
  ½   **cup smooth peanut butter**
  1   **egg, slightly beaten**
  1½ **cups all-purpose flour**
  1   **teaspoon baking powder**
  ¼   **teaspoon salt**
  1   **cup roasted peanuts, chopped**

Microwave butter in a 2-quart casserole at HIGH 30 seconds to soften. Add brown sugar, peanut butter, and egg. Mix well.

Combine flour, baking powder, and salt in a bowl. Add flour and peanuts to brown sugar mixture. Stir until smooth.

Pour into greased 8-inch square baking dish. Microwave at MEDIUM 5 to 7 minutes. Rotate dish ½ turn after 3 minutes. Let stand directly on the counter to cool slightly before cutting into bars.
Yield: 25 bars.

FUDGE-FILLED
PEANUT BUTTER BARS

Power: HIGH/MEDIUM
Microwave Time: 13 to 14 Minutes

½ cup plus 2 tablespoons butter or
    margarine, divided
1 (17½- to 18-ounce) package
    yellow cake mix
1 cup peanut butter
2 eggs
1 (6-ounce) package semisweet
    chocolate morsels
1 (14-ounce) can sweetened
    condensed milk
1 (10-ounce) package coconut
    pecan frosting mix

Microwave ½ cup butter in a 2½-quart glass casserole at HIGH 1 minute. Add cake mix, peanut butter, and eggs. Mix together to form a soft dough. Press dough into the bottom of a 13- x 9-inch glass baking dish.

Microwave chocolate morsels, milk, and 2 tablespoons butter in a 4-cup glass measure at HIGH 1 minute. Stir.

Spread chocolate mixture over dough. Microwave at HIGH 5 minutes. Rotate dish ½ turn. Microwave at MEDIUM 6 to 7 minutes. Cool. Prepare coconut pecan frosting according to directions and frost before cutting.

Yield: 36 bars.

CRUNCHY PEANUT BUTTER-
CHOCOLATE SQUARES

Power: HIGH
Microwave Time: 3½ to 5 Minutes

1 (6-ounce) package semisweet
    chocolate morsels
1 cup light corn syrup, divided
2 tablespoons butter or margarine
4 cups crispy rice or wheat cereal,
    divided
½ cup smooth peanut butter
1 teaspoon vanilla extract
¼ teaspoon salt

Place chocolate morsels, ½ cup corn syrup, and butter in a 2-quart casserole. Microwave at HIGH 2 to 3 minutes. Stir well after 1 minute.

Stir in 2 cups of cereal. Press mixture into a buttered 9-inch square pan.

Combine remaining corn syrup, peanut butter, vanilla, and salt in the 2-quart casserole. Microwave at HIGH 1½ to 2 minutes. Stir after 1 minute.

Stir in remaining cereal. Spread over the chocolate mixture. Cool slightly and chill at least 1 hour before cutting.

Yield: 16 to 20 squares.

PUMPKIN BARS

Power: HIGH/MEDIUM-HIGH
Microwave Time: 10 Minutes

1 (17½- to 18-ounce) package spice
    cake mix, divided
½ cup butter or margarine
3 eggs, divided
1 cup canned pumpkin
½ cup sugar
½ teaspoon grated orange rind
    Dash of salt
½ cup chopped pecans

Measure ⅔ cup dry batter mixture from cake mix. Reserve.

Microwave butter mixture in a 2½-quart glass casserole at HIGH 1 minute. Add remaining dry cake mix and 1 egg. Blend well. Pat mixture into a greased 12- x 8-inch glass baking dish. Microwave at MEDIUM-HIGH 5 minutes. Rotate dish ½ turn after 2½ minutes.

Combine reserved cake mix, pumpkin, sugar, 2 eggs, orange rind, and salt in a large mixer bowl. Beat well. Pour cake batter over first layer. Sprinkle batter with pecans. Microwave at MEDIUM-HIGH 4 minutes. Cover with waxed paper. Cool before serving.

Yield: 24 squares.

RAISIN OR DATE MUMBLES

Power: HIGH
Microwave Time: 11 to 13 Minutes

- ¾ cup butter or margarine
- 1 cup firmly packed brown sugar
- 1¾ cups all-purpose flour
- ½ teaspoon salt
- ½ teaspoon soda
- 1½ cups rolled oats, uncooked
- 2½ cups raisins or dates
- ½ cup sugar
- 2 tablespoons cornstarch
- ¾ cup water
- 3 tablespoons lemon juice

Combine butter, brown sugar, flour, salt, soda, and rolled oats. Press one half of mixture in the bottom of a greased 12- x 8-inch glass baking dish. Reserve remaining half of mixture.

Microwave raisins, sugar, cornstarch, water, and lemon juice in a 2-quart glass casserole at HIGH 5 to 6 minutes. Stir mixture at 1½ minute intervals. Cool.

Spread raisin filling over first layer in baking dish. Pat reserved dry mixture over filling. Microwave at HIGH 6 to 7 minutes. Cool. Cut into squares.

Yield: 24 squares.

WHEAT GERM-CARROT BARS

Power: MEDIUM
Microwave Time: 12 to 14 Minutes

- 1 cup all-purpose flour
- 1 cup plain wheat germ
- 1½ teaspoons baking powder
- ¾ teaspoon salt
- 1 cup sugar
- ⅔ cup butter or margarine
- 2 cups grated carrot
- 2 eggs
- 1 teaspoon vanilla extract
- ¾ cup flaked coconut
- ¾ cup chopped walnuts

Combine flour, wheat germ, baking powder, and salt.

Cream sugar and butter. Add carrot, eggs, and vanilla. Beat well. Blend wheat germ mixture into sugar mixture. Stir in coconut and walnuts.

Spread batter in a greased 13- x 9-inch pan. Microwave at MEDIUM 12 to 14 minutes. Rotate dish ½ turn after 7 minutes. Cool before cutting into squares.

Yield: 36 squares.

DESERTS

If desserts are your weakness now, with a microwave oven you will be in double trouble. Imagine being able to cook a fruit crisp in 12 to 15 minutes, cook a pudding in 5 or 6 minutes with minimal stirring . . . or make really easy baked apples in less than 5 minutes. All of these are possible with a microwave oven.

MICROWAVING CUSTARDS

Because of the delicate ingredients in custards, microwave cooking will usually be done at a MEDIUM power setting to avoid boiling and overcooking. If your oven has only two power settings, start these foods on HIGH, then lower the setting to complete cooking.

Stirring will keep the heated and un-heated portions of puddings and custards well combined. Stir well once or twice to prevent lumps and curdling. A 4-cup glass measure is just the right size container for *most* puddings and stirred custards.

Individual baked custards can be microwaved. Fill custard cups ½ full and arrange in a circle. Microwave at ME-DIUM-LOW and rearrange the cups at least once during cooking. Remove the custards as they cook. Custards should be firm around the edge but shaky in the center. The center will firm as the custards stand and cool.

CHOCOLATE PUDDING
(Conventional Recipe)

      4 cups milk, divided
      4 tablespoons cocoa
      4 tablespoons cornstarch
 1½ cups sugar
      4 eggs, beaten
      1 teaspoon vanilla extract

Heat milk. Combine cocoa and cornstarch. Add a small amount of milk, stirring until smooth. Add sugar and cocoa mixture to heated milk, blending well; then stir in beaten eggs. Bring to a boil, remove from heat, and add vanilla.

Yield: 8 servings.

To Microwave Chocolate Pudding

- Cut ingredients in half. Four servings are quick and easy to microwave.
- Measure milk in a 4-cup glass measure and microwave to scald.
- Add salt to the microwave recipe.
- Combine dry ingredients; stir into the heated milk.
- Add the beaten egg.
- Microwave until thickened.

CHOCOLATE PUDDING

Power: HIGH
Microwave Time: 5 to 8 Minutes

    2 cups milk
    ¾ cup sugar
    2 tablespoons cocoa
    2 tablespoons cornstarch
    ¼ teaspoon salt
    2 eggs, beaten
    ½ teaspoon vanilla extract

Microwave milk in a 4-cup glass measure at HIGH 2 to 3 minutes. Combine sugar, cocoa, cornstarch, and salt in a bowl. Stir into the hot milk mixture; then add the beaten eggs. Microwave at HIGH 3 to 5 minutes or until thickened. Stir once or twice. Add vanilla. Pour into serving dishes and chill before serving.
    Yield: 4 servings.

YOGURT CHOCOLATE MOUSSE

Power: HIGH
Microwave Time: 4 to 5 Minutes

    2 (1-ounce) squares unsweetened
         chocolate
    1 (14-ounce) can sweetened
         condensed milk
    1 teaspoon vanilla extract
    1 (8-ounce) carton commercial
         vanilla or coffee yogurt
    1 (16-ounce) container non-dairy
         whipped topping, divided
    1 baked 9-inch pastry shell
         (optional)

Microwave chocolate squares in a 4-cup glass measure at HIGH 1 to 2 minutes. Stir in milk and vanilla. Microwave at HIGH 3 minutes. Stir mixture at 1 minute intervals. Cool pudding mixture completely.
    Fold in yogurt and ¾ of the non-dairy whipped topping. Pour mixture into a pastry shell, if desired, or individual serving dishes. Garnish with remaining non-dairy whipped topping.
    Yield: one 9-inch pie.

APPLE CRUMB PUDDING

Power: HIGH
Microwave Time: 13 to 14 Minutes

    ⅓ cup butter or margarine
    1 (1-pound) can applesauce
    2 cups toasted bread crumbs
    3 eggs, separated
    ½ teaspoon ground cinnamon
    ⅔ cup sugar, divided
    ⅛ teaspoon salt
    ⅛ teaspoon cream of tartar
    ½ teaspoon vanilla extract

Microwave butter in a 2-quart glass casserole at HIGH 1 minute. Combine butter, applesauce, bread crumbs, beaten egg yolks, cinnamon, and ⅓ cup sugar. Cover with waxed paper. Microwave at HIGH 10 minutes. Stir after 5 minutes.
    Beat egg whites until foamy. Add salt and cream of tartar. When soft peak stage is reached, slowly beat in remaining sugar and vanilla. Beat until stiff. Meringue should be glossy not dry. Spread meringue over pudding in casserole. Microwave at HIGH 2 minutes and 45 seconds. Rotate dish ½ turn after 1 minute. Serve immediately.
    Yield: 6 to 8 servings.

COMPANY BREAD PUDDING

Power: HIGH/MEDIUM
Microwave Time: 9 to 10 Minutes

- ½ cup cocoa
- ⅔ cup sugar
- 2 cups milk
- 3 eggs
- 1½ cups stale white bread, trimmed and crumbled
- 1 teaspoon vanilla extract
  Whipped cream

Combine cocoa and sugar in a mixing bowl. Gradually stir in milk. Add eggs one at a time, beating well after each addition. Stir in bread crumbs and vanilla. Pour into a buttered 1½-quart casserole.

Microwave at HIGH 2 minutes. Stir well. Microwave at MEDIUM 7 to 8 minutes. Let stand 3 to 5 minutes. Serve warm or chilled with whipped cream.

Yield: 6 servings.

OLD-TIME BREAD PUDDING

Power: HIGH/MEDIUM
Microwave Time: 11 to 13 Minutes

- 4 slices buttered bread, toasted
- 2 eggs, lightly beaten
- ½ cup sugar, divided
- ⅛ teaspoon salt
- 1 cup evaporated milk
- 1 cup boiling water
- ½ cup seedless raisins
- 1 teaspoon vanilla extract
- ½ teaspoon ground cinnamon

Cut the toast into cubes and place in a greased 2-quart baking dish.

Combine eggs, ¼ cup sugar, salt, milk, water, raisins, and vanilla in a glass bowl or 4-cup measure. Microwave at HIGH 1 minute. Pour over the bread cubes. Sprinkle with remaining sugar and cinnamon. Microwave at HIGH 2 minutes. Stir thoroughly. Rotate dish ¼ turn. Microwave at MEDIUM 8 to 10 minutes. Let stand directly on counter to cool.

Yield: 6 to 8 servings.

COTTAGE PUDDING

Power: HIGH
Microwave Time: 6 to 7 minutes

- ¼ cup shortening
- 1 cup sugar
- 1 egg
- ¼ teaspoon lemon extract
- 1¾ cups all-purpose flour
- 2½ teaspoons baking powder
- ½ teaspoon salt
- ½ teaspoon ground nutmeg
- ½ teaspoon ground cinnamon
- ⅔ cup milk
  Fruit sauce, custard, or whipped cream

Cream the shortening and sugar in a bowl. Add the egg and lemon extract. Beat well.

Sift flour, baking powder, salt, nutmeg, and cinnamon. Add to the creamed mixture alternately with the milk. Beat well after each addition. Pour into 10-inch round casserole. Microwave at HIGH 6 to 7 minutes. Let stand directly on the counter to cool.

Serve warm or cold with fruit sauce, custard, or whipped cream.

Yield: 6 to 8 servings.

PEACH PUDDING

Power: HIGH
Microwave Time: 8 to 10 Minutes

- 1½ cups sugar
- 3 eggs, beaten
- ¾ cup all-purpose flour
- 2 teaspoons baking powder
- ¼ teaspoon salt
- 2 cups sliced fresh peaches
- 1 teaspoon vanilla extract
- ¾ cup chopped pecans
  Whipped cream or ice cream

Add sugar to beaten eggs and mix well. Sift flour, baking powder, and salt together. Add to egg mixture. Stir just enough to mix. Add peaches and vanilla. Stir lightly. Pour into a buttered 2-quart casserole. Sprinkle chopped pecans on top. Cover with waxed paper. Microwave at HIGH 8 to 10 minutes. Rotate dish ½ turn after 4 minutes.

Serve warm with whipped cream or ice cream.

Yield: 6 servings.

PUDDING FROM A MIX

Power: HIGH
Microwave Time: 5 to 6½ minutes

    1   (3½-ounce) package pudding
          and pie filling
    2   cups milk
    1   baked 9-inch pastry shell
          (optional)

Empty package mix into a 1-quart glass bowl or glass measure. Add enough milk to dissolve pudding; then stir in remaining milk.

Microwave at HIGH 2 to 2½ minutes. Stir to blend well. Microwave at HIGH 3 to 4 minutes longer or until pudding has thickened. Stir well once or twice.

Pour into individual dessert dishes or a baked pastry shell to serve.

Yield: 4 servings.

SOUTHERN RICE PUDDING

Power: HIGH/MEDIUM-LOW
Microwave Time: 20 to 22 Minutes

    2   eggs
    1   (13-ounce) can evaporated milk
    ¾   cup water
    ¾   cup seedless raisins
    ½   cup sugar
    1   teaspoon vanilla extract
    ¼   teaspoon salt
    ½   teaspoon ground cinnamon
    3   cups cooked long grain rice

Combine eggs, milk, water, raisins, sugar, vanilla, salt, and cinnamon in a 2-quart casserole. Stir in rice.

Cover with plastic wrap. Microwave at HIGH 2 minutes. Stir well. Rotate dish ½ turn. Cover. Microwave at MEDIUM-LOW 10 minutes. Stir well. Rotate dish ½ turn. Cover. Microwave at MEDIUM-LOW 8 to 10 minutes. Let stand, covered, 5 to 10 minutes before serving.

Serve warm or chilled.

Yield: 6 to 8 servings.

SURPRISE PUDDING

Power: HIGH/MEDIUM
Microwave Time: 10 to 13 Minutes

    2   cups milk
    3   cups crumbled stale cake
          doughnuts
    ¼   cup butter or margarine, melted
    2   eggs, slightly beaten
    ¼   teaspoon salt
    ½   teaspoon ground cinnamon
    ½   cup seedless raisins

Measure milk into a 4-cup glass measure. Microwave at HIGH 3 to 4 minutes to scald.

Combine doughnut crumbs, butter, eggs, salt, cinnamon, and raisins in a 2-quart casserole. Pour scalded milk over mixture and stir well. Cover with waxed paper.

Microwave at HIGH 2 minutes. Rotate dish ½ turn. Microwave at MEDIUM 5 to 7 minutes. Let stand, covered, 5 minutes to cool slightly and firm.

Yield: 6 servings.

Micronote: Use the microwave oven to heat liqueurs for flaming. Place brandy into a small glass bowl or measuring cup. Microwave at HIGH 15 to 30 seconds. Remove from oven and pour over dessert or other food to flame.

GRATED SWEET POTATO PUDDING ★

Power: HIGH
Microwave Time: 16½ to 18 Minutes

    4 cups grated raw sweet potatoes
    1 cup dark corn syrup
    1 cup sugar
    1 cup milk
    1 teaspoon ground allspice
    ½ teaspoon ground cloves
    ½ cup chopped pecans
    1 cup seedless raisins
    1 teaspoon ground cinnamon
    ½ cup butter or margarine
    3 eggs, beaten
       Half-and-half

Combine sweet potatoes, corn syrup, sugar, milk, allspice, cloves, pecans, raisins, and cinnamon in a 3-quart glass casserole.

Microwave butter in a 1-cup glass measure at HIGH ½ to 1 minute. Pour melted butter over the sweet potato mixture.

Stir in eggs. Cover. Microwave at HIGH 7 minutes. Stir. Uncover. Microwave at HIGH 9 to 10 minutes. Serve warm with half-and-half.

Yield: 8 servings.

SPICED APRICOTS

Power: HIGH
Microwave Time: 13 to 16 Minutes

    1 pound dried apricots
  1½ cups water
    ¼ cup firmly packed brown sugar
    6 whole cloves
    ¼ teaspoon ground cinnamon

Combine apricots, water, sugar, cloves, and cinnamon in a 1½-quart casserole. Stir well. Cover with plastic wrap.

Microwave at HIGH 7 to 8 minutes. Rotate dish ½ turn. Microwave 6 to 8 additional minutes at HIGH or until apricots are tender. Let stand, covered, 4 to 5 minutes before serving.

Serve warm or chilled.
Yield: 4 to 6 servings.

FRESH APPLESAUCE

Power: HIGH
Microwave Time: 6 to 8 Minutes

    6 to 8 medium-sized cooking apples, peeled, cored, and thinly sliced
    ¼ cup water
    ⅓ to ½ cup firmly packed brown sugar
    ⅛ teaspoon salt
    ½ teaspoon ground cinnamon

Combine apples and water in a 1½-quart casserole. Cover with plastic wrap. Microwave at HIGH 6 to 8 minutes, or until apples are tender.

Stir to break the apples apart. Add desired amount of sugar, salt, and cinnamon. Cool.

Yield: about 4 cups.

Micronote: This produces a chunky applesauce. If a finer texture is desired, process in the blender or in a food processor.

COFFEE PARFAIT

Power: HIGH
Microwave Time: 2 to 3 Minutes

    1 cup strong coffee
    1 (16-ounce) package miniature marshmallows
    1 cup whipping cream, whipped
    1 cup chopped nuts

Combine coffee and marshmallows in a large glass mixing bowl. Microwave at HIGH 2 to 3 minutes. Stir to mix well.

Cool to room temperature. Fold into whipped cream. Arrange in layers with the nuts in parfait glasses. Chill before serving.
Yield: 8 servings.

Basic Cheesecake (p.92) becomes an even more delicious dessert when Cherry Topping is added.

BASIC CUSTARD

Power: HIGH/MEDIUM
Microwave Time: 9 to 11 Minutes

½ cup sugar
3 tablespoons all-purpose flour
¼ teaspoon salt
3 cups milk
4 eggs, well beaten
1 teaspoon vanilla extract

Combine sugar, flour, and salt in a 2½-quart casserole. Blend thoroughly. Gradually stir in milk. Microwave at HIGH 4 to 5 minutes or until thick. Stir well at 1 minute intervals.

Add some of the hot custard to beaten eggs. Gradually stir the egg mixture into the hot custard. Add vanilla. Microwave at MEDIUM 5 to 6 minutes, stirring well at least twice. Serve as individual custards or use with recipes calling for cooked pudding.

Yield: 8 servings or 4 cups.

SNOW EGGS WITH CUSTARD SAUCE

Power: HIGH/MEDIUM
Microwave Time: 5½ to 8 Minutes

2 cups milk
3 eggs, separated
½ cup sugar, divided
⅛ teaspoon salt

Measure milk in a 4-cup glass measure. Microwave at HIGH 2 minutes.

Beat egg yolks and ¼ cup sugar in a bowl. Slowly stir in part of the hot milk. Add the egg yolk mixture to the hot milk in the cup.

Microwave at MEDIUM 2 to 4 minutes or until thickened slightly. *Do not boil*. Stir well at 1 minute intervals. Pour into a serving dish.

Fantastic Chocolate Pie (p.141) is perfect for dessert lovers everywhere and is easy to serve anytime. Garnish with whipped cream and grated chocolate.

Cut a grocery bag to a 12- x 14-inch double layered piece. Top with a piece of waxed paper.

Beat egg whites until stiff. Gradually beat in salt and remaining ¼ cup sugar. Beat until whites are stiff and glossy. Drop in oval egg-shaped mounds onto waxed paper.

Microwave at HIGH 1½ to 2 minutes. Meringue mounds will be firm and puffy when done. Drop the cooked meringues onto the custard sauce. Cool before serving in dessert bowls.

Yield: 6 servings.

CARAMEL CUSTARD

Power: HIGH/MEDIUM-LOW
Microwave Time: 18 to 22 Minutes

1 cup sugar
1 tablespoon water
3 whole eggs
5 egg yolks
2 (13-ounce) cans evaporated milk
⅔ cup sugar
2 teaspoons vanilla extract
½ teaspoon salt

Place 1 cup sugar and water in an 8-inch glass baking dish. Microwave, uncovered, at HIGH 8 minutes. Stir often until sugar turns light brown. Rotate pan until bottom is completely covered with caramel.

Mix remaining ingredients in a large bowl until well blended. Pour egg mixture into caramel-coated dish. Microwave, uncovered, at HIGH 2 minutes. Stir lightly with a rubber spatula to move heated portion toward center of the dish. Microwave at MEDIUM-LOW 4 to 6 minutes. Rotate dish ½ turn. Microwave at MEDIUM-LOW 4 to 6 minutes or until done.

Custard is done when a knife inserted near center comes out clear. Let stand directly on the counter to cool. Chill thoroughly to serve.

Yield: 6 to 8 servings.

BAKED CUSTARD

Power: HIGH
Microwave Time: 7 Minutes

  3   eggs, slightly beaten
  4   tablespoons sugar
  ¼   teaspoon salt
  ½   teaspoon vanilla extract
  1⅔ cups milk
  1½ cups boiling water

Combine eggs, sugar, salt, and vanilla in a
1-quart casserole. Mix well. Microwave
milk in a 4-cup glass measure at HIGH 2
minutes. Stir slowly into the egg mixture.
Pour 1½ cups boiling water into a 2-quart
casserole. Place the 1-quart casserole containing custard in the boiling water. Cover
the 1-quart casserole with waxed paper.
Microwave at HIGH 5 minutes. Let stand,
covered, until cool. Center of custard will
become firm upon cooling.
　　Yield: 6 servings.

GRAHAM-MARSHMALLOW
CUSTARD

Power: HIGH/MEDIUM-HIGH
Microwave Time: 10 to 11 Minutes

  1½ cups milk, scalded
  3   double honey graham crackers
  2   eggs, beaten
  3   tablespoons sugar
  ¼   teaspoon salt
  ½   teaspoon vanilla extract
  8   large marshmallows, quartered

Measure milk in a 2-cup glass measure or
glass mixing bowl. Microwave at HIGH 4
minutes.
　　Crumble the graham crackers into a mixing bowl. Pour the hot milk over crackers.
　　Combine eggs, sugar, salt, and vanilla.
Stir into the milk and crackers. Fold in
marshmallows. Pour into a 9-inch round
baking dish or casserole. Microwave at
MEDIUM-HIGH 3 minutes. Rotate dish ¼
turn. Microwave at MEDIUM-HIGH 3 to 4
minutes. Let stand 5 minutes. Serve either
warm or cold.
　　Yield: 6 servings.

BASIC CHEESECAKE

Power: HIGH/MEDIUM
Microwave Time: 22 to 27 Minutes

  ¼   cup butter or margarine
  1½ tablespoons sugar
  1   cup fine crumbs (graham
        crackers or vanilla wafers)
  ¼   teaspoon ground nutmeg
  2   (8-ounce) packages cream
        cheese, softened
  ¾   cup sugar
  3   eggs
  1   tablespoon fresh lemon juice
  ½   teaspoon vanilla extract

Microwave butter at HIGH 1 minute to melt
in an 8-inch round glass cake pan. Stir in 1½
tablespoons sugar, crumbs, and nutmeg.
Press mixture evenly on bottom and sides
of dish. Microwave at HIGH 2 minutes.
Cool slightly and chill.
　　Beat cream cheese until fluffy. Add ¾
cup sugar, eggs, lemon juice, and vanilla.
Beat well. Pour into chilled crust.
　　Microwave at MEDIUM 20 to 25 minutes.
Rotate dish ¼ turn at 5 to 6 minute inter-
vals. Center will be slightly soft, but will
firm when chilled.
　　To serve, top with any of the topping
ideas given.
　　Yield: one 8-inch cheesecake.

Cherry Cheesecake:

  1   (16-ounce) can whole cherry pie
        filling

Spread pie filling over the cooked, chilled
cheesecake. Chill thoroughly before
serving.

Strawberry Cheesecake:

  1½ cups ripe firm whole
        strawberries
        Strawberry Topping (see p. 167)

Arrange whole strawberries over the cheesecake. Pour cooked topping over the strawberries. Chill thoroughly before serving.

Melba Cheesecake:

Pour Melba Sauce (see p. 166) over individual servings.

BLACK FOREST CHEESECAKE
Power: HIGH/MEDIUM-HIGH
Microwave Time: 7 to 8½ Minutes

Crust:

- 1 cup crushed chocolate wafers
- 2 tablespoons sugar
- ¼ cup butter

Mix crushed chocolate wafers and sugar. Cut in butter until mixture resembles fine meal. Line the bottom of a 9-inch glass pie plate with crumb mixture. Microwave at HIGH 2 minutes. Rotate dish after 1 minute. Cool.

Filling:

- 4 (3-ounce) packages cream cheese, softened
- 2 eggs
- ½ cup sugar
- 1 teaspoon vanilla extract
- ⅓ cup semisweet chocolate morsels
- 1 (22-ounce) can cherry pie filling
  Whipped cream
  Maraschino cherries

Cream together cream cheese, eggs, sugar, and vanilla until light and fluffy.

Microwave chocolate morsels in a 1-cup glass measure at HIGH 1 to 1½ minutes. Lightly swirl melted chocolate into cream cheese mixture. Pour filling over crumb mixture. Microwave at MEDIUM-HIGH 4 to 5 minutes. Rotate dish ¼ turn at 1 minute intervals. Outer edge of filling should be set. Cool to room temperature.

Spread cherry pie filling over cream cheese mixture. Chill thoroughly before serving.

Garnish with whipped cream and maraschino cherries.
Yield: one 9-inch pie.

MARBLE CHEESECAKE
Power: HIGH/MEDIUM/
MEDIUM-HIGH
Microwave Time: 9½ to 11½ Minutes

- ¼ cup butter or margarine
- 1 cup crushed vanilla wafer crumbs
- ¼ cup sugar
- 4 (3-ounce) packages cream cheese, softened
- 2 eggs
- ½ cup sugar
- 1 teaspoon vanilla extract
- ⅓ cup semisweet chocolate morsels

Place butter in a 9-inch glass pie plate. Microwave at HIGH 30 seconds to melt. Stir the crumbs and ¼ cup sugar into the melted butter. Press evenly over sides and bottom of the pie plate. Microwave at HIGH 1 to 2 minutes. Rotate ½ turn after 1 minute. Let crust cool while preparing filling.

Combine cream cheese, eggs, ½ cup sugar, and vanilla in a large mixer bowl. Beat until smooth and creamy. Pour the cream cheese mixture into the cooked pie shell.

Measure chocolate morsels in a 1-cup glass measure or custard cup. Microwave at MEDIUM 2 to 3 minutes. Stir to blend. Spoon in "dabs" over the filling. Swirl the chocolate lightly into the filling with a fork.

Microwave at MEDIUM-HIGH 3 minutes. Rotate ¼ turn. Microwave at MEDIUM-HIGH 3 minutes. Let stand to cool slightly.
Yield: one 9-inch pie.

PEACH ALMONDINE ★

Power: HIGH
Microwave Time: 5 to 6 Minutes

 1 **tablespoon water**
 ¼ **cup sugar**
 1 **(3-ounce) package slivered almonds**
 1 **(29-ounce) can peach halves, drained**
 1 **teaspoon lemon juice**
 2 **tablespoons dry sherry**
 ½ **teaspoon ground cinnamon**
 Vanilla ice cream

Combine water and sugar in a 9-inch glass pie plate. Mix well. Stir in almonds. Microwave at HIGH 2 minutes. Pour on waxed paper to cool; then crush.

Place peach halves, cut side up, in an 8-inch glass baking dish. Combine lemon juice, sherry, and cinnamon in a small dish. Drizzle over the peach halves. Cover with waxed paper. Microwave at HIGH 3 to 4 minutes.

Place hot peaches in individual serving dishes. Top with ice cream and sprinkle crumbled almond mixture over ice cream.

Yield: 5 to 6 servings.

Micronote: Place peach halves in individual glass serving dishes before filling. Follow above directions; then arrange dishes in a circle in the microwave oven. Microwave at HIGH 3 to 4 minutes and serve according to above instructions.

PEACH DELIGHT

Power: HIGH
Microwave Time: 15 to 16 Minutes

 ¼ **cup butter or margarine**
 1 **(29-ounce) can sliced peaches or 3 cups sliced fresh peaches**
 ¾ **cup all-purpose flour**
 ¾ **cup sugar**
 ¼ **teaspoon salt**
 1½ **teaspoons baking powder**
 ¾ **cup milk**
 Dash of ground nutmeg

Microwave butter in a 1½-quart glass baking dish at HIGH ½ to 1 minute. Add fruit with juice to melted butter. *Do not stir.* Combine flour, sugar, salt, and baking powder. Stir in milk. Pour mixture over peaches. *Do not stir.* Microwave at HIGH 15 minutes. Sprinkle with nutmeg. Serve warm.

Yield: 6 to 8 servings.

ENGLISH TRIFLE

Power: HIGH
Microwave Time: 5 to 7 Minutes,
  excluding custard

 ½ **cup slivered almonds**
 1 **tablespoon butter or margarine**
 1 **(8- to 9-inch) yellow cake layer, baked**
 1 **cup raspberry jam, divided**
 ½ **cup sherry, divided**
 1 **recipe Basic Custard, cooled slightly (see p. 91)**
 1 **to 2 cups whipping cream**
 4 **tablespoons sugar**

Place almonds and butter in a 9-inch glass pie plate. Microwave at HIGH 4 to 5 minutes or until toasted, stirring once. Set aside.

Slice cake layer into 12 to 15 strips. Layer ⅓ of the cake strips in a 3-quart serving bowl.

Be sure to *remove* lid from jam jar and microwave at HIGH 1 to 1½ minutes or until heated. Drizzle ⅓ of the warm jam over cake. Sprinkle with ⅓ of sherry. Repeat with remaining cake, jam, and sherry, making 2 more layers.

Pour Basic Custard over the cake layers. Cover and chill several hours.

Just before serving, whip cream until thickened. Add sugar. Spoon over top of cake. Sprinkle with toasted almonds.

Yield: 10 to 12 servings.

EGGS AND CHEESE

Eggs can be difficult to cook whether cooking them by a conventional heat method or with microwave energy. Because fat foods absorb microwave energy at a different rate from other foods, the egg yolk, which is higher in fat, cooks faster than the white of the egg. But, since the white surrounds the yolk, it absorbs energy first and makes microwave "fried" eggs possible.

Because of the delicate nature of eggs, if HIGH power is used, it should be for a short part of the total cooking time. Select MEDIUM-HIGH or MEDIUM to finish cooking eggs started with a short period of HIGH power cooking.

BASIC EGG COOKING TECHNIQUES

Eggs can be microwaved a variety of ways with good results. Use the microwave oven for fried, poached, "baked," or scrambled eggs, but not for hard-cooked eggs. The shell on the egg traps heat, which builds up inside, and the egg then bursts from the pressure of the steam.

Good results can be achieved when following recommended techniques for eggs cooked any way other than in the shell.

Eggs also combine well with cheese, milk, cream soup, or other ingredients.

For basic eggs cooked the way you like them follow these basic instructions:

Scrambled: Place butter in glass bowl or measure. Microwave to melt. Then beat in the eggs. Microwave, covered with waxed paper, until only slightly firm. Stir well and set aside to allow cooking to continue.

Fried: Place butter in flat dish or custard cup. Microwave to melt. Break eggs into butter. Pierce the yolk. Cover dish with waxed paper. Microwave at MEDIUM-HIGH.

Poached: Measure needed amount of water into a glass or plastic ring mold or a casserole. Microwave at HIGH to boil. Then carefully break each egg into boiling water, being careful to keep each one separate. Cover with plastic wrap and microwave at MEDIUM-HIGH ¾ to 1 minute per egg. Let stand, covered, for cooking to continue.

Baked: Eggs can be placed over other ingredients such as cream or heated hash or other cooked meats to make a baked-type egg. Pierce the yolk, cover with plastic wrap, and microwave at MEDIUM-HIGH or MEDIUM.

CONTAINERS FOR MICROWAVING EGGS

Many of the containers used for microwave egg cookery are already used for

other conventional cooking activities. Among the most popular are:
• 2- or 4-cup glass measure
• Cereal bowl
• Saucers, if they are of safe-for-microwave material
• Custard cups, either plastic or oven glass
• Mixing bowls
• Casseroles
Use either the newer, safe-for-microwave plastic or glass ring for poached eggs. It helps hold them in a circle which makes for more even cooking.

MICROWAVING COMBINATION EGG DISHES

When combining eggs with other ingredients for quiche or strata-type dishes, we recommend heating the egg and milk slightly first. This simple technique gives more even cooking results.

Because eggs are included in these dishes, we recommend using HIGH for a short part of the total time to start these foods cooking, then MEDIUM-HIGH or MEDIUM to complete the cooking process.

FRESH CORN-CHEESE QUICHE
(Conventional Recipe)

4 ears fresh corn
5 eggs, beaten
1½ cups half-and-half
¼ cup grated Parmesan cheese
2 tablespoons finely chopped onion
2 tablespoons chopped pimiento
1 teaspoon salt
⅛ teaspoon pepper
1 unbaked 9-inch pastry shell
6 strips crisp bacon

Preheat oven to 400°. Cut the corn kernels off cobs and set aside. Blend the eggs with half-and-half in a bowl. Add the cheese, onion, pimiento, salt, and pepper and mix well. Stir in the corn kernels and pour into pastry shell. Bake for 25 minutes. Reduce temperature to 350°. Arrange bacon over

corn mixture and bake for 20 minutes longer or until a knife inserted in center comes out clean.
Yield: 6 servings.

To Microwave Fresh Corn-Cheese Quiche

• Cook pastry shell and bacon. Set aside.
• Cut corn off cob.
• Combine eggs and other ingredients in a glass bowl. Heat before adding to the baked pie shell.
• Sprinkle with paprika and parsley and top with crisp bacon before serving.

FRESH CORN-CHEESE QUICHE
Power: HIGH/MEDIUM
Microwave Time: 20 to 27 Minutes

6 slices bacon
4 ears fresh corn
5 eggs
1¼ cups milk
½ cup grated Parmesan cheese
2 tablespoon chopped pimiento
1 teaspoon salt
⅛ teaspoon pepper
1 baked 9-inch pastry shell (in a glass pie plate)
Paprika
Parsley

Place bacon slices on paper plate or on a microwave roasting rack placed in a 12- x 8-inch glass baking dish. Cover with paper towel. Microwave at HIGH 5 to 7 minutes or until crisp. Set aside.

Cut corn off the cob and set aside. Beat eggs in a glass bowl. Add milk, cheese, pimiento, salt, and pepper. Microwave at MEDIUM 2 to 3 minutes or until heated through. Stir well and add corn.

Pour egg and corn mixture into the baked pastry shell. Microwave at MEDIUM 13 to 17 minutes or until firm around edges. Center should be slightly soft, but will firm on standing. Sprinkle top with paprika. Arrange bacon slices over top and garnish with parsley.
Yield: 6 to 8 servings.

CRUSTLESS ONION SOUP QUICHE

Power: HIGH/MEDIUM
Microwave Time: 14 to 15 Minutes

> 10 slices bacon, cooked, crumbled, and divided
> 1 cup grated Swiss cheese, divided
> 4 eggs
> 1 (13-ounce) can evaporated milk
> 1 (1⅜-ounce) packet dry onion soup mix
> Parsley

Reserve 2 tablespoons of bacon for garnish. Sprinkle remaining bacon in bottom of 9-inch glass pie plate. Spread ½ cup of cheese over bacon.

Beat eggs well. Add milk, dry soup mix, and remaining cheese. Stir to blend. Pour over bacon and cheese.

Microwave at HIGH 2 minutes. Rotate dish ½ turn. Microwave at MEDIUM 12 to 13 minutes. Outside edges will puff and center will be slightly soft. When cooked to desired doneness, let stand, covered with waxed paper, 7 to 10 minutes.

To serve, garnish with reserved bacon and fresh parsley.

Yield: 4 to 6 servings.

SHRIMP ONION QUICHE

Power: HIGH/MEDIUM
Microwave Time: 12 to 14 Minutes

> 1 unbaked 9-inch pastry shell
> 2 slices bacon
> ½ cup chopped green onion
> ½ cup frozen shrimp
> 1 cup grated Swiss cheese
> 1 egg
> ½ cup half-and-half
> ½ teaspoon salt
> ⅛ teaspoon cayenne pepper
> Paprika

If using a frozen pastry shell, remove from metal pan to glass pan. Prick lightly with a fork. Microwave at HIGH 4 to 6 minutes or until dry-looking on bottom. Set aside.

Place bacon on paper towels. Microwave at HIGH 1½ to 2 minutes. Crumble into cooked crust.

Combine onion and shrimp in a small bowl. Cover. Microwave at HIGH 1½ to 2 minutes. Drain. Spread over bacon in crust. Top with cheese.

Beat egg well in a small glass bowl. Stir in half-and-half, salt, and pepper. Cover with waxed paper. Microwave at HIGH 1 minute. Pour over other ingredients in crust. Microwave, covered, at HIGH 1 minute. Rotate dish ½ turn. Microwave at MEDIUM 3 minutes.

Sprinkle with paprika. Let stand, covered, 1 minute before serving.

Yield: 6 servings.

SHRIMP QUICHE SPECIALITY

Power: HIGH
Microwave Time: 11 to 13 Minutes

> 4 eggs
> 1 cup half-and-half or evaporated milk
> ½ teaspoon seasoned salt
> 1 tablespoon dried parsley
> 2 cups shredded Swiss cheese
> ¼ cup Parmesan cheese
> 1 (4½-ounce) can shrimp, drained
> 1 baked 9-inch pastry shell (in a glass pie plate)
> 2 teaspoons soy sauce
> 1 (12-ounce) can asparagus spears, drained
> 1 (2-ounce) jar pimiento, drained

Mix eggs, cream, and salt in a 4-cup glass measure. Microwave at HIGH 1 minute. Stir in parsley, Swiss cheese, Parmesan cheese, and shrimp.

Brush baked pastry shell with soy sauce. Pour filling mixture into pie crust. Cover with waxed paper. Microwave at HIGH 8 to 10 minutes.

Arrange drained asparagus spears and pimiento in a spoke design on pie filling. Cover with waxed paper. Microwave at HIGH 1 minute. Let pie stand, covered, 2 minutes before serving.

Yield: 6 to 8 servings.

SPINACH QUICHE ★

Power: HIGH/MEDIUM-HIGH
Microwave Time: 20 to 22 Minutes

>   2 (10-ounce) packages frozen
>   chopped spinach
> ¼ cup butter or margarine
>   1 small onion, chopped
>   4 eggs
> ½ cup commercial biscuit mix
>   2 cups half-and-half
> ½ teaspoon basil
> ½ teaspoon salt
> ⅛ teaspoon ground nutmeg
>   Dash of pepper
>   1 cup shredded Swiss cheese
>   Dash of paprika

Pierce packages of spinach several times with a fork. Place on a paper plate. Microwave each at HIGH 2 minutes. Drain.

Combine butter and chopped onion in a 2-cup glass bowl. Microwave at HIGH 2 minutes.

Combine eggs, biscuit mix, half-and-half, basil, salt, nutmeg, and pepper in a blender jar. Process on Low Speed for 3 minutes. Pour mixture into a 10-inch quiche dish.

Sprinkle shredded cheese over the cream mixture. Combine onion and butter mixture with drained spinach. Add spinach mixture to cream and cheese mixture. Garnish with paprika.

Microwave quiche at MEDIUM-HIGH 14 to 16 minutes. Rotate dish ¼ turn at 3½ to 4 minute intervals.

Quiche is cooked when a knife comes out clean when inserted in the center of pie. Center may be slightly soft, but will firm on standing 2 to 3 minutes.

Yield: 8 to 10 servings.

MICROWAVE 'FRIED' EGGS

Power: MEDIUM
Microwave Time: see below

>   1 teaspoon butter or margarine per
>   egg
>   Eggs

Place butter in custard cups, one for each egg. Break one egg into each custard cup. Pierce the yolk with a toothpick. Cover with plastic wrap. Microwave at MEDIUM 30 seconds per egg. Rotate each dish ¼ turn about halfway through microwaving. Let stand, covered, 1 minute to complete cooking.

Yield: 1 to 6 eggs.

Eggs	Teaspoons Butter	Microwave Time
1	1	30 seconds
2	2	45 to 60 seconds
3	3	1 to 1½ minutes
4	4	1½ to 2 minutes
5	5	1¾ to 2½ minutes
6	6	2 to 3 minutes

TRADITIONAL FRIED EGGS

Power: HIGH
Microwave Time: 45 Seconds for 1 egg

>   1 teaspoon butter per egg
>   1 to 4 eggs

Follow manufacturer's directions to preheat browning skillet. Add butter and break eggs into the preheated skillet. Cover with the glass lid. Microwave at HIGH 45 seconds per egg.

Yield: 1 to 4 eggs.

POACHED EGGS

Power: HIGH/MEDIUM-HIGH
Microwave Time: 4 to 6 Minutes plus ¾
  to 1 Minute per egg

>   1 teaspoon vinegar
>   2 cups hot tap water
>   4 eggs

Add vinegar to water in 2-quart casserole. Microwave at HIGH 4 to 6 minutes, or until boiling.

Break eggs into a saucer. Puncture membrane by piercing with a toothpick. Gently ease eggs, one at a time, into the boiling

water. Cover with waxed paper. Microwave at MEDIUM-HIGH ¾ to 1 minute per egg depending on doneness desired.
Yield: 4 eggs.

SCRAMBLED EGGS

Power: MEDIUM-HIGH
Microwave Time: see below

- 1 teaspoon butter or margarine per egg
- 1 egg
- 1 tablespoon milk per egg
  Salt
  Pepper

Place butter in casserole. Add desired number of eggs and amount of milk. Beat with a fork until blended. Cover with waxed paper. Microwave, following times below, at MEDIUM-HIGH until eggs are set, but still moist. Stir once or twice during cooking time.

Eggs	Microwave Time
1	1 to 1½ minutes
2	1½ to 2½ minutes
4	4 to 5½ minutes
6	6 to 7½ minutes

Season with salt and pepper.
Yield: 1 serving per egg.

ELEGANT SCRAMBLED EGGS

Power: HIGH/MEDIUM-HIGH
Microwave Time: 13 to 16½ Minutes

- 6 slices bacon
- 2 tablespoons butter or margarine
- 4 tablespoons chopped green pepper
- 4 to 6 eggs
- 4 tablespoons milk
- 3 English muffins, split and toasted, or 6 slices toast
- 1 medium-sized tomato cut into wedges

Place bacon on paper towel in 12- x 8-inch baking dish. Cover with paper towel. Microwave at HIGH 6 to 7 minutes. Cool and crumble. Set aside.

Place butter and green pepper in a 1½-quart casserole. Microwave at HIGH 2 minutes. Stir in eggs and milk. Cover with waxed paper. Microwave at MEDIUM-HIGH 5 to 7½ minutes. Stir well at 1 minute intervals.

Stir in crumbled bacon. Spoon over toast or English muffins. Garnish with tomato wedges.
Yield: 4 to 6 servings.

SPECIAL SCRAMBLED EGGS

Power: HIGH/MEDIUM
Microwave Time: 8 to 13 Minutes

- 2 tablespoons butter or margarine
- ½ cup chopped green onion
- 5 slices bacon, cooked and crumbled
- 4 eggs
- 1 cup evaporated milk
- ⅛ teaspoon hot sauce
- ½ teaspoon salt
- ⅛ teaspoon pepper
- ¾ cup shredded sharp Cheddar cheese

Place butter and onion in a 9-inch glass pie plate. Microwave at HIGH 1 to 2 minutes. Sprinkle bacon pieces over cooked onion.

Beat eggs. Add milk, hot sauce, salt, and pepper. Pour over bacon and onion.

Cover with waxed paper. Microwave at HIGH 1 to 2 minutes. Stir to mix lightly. Microwave at MEDIUM 5 to 7 minutes. Rotate dish ½ turn after 3 minutes.

Sprinkle cheese over eggs. Microwave at MEDIUM 1 to 2 minutes or until cheese is melted. Let stand, covered, 1 minute before serving.
Yield: 4 to 5 servings.

GUEST EGGS

Power: HIGH
Microwave Time: 9 to 11½ Minutes

>   4 slices bacon
>   2 tablespoons bacon drippings
>   ¼ cup chopped green pepper
>   6 eggs
>   ¼ teaspoon salt
>   ⅛ teaspoon pepper
>   ⅓ cup water
>   1 (10¾-ounce) can cream of
>   mushroom soup, undiluted
>   ¼ cup grated sharp Cheddar cheese

Place bacon in a 1½-quart casserole. Cover with paper towel. Microwave at HIGH 3 to 4 minutes. Remove bacon and crumble. Set aside.

Leave 2 tablespoons bacon drippings in the casserole. Stir in green pepper. Cover with waxed paper. Microwave at HIGH 1 to 1½ minutes.

Beat eggs, salt, and pepper well. Stir in water and soup. Pour egg mixture over green pepper. Cover with plastic wrap.

Microwave at HIGH 4 to 5 minutes. Stir lightly at 1 minute intervals. While still slightly moist, stir in crumbled bacon and cheese. Microwave at HIGH 1 minute. Let stand, covered, 1 minute before serving.

Yield: 6 servings.

BRUNCH EGGS

Power: HIGH/MEDIUM
Microwave Time: 17½ to 22½ Minutes

>   2 tablespoons butter or margarine
>   2 tablespoons all-purpose flour
> 1¼ cups milk
>   ¼ cup chopped onion
>   1 cup shredded sharp Cheddar
>   cheese
>   ½ teaspoon salt
>   ¼ teaspoon pepper
>   6 hard-cooked eggs, chopped
>   1 cup crushed potato chips
>   12 slices bacon, cooked and
>   crumbled

Place butter in a 2-quart casserole. Microwave at HIGH 30 seconds. Stir flour into melted butter to make a smooth paste. Add milk gradually, stirring well.

Microwave at HIGH 4 to 5 minutes, stirring well at 1 minute intervals. When thick and smooth, add onion, cheese, salt, and pepper. Microwave at HIGH 1 to 2 minutes or until bubbly.

Alternate layers of cheese sauce, eggs, potato chips, and bacon in a 10-inch round casserole.

Cover with waxed paper. Microwave at MEDIUM 12 to 15 minutes. Let stand, covered, 2 minutes before serving.

Yield: 6 servings.

EGGS RANCHEROS

Power: HIGH/MEDIUM
Microwave Time: 5 to 6 Minutes

>   1 (8-ounce) can mild taco sauce,
>   divided
>   4 eggs
>   2 cups shredded medium-sharp
>   Cheddar cheese
>   Toast or cornbread

Pour half the taco sauce into an 8-inch glass pie plate. Break eggs and place one at a time into the sauce. Carefully pour remaining sauce over eggs.

Cover with waxed paper. Microwave at HIGH 1 minute. Rotate dish ½ turn. Microwave at MEDIUM 3 to 4 minutes or until whites are firm. Sprinkle cheese over eggs. Microwave at MEDIUM 1 minute or until cheese is melted. Serve immediately over toast or cornbread.

Yield: 2 to 4 servings.

Micronote: If eggs cool before serving, return them to the microwave oven and microwave at HIGH about 10 to 15 seconds per egg or to serving temperature.

CREAMED EGGS

Power: MEDIUM
Microwave Time: 2 to 3 Minutes

    4   to 6 hard-cooked eggs
    ⅛   teaspoon pepper
    2   cups Basic White Sauce (see p.
        164)
    3   to 4 pieces toast
    ¼   cup grated Parmesan cheese
        Paprika

Cut eggs into ½-inch pieces. Stir eggs and pepper into white sauce. Cover with plastic wrap. Microwave at MEDIUM 2 to 3 minutes. Serve on strips of toast. Sprinkle with grated cheese and paprika to serve.

Yield: 4 to 6 servings.

Micronote: Since boiled eggs cannot be prepared, try the microwave "fried" egg technique for eggs to be chopped. Cooked and chilled, they work well for salads, creamed eggs, or as a garnish.

CREOLE RAREBIT

Power: HIGH
Microwave Time: 11 to 13 Minutes

    3   tablespoons butter or margarine
    ¾   cup minced onion
    ¾   cup chopped green pepper
    ½   cup milk
    ¾   cup tomato soup, undiluted
    1½   cups pimiento cheese spread
    1½   cups shredded sharp Cheddar
         cheese
    3   egg yolks
         Toast or crackers

Place butter, onion, and green pepper in a 2-quart casserole. Microwave at HIGH 5 to 6 minutes. Stir once after 2 minutes. Add milk and soup. Stir well. Microwave at HIGH 2 minutes. Stir in cheese spread and shredded cheese. Microwave at HIGH 2 to 3 minutes.

Beat egg yolks. Add some of the hot mixture to beaten egg yolks. Stir the egg yolk mixture into the hot cheese mixture. Microwave at HIGH 2 minutes.

Serve over toast as a main dish or use as a hot dip for crackers.

Yield: approximately 6 cups or 8 main dish servings.

CHEESE SOUFFLÉ

Power: HIGH/MEDIUM
Microwave Time: 18 to 21 Minutes

    6   slices white bread, crust
         removed
    ½   pound sharp Cheddar cheese,
         shredded
    4   eggs
    1   teaspoon salt
    2   tablespoons grated Parmesan
         cheese
    2   cups milk
    2   teaspoons dry mustard
    ¼   teaspoon hot sauce

Place trimmed bread in a single layer in a 13- x 9-inch baking dish. Sprinkle shredded cheese over bread. Combine thoroughly the eggs, salt, Parmesan cheese, milk, mustard, and hot sauce. Slowly pour egg mixture over cheese and bread. Cover with plastic wrap. Chill at least 1 hour or up to 24 hours.

When ready to cook, cover with waxed paper. Microwave at HIGH 5 minutes. Rotate dish ¼ turn. Microwave at MEDIUM 12 to 14 minutes. Rotate ½ turn halfway through microwaving. Soufflé will be puffy and set around the edge. If still soft in spots, microwave at MEDIUM 1 or 2 minutes. Cover wet spots with waxed paper placed directly on the surface. Serve immediately.

Yield: 6 to 8 servings.

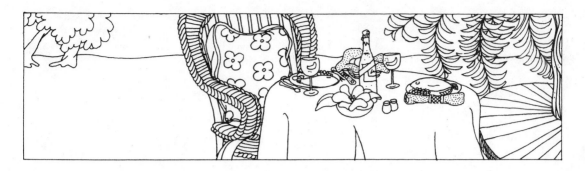

FISH AND SHELLFISH

Almost every variety of seafood (either fish or shellfish) is an excellent choice for microwaving. Naturally juicy, fish and shellfish can be poached, steamed, or microwaved in a sauce or served plain with lemon juice for a low calorie meal. Because of its high moisture content fish cooks quickly, retains its natural flavor, and can be microwaved at HIGH power.

Fish cooks in about 4 to 5 minutes per pound and should be completely defrosted at MEDIUM or MEDIUM-LOW power for 3½ to 4 minutes per pound before cooking. This will prevent overcooking. Allow fish and shellfish to rest about 5 minutes before cooking.

Whole fish can be baked in the microwave oven if the thin parts and the tail are covered with small pieces of foil to prevent overcooking. Cover whole fish with waxed paper to microwave. Whole baked fish can be served attractively garnished with lemon slices or with Hot Lemon Butter (see p. 49) to pass as a topping.

Shellfish, such as shrimp, clams, and oysters, microwave best when arranged in a single layer and covered with plastic wrap. When clams and oysters are done, their shells will open, usually in about 2 or 3 minutes per dozen. Remove each item as it cooks and allow to stand to continue cooking. HIGH power works well when microwaving these seafoods.

Whole lobster can be microwave-steamed in just a few minutes. Combine wine, broth, or water to make about ½ cup. Microwave at HIGH to boil, then add lobster. Cover with plastic wrap and microwave at HIGH until the shell turns red and the meat is white, juicy, and tender. Eat and enjoy with Hot Lemon Butter (see p. 49).

CONTAINERS FOR SEAFOOD

Individual portions of fish can be microwaved in custard cups, saucers, bowls, seafood shells, and other safe-for-microwave serving dishes. Whole fish and lobster can be microwaved in flat, shallow casseroles. Plastic wrap, placed over the casserole, will hold in the steam and help make cooking even for lobster, shrimp, and rolled fillets.

Several servings of fish fillets should be arranged with the thicker part toward the outside of the dish. Use a glass or plastic ring mold for cooking individual rolled-up fish fillets. If you don't have a ring mold, arrange the rolled fillets around the inner outside rim of a round baking dish, leaving the center open.

If you plan to serve the fish with a sauce, prepare the sauce first in a glass measure. Press plastic wrap directly over the top of the sauce to prevent a "skin" from forming. Reheat, if necessary, before pouring over the seafood.

TEST FOR DONENESS

Because fish cooks very quickly, watch it carefully to prevent overcooking when microwaving. Fish is done when it turns opaque and will flake easily. Allow fish to stand covered 4 or 5 minutes for cooking to continue and internal temperatures to even out. Shellfish, like lobster and shrimp, will be milky and opaque when done.

A CROWN OF FLOUNDER
(Conventional Recipe)

 6   strips bacon
 1   (8-ounce) package herb-seasoned stuffing mix
     Butter or margarine, melted
 2   tablespoons minced parsley
 ¼   cup minced onion
 6   thin flounder fillets (or any white fish)
     Mushroom Caper Sauce

Fry bacon crisp; drain; measure drippings; crumble bacon. Prepare stuffing mix as directed on package, adding enough melted butter or margarine to bacon drippings to equal amount of moistening called for. Stir in bacon, parsley, and onion; mix well.

Spread equal amount of stuffing on each fillet; roll up; secure with wooden toothpicks. Place each roll-up upright in well-greased muffin cups. Brush with additional melted butter or margarine. Bake at 375° for 30 minutes. If necessary, brush again with melted butter; run under broiler to brown. Serve with Mushroom Caper Sauce.

Yield: 6 servings.

Mushroom Caper Sauce:

 1   (3-ounce) can broiled, sliced mushrooms
     Milk or half-and-half
 1   (10¾-ounce) can cream of mushroom soup, undiluted
 2   tablespoons capers

Drain mushrooms; measure broth; add enough milk or cream to measure ⅓ cup. Blend with soup. Add mushrooms and capers. Heat and serve warm over flounder.
Yield: 2½ to 3 cups.

To Microwave A Crown Of Flounder

• Cook bacon; set aside.
• Use only half the stuffing, parsley, and onion.
• Arrange the prepared flounder rolls around the inside edge of a 9-inch glass casserole.

To Microwave Mushroom Caper Sauce

• Combine all ingredients in a 4-cup glass measure.
• Microwave to heat.

A CROWN OF FLOUNDER

Power: HIGH/MEDIUM
Microwave Time: 18 Minutes

- 4 tablespoons butter or margarine
- 6 slices bacon
- ½ cup water
- 1 tablespoon minced parsley
- 2 tablespoons minced onion
- 4 ounces herb-seasoned stuffing mix
- 6 flounder fillets
  Mushroom Caper Sauce

Microwave butter in a 2-cup glass measure at HIGH 1 minute.

Microwave bacon slices on roasting rack in a 12- x 8-inch glass baking dish at HIGH 6 minutes. Remove and measure drippings. Add enough melted butter to make ¼ cup. Crumble bacon.

Microwave water in a 1-cup glass measure at HIGH 2 minutes. Add water, bacon drippings, crumbled bacon, parsley, and onion to herb stuffing. Mix well.

Spread an equal amount of stuffing mix on each flounder fillet. Roll fillet like a jelly roll. Secure roll with wooden toothpicks. Arrange rolls on end in a 9-inch round glass baking dish. Pour remaining butter over roll-ups. Cover with waxed paper. Microwave at MEDIUM 9 minutes. Rotate dish ¼ turn at 2 minute intervals.

Let flounder stand, covered, 3 to 5 minutes before serving. Serve with Mushroom Caper Sauce.

Yield: 6 servings.

Mushroom Caper Sauce:

Power: MEDIUM
Microwave Time: 4 to 5 Minutes

- 1 (3-ounce) can broiled, sliced mushrooms
- 3 tablespoons milk or half-and-half
- 1 (10¾-ounce) can cream of mushroom soup, undiluted
- 2 tablespoons capers

Drain mushrooms, reserving the liquid. Pour liquid in a 4-cup glass measure. Add milk, soup, mushrooms, and capers. Microwave at MEDIUM 4 to 5 minutes. Stir mixture after 2 minutes of microwaving. Serve warm over flounder.

Yield: 2½ to 3 cups.

CRABMEAT ELEANOR

Power: HIGH
Microwave Time: 12 to 14 Minutes

- 1 (4-ounce) can button mushrooms, drained
- 1 small green pepper, cut in thin strips
- 2 tablespoons butter or margarine
- ¼ cup slivered, blanched almonds, toasted
- 1 tablespoon orange juice
- 1 teaspoon lemon juice
- 2 (10½-ounce) cans cream of celery soup, undiluted
- ½ teaspoon celery salt
- ¼ cup quartered ripe olives
- ¼ cup chopped pimiento, drained
- 2 tablespoons chopped parsley
  Dash of hot sauce
- 2 (6-ounce) cans crabmeat, drained
  Dash of salt
  Dash of pepper
  Cooked rice or Chinese noodles

Combine mushrooms, green pepper, and butter in a 2½-quart casserole. Cover with plastic wrap. Microwave at HIGH 2 minutes. Add remaining ingredients, except rice or noodles. Stir lightly to mix.

Cover with waxed paper. Microwave at HIGH 10 to 12 minutes. Stir lightly after 6 minutes. Let stand, covered, 3 to 5 minutes. Serve over hot rice or Chinese noodles.

Yield: 8 servings.

CRAB DELUXE

Power: HIGH
Microwave Time: 11½ to 12½ Minutes

>   4   tablespoons butter or margarine,
>   divided
>   2   tablespoons cornstarch
>   1   cup milk
>   1   (6½-ounce) can crabmeat,
>   drained
>   2   teaspoons lemon juice
>   1   teaspoon salt
>   1   teaspoon prepared mustard
>   ¼   cup mayonnaise
>   2   teaspoons minced onion
>   2   hard-cooked eggs, chopped
>   Dash of pepper
>   ¾   cup buttered bread crumbs

Microwave 2 tablespoons butter in a 2-cup glass measure at HIGH 30 seconds. Blend in cornstarch until smooth. Gradually stir in milk. Microwave milk mixture at HIGH 3 to 4 minutes. Stir at 1 minute intervals until mixture is thick.

Microwave remaining 2 tablespoons butter in a 1-quart glass casserole at HIGH 1 minute. Combine with crabmeat, lemon juice, salt, mustard, mayonnaise, onion, eggs, and pepper. Stir in white sauce. Spread bread crumbs on top of casserole. Cover with waxed paper. Microwave at HIGH 7 minutes.

Yield: 4 to 6 servings.

CRABMEAT-BROCCOLI CASSEROLE

Power: HIGH/MEDIUM
Microwave Time: 16 Minutes

>   1   (10-ounce) package frozen
>   chopped broccoli
>   1   (6-ounce) package frozen
>   crabmeat
>   ½   cup commercial sour cream
>   ¼   cup chili sauce
>   1   medium-sized onion, chopped
>   2   tablespoons lemon juice
>   1   tablespoon lemon rind
>   1   cup shredded sharp Cheddar
>   cheese

Pierce package of broccoli several times and place on a paper plate. Microwave at HIGH 4 minutes.

Microwave crabmeat in a 1½-quart casserole at MEDIUM 2 minutes. Combine crabmeat with broccoli, sour cream, chili sauce, onion, lemon juice, lemon rind, and cheese. Cover with waxed paper. Microwave at HIGH 5 minutes. Rotate casserole ½ turn. Microwave at MEDIUM 5 more minutes.

Yield: 6 to 8 servings.

DELUXE SEAFOOD CASSEROLE

Power: HIGH
Microwave Time: 12 Minutes

>   2   (6½-ounce) packages frozen
>   crabmeat, thawed
>   2   (10¾-ounce) cans cream of
>   mushroom soup, undiluted
>   and divided
>   2   cups cooked shrimp
>   1½ cups sliced fresh mushrooms
>   1   (7½-ounce) can white tuna fish
>   1½ cups shredded sharp Cheddar
>   cheese
>   2   hard-cooked eggs, sliced

Spread crabmeat on bottom of a 12- x 8-inch glass casserole dish. Cover crabmeat with ⅓ of mushroom soup. Spread shrimp over soup layer. Cover shrimp with ⅓ of mushroom soup. Spread mushrooms and tuna fish over second soup layer. Spread remaining ⅓ soup over tuna and mushrooms. Cover with waxed paper. Microwave at HIGH 12 minutes.

Top casserole with cheese and sliced eggs. Let stand at least 2 minutes before serving.

Yield: 10 to 12 servings.

FISH MARGUERY IN PAPER ★ ★

Power: HIGH
Microwave Time: 11¼ to 15½ Minutes

- 1 **pound fish fillets (any mild**
       white fish)
- ¼ **cup dry white wine**
- 2 **teaspoons lemon juice**
- ⅛ **teaspoon salt**
    Dash of pepper
- 5 **tablespoons butter or margarine**
- ½ **cup mushrooms, sliced**
- 1½ **cups cooked shrimp, crabmeat,**
       or lobster
- ½ **teaspoon salt**
- ⅛ **teaspoon pepper**
- ¼ **cup water chestnuts, drained**
       and sliced
- 2 **tablespoons all-purpose flour**
- 1 **cup liquid (fish juices from**
       cooking plus additional wine)
- 1 **egg yolk, beaten**
- 2 **tablespoons half-and-half**
- 1 **teaspoon brown mustard**
    Dash of hot sauce
- 2 **sprigs parsley, chopped**

Place fish in 12- x 8-inch baking dish. Add wine, lemon juice, salt, and pepper. Dot with 1 tablespoon of butter. Microwave at HIGH 3 minutes or until butter melts. Remove fish and reserve liquid.

Cut four 12- x 15-inch pieces of parchment paper. Butter each well. Divide fish into 4 equal portions and place 1 portion on each of the pieces of paper. Place the parchment paper and fish into a flat baking dish. Set aside while making sauce.

Combine mushrooms, seafood, 2 tablespoons of butter, salt, and pepper in a 2-cup glass measure. Microwave at HIGH 1 to 2 minutes or until hot. Spoon this mixture over the fish. Spread water chestnuts over the seafood. Add these juices to reserved fish liquid.

Microwave 2 tablespoons of butter at HIGH 1 minute to melt in a 2-cup glass measure. Stir in flour. Slowly add reserved liquid and microwave at HIGH 2 to 3 minutes or until thickened. Stir 2 or 3 times during microwaving.

Blend ¼ cup of the thickened sauce with egg yolk, half-and-half, mustard, and hot sauce. Return to cooked sauce, stirring to blend well. Microwave at HIGH 15 to 30 seconds. Spoon the sauce over the fish and other ingredients on the parchment paper. Garnish with parsley.

Fold the paper loosely over the top and ends. Microwave at HIGH 4 to 6 minutes or until very hot. Rotate dish after 2 to 3 minutes.

Yield: 4 servings.

FISH MOZZARELLA

Power: HIGH
Microwave Time: 4 to 5 Minutes

- 1 **pound mild white fish**
- ¼ **teaspoon seasoned salt**
- 2 **tablespoons butter or margarine**
- ⅓ **cup commercial sour cream**
- 3 **ounces Mozzarella cheese,**
       shredded
- 1 **tablespoon chopped parsley**

Wipe and dry fish. Arrange fish in a 12- x 8-inch glass baking dish. Sprinkle with seasoned salt. Dot with butter; then cover with waxed paper. Microwave at HIGH 2 minutes.

Blend sour cream and cheese. Spread mixture on fish. Sprinkle with parsley. Cover with waxed paper. Microwave at HIGH 2 to 3 minutes.

Yield: 3 to 4 servings.

FISH PARMESAN

Power: HIGH
Microwave Time: 4 to 5 Minutes

- 1 **pound mild white fish**
- ¼ **teaspoon seasoned salt**
- 2 **tablespoons butter or margarine**
- ½ **cup grated Parmesan cheese**
- ½ **cup mayonnaise**
- 2 **tablespoons chopped green onions**
  Paprika

Wipe and dry fish. Arrange fish in a 12- x 8-inch glass baking dish. Sprinkle with seasoned salt. Dot with butter. Cover with waxed paper. Microwave at HIGH 2 minutes.

Blend Parmesan cheese, mayonnaise, and onions. Spread cheese mixture over fish. Cover with waxed paper. Microwave at HIGH 2 to 3 minutes.

Sprinkle with paprika before serving.
Yield: 3 to 4 servings.

SALMON LOAF

Power: HIGH/MEDIUM
Microwave Time: 12 to 13 Minutes

- 1 **(16-ounce) can salmon, drained**
- 1½ **cups whole wheat fresh bread crumbs**
- ½ **cup commercial sour cream**
- ½ **cup chopped onion**
- ¼ **cup chopped celery**
- ¼ **cup chicken broth**
- 2 **eggs**
- 1 **teaspoon Worcestershire sauce**
- ½ **teaspoon salt**
  Dash of pepper

Combine all ingredients in a mixing bowl.

Spoon mixture into a 10-inch microwave tube pan. Cover. Microwave at HIGH 5 minutes. Rotate dish. Microwave at MEDIUM 7 to 8 minutes.

Yield: 4 to 6 servings.

COQUILLE ST. JACQUES

Power: HIGH/MEDIUM-HIGH
Microwave Time: 17 to 23 Minutes

- 2 **tablespoons butter, or margarine, divided**
- ⅓ **cup finely chopped celery**
- 1 **(4-ounce) can sliced mushrooms, drained**
- ½ **teaspoon salt**
- 2 **tablespoons all-purpose flour**
- 1 **tablespoon grated lemon rind**
- 1 **pound fresh raw scallops**
- ½ **cup dry white wine**
- ½ **cup half-and-half**
- 3 **tablespoons butter, melted**
- ¼ **cup fine dry bread crumbs**
- 2 **tablespoons grated Parmesan cheese**

Place 2 tablespoons butter, celery, and mushrooms in a 2-quart casserole. Microwave at HIGH 2 to 3 minutes. Stir well at 1 minute intervals. Stir in salt, flour, and lemon rind. Add scallops and wine.

Microwave at HIGH 5 to 6 minutes or until thickened. Stir after 2 or 3 minutes. Carefully stir in half-and-half. Microwave at HIGH 3 to 4 minutes. Stir well after 2 minutes.

Microwave 3 tablespoons butter at HIGH 1 minute in a 2-cup glass measure. Combine melted butter, crumbs, and cheese. Set aside.

Divide scallop mixture among 4 individual ramekins or 4 clean scallop shells. Top with crumb mixture. Cover with waxed paper. Microwave at MEDIUM-HIGH 6 to 9 minutes. Rearrange or rotate after 3 or 4 minutes. Let stand, covered, 3 to 5 minutes before serving.

Yield: 4 servings.

Micronote: Place the filled ramekins or shells on a safe-for-microwave tray or platter so that they can be easily rotated or rearranged during microwaving.

SEAFOOD CREOLE

Power: HIGH
Microwave Time: 32 to 41 Minutes

- 3 stalks celery, chopped
- ½ pound mushrooms, sliced
- 3 green onions, chopped
- 1 clove garlic, minced
- 4 tablespoons butter or margarine
- 2 (16-ounce) cans tomato wedges, drained
- 1 tablespoon Worcestershire sauce
- 1 teaspoon hot sauce
- 1 teaspoon salt
- ⅛ teaspoon pepper
- 1 pound flounder or other white fish, partially thawed and cut in pieces
- ½ pound frozen shrimp
  Hot cooked rice
  Parsley

Combine celery, mushrooms, onion, garlic, and butter in a 2½-quart casserole. Cover with waxed paper. Microwave at HIGH 6 to 8 minutes or until vegetables are crisp-tender. Stir well.

Add all other ingredients except fish, shrimp, rice, and parsley. Cover with waxed paper and microwave at HIGH 20 to 25 minutes. Stir once or twice during microwaving.

Add fish and frozen shrimp. Stir well and microwave at HIGH 6 to 8 minutes or until fish and shrimp are cooked. Serve immediately over a bed of hot cooked rice. Garnish with parsley.

Yield: 6 to 8 servings.

SHRIMP

Power: HIGH
Microwave Time: 4 to 5 minutes per pound

Fresh Shrimp

Peel and devein shrimp. Arrange the shrimp around the outside edge of a glass pie plate or other flat round dish. Cover with plastic wrap. Turn a corner back to form a vent. Microwave at HIGH approximately 5 minutes per pound. Watch carefully to prevent overcooking. Shrimp are done when they are pink. Let stand 3 to 5 minutes.

Use in recipes calling for cooked shrimp or serve alone, either hot or cold.

SHRIMP CREOLE

Power: HIGH
Microwave Time: 23 to 29 Minutes

- 1 (16-ounce) can tomato wedges
- 1 zucchini, cubed
- 2 medium-size onions, chopped
- 1 large green pepper, diced
- 1 (10-ounce) package frozen okra, thawed
- 1 cup chopped celery
- 1 tablespoon Worcestershire sauce
- 2 teaspoons hot sauce
- ½ teaspoon pepper
- 1 teaspoon salt
- 2 tablespoons cornstarch
- 1 (12-ounce) package frozen shrimp, thawed and drained

Drain tomatoes, reserving juice.

Combine tomato wedges, zucchini, onions, green pepper, okra, celery, Worcestershire sauce, hot sauce, pepper, and salt in a 2-quart glass casserole. Cover with plastic wrap. Microwave at HIGH 20 to 25 minutes.

Measure ½ cup reserved tomato juice. Combine cornstarch and tomato juice. Stir to dissolve and add shrimp. Add shrimp mixture to vegetable mixture. Cover with waxed paper or lid. Microwave at HIGH 3 to 4 minutes. Let Creole stand, covered, 4 minutes before serving.

Yield: 4 servings.

Cream of Broccoli Soup (p.169) and many other types of soups can be heated to the perfect serving temperature using the microwave oven. Serve soup as an appetizer with any seafood for a midnight supper.

SHRIMP AND ARTICHOKES

Power: HIGH/MEDIUM
Microwave Time: 13 to 17 Minutes

- 1 (10-ounce) package frozen
    artichoke hearts
- 1 tablespoon Worcestershire sauce
- ¼ cup dry sherry
- 1 (10¾-ounce) can cream of
    mushroom soup, undiluted
- ½ teaspoon salt
- ¼ teaspoon pepper
- ¾ pound cooked shrimp
- ¼ pound fresh mushrooms, sliced
- 2 tablespoons butter or margarine
- ¼ cup grated Parmesan cheese
    Paprika

Pierce artichoke package with a fork. Place on a paper plate. Microwave at HIGH 3 to 5 minutes. Let stand to cool slightly. Drain, if necessary.

Combine Worcestershire sauce, sherry, soup, salt, and pepper in a bowl.

Arrange the artichoke hearts, shrimp, and mushroom slices in a 1½-quart casserole. Dot with butter. Pour the sauce ingredients over top. Sprinkle with cheese and paprika.

Microwave at HIGH 5 minutes. Rotate dish ½ turn. Microwave at MEDIUM 5 to 7 minutes. Let stand, covered, 2 minutes before serving.

Yield: 4 to 6 servings.

SHRIMP VINO ★

Power: MEDIUM/HIGH
Microwave Time: 6 Minutes

- 1 (8-ounce) package frozen
    shrimp, peeled and deveined
- 1 (10¾-ounce) can Cheddar cheese
    soup, undiluted
- 2 tablespoons dry white wine
- 4 large fresh mushrooms, sliced
- 2 cups cooked rice

As a new way to serve shrimp, combine with cooked rice and chopped vegetables for Shrimp Rice Salad (p.109). We served it cold, but it is also good hot.

Spread shrimp in a 2-quart glass casserole. Microwave at MEDIUM 1 minute. Rearrange shrimp. Microwave again at MEDIUM 1 minute.

Stir in soup, wine, and mushrooms. Cover with waxed paper. Microwave at HIGH 4 minutes.

Serve over hot rice.

Yield: 4 to 6 servings.

SHRIMP RICE SALAD

Power: HIGH
Microwave Time: 5 Minutes

- 1 pound shrimp, peeled and
    deveined
- 2 cups cooked rice
- ½ cup thinly sliced celery
- ¼ cup thinly sliced olives
- ¼ cup chopped green pepper
- ¼ cup chopped pimiento
- ¼ cup minced onion
- ⅛ teaspoon garlic salt
- ⅛ teaspoon celery salt
- ¼ teaspoon pepper
- 3 to 4 tablespoons commercial
    French dressing
    Lettuce
    Tomato wedges
    Celery leaves

Arrange peeled shrimp around outside edge of flat round baking dish. Cover with plastic wrap. Microwave at HIGH 5 minutes. Let stand, covered, 3 to 5 minutes. Drain well.

Combine cooked shrimp with rice, celery, olives, green pepper, pimiento, onion, garlic and celery salt, pepper, and French dressing. Toss lightly to combine. Chill thoroughly.

Serve on lettuce and garnish with tomato wedges and celery leaves.

Yield: 4 servings.

SOLE VERONIQUE

Power: HIGH
Microwave Time: 8 Minutes

- **1 pound fillet of sole**
- **1 cup dry white wine, divided**
- **¼ cup butter or margarine**
- **1 tablespoon cornstarch**
- **⅔ cup half-and-half**
- **1 cup seedless grapes**

Arrange sole in a 12- x 8-inch baking dish. Pour ⅔ cup wine over fish. Reserve ⅓ cup wine. Cover fish with plastic wrap. Microwave at HIGH 4 minutes. Rotate dish ½ turn after 2 minutes. Drain fillets.

Place butter in a 4-cup glass measure. Microwave at HIGH 1 minute. Dissolve cornstarch in half-and-half. Stir mixture into melted butter. Add remaining wine to cream mixture. Microwave at HIGH 2½ minutes. Stir mixture at 30 second intervals. Add grapes to cream mixture.

Arrange cooked sole on a serving platter suitable for the microwave. Pour cream sauce over fillets. Microwave at HIGH 30 seconds.

Yield: 3 to 4 servings.

BAKED STUFFED TROUT

Power: HIGH
Microwave Time: 10½ to 12½ Minutes

- **4 to 5 (2½-pounds) trout**
- **¼ cup butter or margarine**
- **¼ teaspoon salt**
- **2 cups stuffing mix, prepared according to directions**
- **¼ teaspoon pepper**
- **¼ teaspoon onion powder**
- **¼ teaspoon paprika**

Wipe and dry fish. Microwave butter in a 1-cup glass measure at HIGH 30 seconds. Brush inside of fish with ½ of the butter. Lightly salt inside of fish. Fill fish with stuffing mix. Brush outside of fish with remaining butter. Sprinkle fish with pepper, onion powder, and paprika.

Arrange fish in a 12- x 8-inch baking dish. Microwave at HIGH 10 to 12 minutes. Rotate dish ½ turn after 5 minutes.

Yield: 4 to 5 servings.

HOT TUNA BAKE

Power: HIGH/MEDIUM
Microwave Time: 18 to 20 Minutes

- **8 slices bread (trim crust), divided**
- **¼ cup butter or margarine**
- **1 (7-ounce) can tuna fish, drained**
- **1 cup shredded sharp Cheddar cheese**
- **3 eggs, beaten**
- **1 cup milk**
- **½ teaspoon salt**
- **1 (10-ounce) can cream of shrimp soup, undiluted**
- **½ cup commercial sour cream**
- **¼ teaspoon seasoned salt**
- **1 hard-cooked egg, sliced**
  Paprika
  Chopped parsley

Spread bread slices with butter. Place 4 slices in an 8-inch square baking dish. Spread tuna fish and cheese over bread slices. Top with remaining 4 bread slices.

Combine eggs, milk, and salt. Pour over bread in baking dish. Chill for 8 to 24 hours.

Before microwaving, bring bread mixture to room temperature. Combine shrimp soup, sour cream, and salt in a 2-cup glass measure. Microwave at HIGH 3 minutes. Pour soup mixture over sandwiches. Cover with waxed paper or lid. Microwave at MEDIUM 15 to 17 minutes. Garnish with sliced eggs, paprika, and chopped parsley.

Yield: 4 to 6 servings.

TUNA PUFFS IN CHEESE SAUCE

Power: HIGH
Microwave Time: 8 to 9½ Minutes

- 1 cup instant mashed potato flakes
- 1 (9¼-ounce) can tuna fish, drained
- 2 eggs
- ⅓ cup finely chopped celery
- 3 tablespoons chopped pimiento
- 1 tablespoon instant minced onion
- ¼ teaspoon salt
- ½ cup crushed corn flakes
- 1 teaspoon crushed parsley
- 1 (10½-ounce) can Cheddar cheese soup, undiluted
- ⅓ cup milk
  Dash of cayenne pepper

Combine potato flakes, tuna fish, eggs, celery, pimiento, onion, and salt. Mix well. Form mixture into 12 balls, 2 inches in diameter.

Mix corn flakes and parsley. Coat tuna balls with corn flake mixture. Arrange tuna balls in an 8-inch round glass baking dish. Microwave at HIGH 6 to 7 minutes. Turn tuna puffs at 2 minute intervals.

Microwave soup, milk, and cayenne pepper in a 4-cup glass measure at HIGH 2 to 2½ minutes. Stir. Serve over tuna puffs.

Yield: 12 servings.

HOT CHEESE TUNA SALAD

Power: HIGH
Microwave Time: 3 to 4 Minutes

- 1 cup shredded Cheddar cheese
- 3 hard-cooked eggs, chopped
- 1 (7-ounce) can tuna fish, drained
- 2 tablespoons chopped green pepper
- 2 tablespoons chopped onion
- 2 tablespoons chopped stuffed olives
- 2 tablespoons chopped sweet pickle
- ½ cup mayonnaise
  Crackers or buns

Combine cheese, eggs, tuna fish, green pepper, onion, olives, pickle, and mayonnaise in a 1-quart glass bowl. Stir until blended. Microwave at HIGH 3 minutes. Stir after 1 minute.

Let mixture stand 1 minute before serving. Serve with crackers or buns.

Yield: 2 cups.

PARADE-DRESSED WHITEFISH

Power: HIGH
Microwave Time: 8½ to 9 Minutes

- 2 pounds whitefish fillets, divided
- ½ cup butter or margarine, divided
- 1 cup chopped onion
- 2 cups toasted bread cubes
- 1 cup shredded Cheddar cheese
- 2 tablespoons chopped parsley
- 2 teaspoons dry mustard
- ¼ teaspoon salt
  Dash of pepper
- 2 tablespoons lemon juice, divided
- ¼ teaspoon paprika

Arrange 1 pound fish fillets in a greased 2-quart glass casserole.

Microwave ¼ cup butter in a 2-quart casserole at HIGH 1 minute. Add chopped onions to melted butter. Microwave at HIGH 2 minutes. Mix in bread cubes, cheese, parsley, mustard, salt, pepper, and 1 tablespoon lemon juice. Spread stuffing mixture over fish fillets in casserole. Cover with remaining 1 pound fish fillets.

Microwave remaining ¼ cup butter in a 1-cup glass measure at HIGH 30 seconds. Stir in remaining 1 tablespoon of lemon juice. Brush fillets with lemon butter. Sprinkle with paprika.

Cover stuffed fillets with waxed paper. Microwave at HIGH 5 minutes. Rotate dish ½ turn after 3 minutes. Let casserole stand for 5 minutes before serving.

Yield: 6 to 8 servings.

GRAINS AND PASTAS

Pastas and grains like rice, grits, and oatmeal are favorite foods. Frequently prepared in all parts of the country, these foods can be used in a variety of ways.

Oatmeal, cream of wheat, and grits are traditionally served in different regions of the country as breakfast foods. Rice and pastas are served hot with butter and seasonings, topped with a sauce or combined with other ingredients as a casserole.

Because these foods are a dry food they require a certain amount of time to rehydrate or absorb moisture. This time will be about the same whether cooking conventionally or microwaving.

BASICS FOR MICROWAVED RICE
- Use a 2- to 3-quart casserole when cooking regular rice to allow room for the water to expand during boiling.
- Combine water, salt, and butter. Bring to boil at HIGH; then stir in rice and complete cooking at MEDIUM.
- Cover with glass lid or plastic wrap. Turn a small portion of the plastic wrap back at one corner to form a vent.
- Microwave according to times given on the chart.
- Stir or rearrange after half the cooking time.
- Let stand, covered, several minutes before serving.

BASICS FOR MICROWAVED CEREALS
Grits, oatmeals, and other cooked cereals are easy to prepare in the microwave oven. They cook in a simple process right in the bowl, so you may find yourself enjoying and preparing cooked cereals more. There is no messy pot to clean up, and you can prepare individual or several servings.

To microwave cereals:
- Combine cereal and hot tap water in an appropriate large-sized bowl.
- Microwave at HIGH according to times given on the chart.
- Stir well after half the cooking time.
- Serve immediately for a firm-textured cereal or let stand several minutes if you like a softer texture cereal.

BASICS FOR MICROWAVED PASTAS
As is true of rice, pasta requires the same length of time to microwave as to cook conventionally. To microwave pasta:
- Use a cooking dish large enough to allow the pasta to be completely covered with water during microwaving. A flat 12- x 8-inch or 13- x 9-inch dish works well for

long flat pasta, and a 2- or 3-quart casserole is a good size for macaroni, rotini, and other smaller-type pasta.
- A tight cover of plastic wrap works best to hold in the steam. Turn a small portion of the plastic wrap back at one corner to form a vent.

- Combine water, oil, and salt in the casserole.
- Microwave at HIGH to boil; then add the pasta.
- Microwave at MEDIUM to cook. Drain immediately and serve or combine with other ingredients.

PASTA COOKING CHART

Type	Raw Pasta	Water	Tablespoon of Oil	Casserole	Yield Cooked	Minutes at HIGH to Boil Water	Minutes at MEDIUM to Cook Pasta
Egg Noodles	2 cups	3 cups	1	3-quart	2½ cups	7 to 9	9 to 11
Macaroni	3 cups	3 cups	1	3-quart	4 cups	7 to 9	11 to 13
Spaghetti	7- to 8-ounce package	4 cups	1	3-quart	4 cups	8 to 10	11 to 13
Lasagna Noodles	8-ounce package	6 cups	1	13- x 9-inch	4 cups	11 to 13	14 to 16
Macaroni and Cheese Mix	7¼-ounce package	2 cups	none	2-quart	3 cups	4 to 5	15 to 17

CEREAL COOKING CHART

Type	Raw Cereal	Hot Tap Water	Salt	Casserole	Yield Cooked	Minutes at HIGH
Oatmeal						
Quick-cooking	⅔ cup	1½ cups	½ teaspoon	2-quart	2 servings	2 to 3
	1⅓ cups	3 cups	¾ teaspoon	2½-quart	4 servings	5 to 6
Old-fashioned	⅔ cup	1½ cups	½ teaspoon	2-quart	2 servings	6 to 7
	1⅓ cups	3 cups	¾ teaspoon	3-quart	4 servings	8 to 9
Cream of Wheat	⅓ cup	1¾ cups	¼ teaspoon	2-quart	2 servings	5 to 6
	⅔ cup	3½ cups	½ teaspoon	3-quart	4 servings	7 to 8
Grits						
Quick-cooking	⅓ cup	1⅓ cups	¼ teaspoon	2-quart	2 servings	6 to 7
Instant	1-ounce packets	water and salt as directions call for			1 serving	1

To serve cooked cereals, stir butter and other spices, seasonings, and flavorings into the hot cereal as desired.

Oatmeal toppings
- Brown sugar
- Raisins
- Chopped dates

Grits seasonings
- Shredded cheese
- Garlic powder
- Finely chopped green onion
- Crumbled bacon

RICE COOKING CHART

Type	Raw Rice	Water	Casser- role	Yield Cooked	Minutes at	
					HIGH to Boil Water	MEDIUM to Cook Rice
Long grain white	1 cup	2 cups	2-quart	3 cups	4 to 5	14 to 17
Long grain white	1½ cups	3 cups	3-quart	4½ cups	6 to 7	14 to 18
Brown rice	1 cup	3 cups	3-quart	4 cups	6 to 7	30 to 35
Long grain white and wild rice mix	6-oz. pkg.	2½ cups	2-quart	3 cups	5 to 6	25 to 30
Precooked rice	1 cup	2 cups	1-quart	2 cups	3 to 4	Let stand covered 5 to 10

RICE ROMANOFF
(Conventional Recipe)

   3   **cups cooked rice**
   2   **green onions, finely chopped**
   1   **(12-ounce) carton large curd**
         cottage cheese
   1   **(8-ounce) carton commercial sour**
         cream
  ¼   **cup milk**
  ¼   **teaspoon hot sauce**
  ½   **teaspoon salt**
  ½   **cup grated Parmesan cheese**

Combine rice and onion; set aside. Combine cottage cheese, sour cream, milk, hot sauce, and salt; stir into rice. Spoon mixture into a greased 1½-quart casserole, sprinkle with Parmesan cheese, and bake at 350° for 25 minutes.

Yield: 6 to 8 servings.

To Microwave Rice Romanoff

- Cut down on amount of cottage cheese.
- Omit milk.
- Add Worcestershire sauce and double amount of cheese for flavor enhancer and color.
- Use a slightly larger casserole.
- Wait until near the end of cooking time to add cheese.

RICE ROMANOFF

Power: HIGH
Microwave Time: 10 to 11 Minutes

   3   **cups cooked rice**
   1   **cup large curd cottage cheese**
   1   **(8-ounce) carton commercial sour**
         cream
  ¼   **teaspoon hot sauce**
  ½   **teaspoon salt**
  ½   **teaspoon Worcestershire sauce**
   1   **cup grated Parmesan cheese**

Place cooked rice in 2-quart casserole. Combine cottage cheese, sour cream, hot sauce, salt, and Worcestershire sauce. Stir into the rice to mix well. Cover. Microwave at HIGH 8 minutes, stirring after 4 minutes.

Sprinkle cheese on top. Microwave at HIGH, uncovered, 2 to 3 minutes.

Yield: 6 to 8 servings.

RICE

Power: HIGH/MEDIUM
Microwave Time: 18 to 22 Minutes

   2   **cups hot water**
   1   **teaspoon salt**
   1   **cup long grain rice, uncooked**

Combine water and salt in a 2½-quart casserole. Microwave at HIGH 4 to 5 minutes or until boiling. Stir in the rice. Cover with plastic wrap.

Microwave at MEDIUM 14 to 17 minutes. Stir once after 8 minutes. Let stand, covered, 5 to 6 minutes.

Yield: 4 to 6 servings.

BAKED RICE DELUXE

Power: HIGH/MEDIUM
Microwave Time: 15 to 17 Minutes

  1 **cup chopped onion**
  2 **tablespoons butter or margarine**
1½ **cups quick-cooking rice, uncooked**
 ½ **teaspoon salt**
1½ **cups water**
  1 **(10-ounce) package frozen chopped spinach**
  1 **(5-ounce) jar sharp process cheese spread**
  1 **(10¾-ounce) can cream of mushroom soup, undiluted**
 ¼ **teaspoon ground nutmeg**

Combine onion and butter in 2-quart casserole. Cover with plastic wrap. Microwave at HIGH 3 minutes. Stir after 2 minutes. Add rice, salt, and water. Cover with plastic wrap. Microwave at HIGH 3 minutes. Let stand, covered.

Pierce spinach package with a fork and place on paper plate. Microwave spinach at HIGH 5 minutes, or until thawed. Drain well. Add to rice mixture. Stir in cheese. Mix well. Stir in soup and nutmeg. Microwave at MEDIUM 4 to 6 minutes. Let stand several minutes before serving.

Yield: 6 servings.

HERBED RICE

Power: HIGH
Microwave Time: 7 to 10 Minutes

  1 **cup chopped onion**
  3 **tablespoons butter or margarine**
  1 **teaspoon garlic powder**
 ¼ **cup finely minced parsley**
 ¼ **teaspoon cayenne pepper**
  3 **cups cooked rice**

Combine onion and butter in a 2½-quart casserole. Cover. Microwave at HIGH 4 to 5 minutes.

Add other ingredients and toss lightly to mix rice well. Cover. Microwave at HIGH 3 to 5 minutes or until thoroughly heated. Stir well after 2 minutes. Let stand several minutes before serving.

Yield: 6 servings.

ORANGE RICE

Power: HIGH
Microwaving Time: 12 to 13 Minutes

  1 **cup chopped celery**
 ¼ **cup chopped onion**
 ¼ **cup butter or margarine**
  1 **cup water**
 ¼ **cup frozen orange juice concentrate, undiluted**
 ½ **teaspoon salt**
1⅓ **cups packaged precooked rice**

Combine celery, onion, and butter in a 1½-quart casserole. Cover. Microwave at HIGH 5 minutes or until celery is soft.

Stir in water, juice concentrate, and salt. Cover. Microwave at HIGH 7 to 8 minutes or until boiling.

Stir in rice. Let stand, covered, 5 to 10 minutes. Fluff with fork before serving.

Yield: 4 servings.

ONE-DISH RICE FROM A MIX

Power: HIGH/MEDIUM-LOW
Microwave Time: see below

  1 **package rice mix**
    Water

Measure the amount of water required by the package directions. Pour into a 2½- or 3-quart casserole. Cover with plastic wrap. Microwave at HIGH until boiling.

Stir in rice and seasonings. Cover with plastic wrap. Microwave at MEDIUM-LOW until rice is tender, usually about the same time as conventional time given in package directions.

Yield: see package.

BAKED WILD RICE

Power: HIGH/MEDIUM-HIGH
Microwave Time: 15 Minutes

    1   (6-ounce) package wild rice mix
          with spices
    2½ cups water
    ½   cup milk
    ⅛   teaspoon pepper
    ¼   teaspoon salt
    2   cups shredded sharp Cheddar
          cheese
    ¼   cup chopped ripe olives

Combine rice, package of spices, and water in a 2-quart casserole. Cover with plastic wrap. Microwave at HIGH 10 minutes. Let stand, covered, 10 minutes.

Combine milk, pepper, salt, and cheese in a 4-cup glass measure. Cover and microwave at HIGH 1 minute. Add olives.

Stir the milk mixture into the cooked rice. Microwave at MEDIUM-HIGH 4 minutes. Let stand, covered, 4 to 5 minutes before serving.

Yield: 6 to 8 servings.

SOUTHERN GRITS CASSEROLE

Power: HIGH
Microwave Time: 12 Minutes

    2½ cups water
    1   cup quick-cooking grits,
          uncooked
    3   tablespoons butter or margarine
    1½ teaspoons salt
    ½   teaspoon white pepper
    ½   teaspoon cayenne pepper
    3   eggs, beaten
    1½ cups shredded Cheddar cheese,
          divided

Microwave the water at HIGH until boiling in a 1½-quart casserole, or use the conventional range to boil.

Add grits, butter, salt, and peppers to the water. Cover with waxed paper. Microwave at HIGH 5 minutes, stirring twice. Stir some of the hot grits into the beaten eggs. Stir in 1 cup of cheese and add egg-cheese mixture to grits. Stir well to mix. Microwave

at HIGH 5 minutes. Rotate dish ½ turn after 2 minutes.

Sprinkle the reserved ½ cup cheese on top of mixture. Cover. Microwave at HIGH 2 minutes or until cheese melts. Let stand 3 to 4 minutes before serving. Serve hot.

Yield: 6 to 8 servings.

MACARONI DELIGHT

Power: MEDIUM-HIGH
Microwave Time: 13 to 16 Minutes

    1   (10¾-ounce) can cream of onion
          soup, undiluted
    1½ cups shredded mild Cheddar
          cheese, divided
    ¼   cup chopped green onion
    5   tablespoons finely chopped
          parsley, divided
    ½   cup milk
    1   tablespoon butter or margarine
    1   tablespoon Worcestershire sauce
    1   teaspoon salt
    ¼   teaspoon pepper
    3   cups cooked macaroni

Combine soup, 1 cup of cheese, onion, 3 tablespoons parsley, milk, butter, Worcestershire sauce, salt, and pepper in a 2-quart casserole. Microwave at MEDIUM-HIGH 5 to 6 minutes.

Stir in cooked macaroni. Cover. Microwave at MEDIUM-HIGH 8 to 10 minutes. Stir well after 5 minutes.

Sprinkle remaining cheese and parsley over top. Let stand, covered, 3 to 4 minutes before serving.

Yield: 4 to 6 servings.

Micronote: Remove stems from fresh parsley, chives, basil, sage, and other herbs. Rinse and pat dry. Spread ½ to 1 cup of the rinsed herbs between two sheets of paper towel. Microwave at HIGH 2 to 2½ minutes. Crumble or break as desired and store in an airtight container.

MEATS

Because meats require a little more attention whether cooking conventionally or with microwave many people are hesitant to use their microwave oven for roasting meats. It is possible to get good results, especially when roasting tender cuts of meat, if basic rules are followed.

WHAT IS NEEDED
FOR MICROWAVE ROASTING

In microwaving meats certain accessories are a must. Here are the needed items:
- A 12- by 8-inch flat glass casserole.
- A microwave plastic roasting rack or a glass lid or saucers to use as a trivet.
- Aluminum foil to use as shielding and to cover the roast while it is standing.
- A good thermometer; conventional thermometers can be used to test for doneness while the meat is outside the oven, and a microwave thermometer can be left in the meat while it is in the oven.
- Either waxed paper or paper towels to prevent spattering.
- Oven cooking bags, which are useful when cooking pork and other foods that need steam to tenderize and stay juicy.

MICROWAVING LESS
TENDER PIECES OF MEAT

This category includes pot roasts, braised beef, stew meats, and other meats which require long, slow cooking in order to tenderize. Usually these meats should be microwaved in deeper containers and casseroles, with some liquid added to create steam, and should be covered with plastic wrap to hold in the steam. Oven cooking bags can also be used to form a tight covering for roasts and other less tender cuts of meat.

The meat can be pre-browned on top of the range, in a browning dish, or by adding commercial brown bouquet sauce for color, if desired.

Cook the meat until tender; then add other ingredients such as vegetables for stews and boiled dinners.

BASIC BROWNING SAUCE

- 1 egg, slightly beaten
- 1 teaspoon commercial brown bouquet sauce
- ¾ teaspoon ground sage
- ½ teaspoon pepper

Combine all ingredients in a jar with a tight lid. Mix thoroughly. Spread on meats at the end of the microwaving to add additional color, if desired.

Basic Browning Sauce can be stored, tightly covered, in the refrigerator up to a week.

117

TENDER BEEF ROASTS

The lower and variable power settings now available on some microwave ovens make rolled or standing rib roasts simple and easy to prepare. Follow these steps for best results:

- Select evenly shaped roasts or form into an even shape by tying with heavy string.
- Completely defrost a frozen roast.
- Place roast on a microwave roasting rack in a flat baking dish.
- If desired, brush Basic Browning Sauce over the entire roast.
- Cover roast with waxed paper. This holds the heat close to the meat.
- Microwave at MEDIUM to desired doneness.
- To avoid overcooking, pay attention to the internal temperature of the meat. Use the temperature sensor probe if your oven has one.
- Check for doneness by inserting the thermometer into the thickest part of the meat, avoiding contact with bone or fat.
- If you use a standard meat thermometer, remove roast from oven and insert thermometer into the thickest part of the meat. Remove thermometer before returning meat to the microwave oven.
- Meat temperature may rise 5° to 10° while standing.
- Check at minimum cooking time.
- At the end of microwaving time, cover roast with a foil tent and let stand 10 to 15 minutes.

MICROWAVING GROUND MEATS

All types of ground meats can be microwaved with very good results. Ground beef can be shaped into patties, loaves, or meatballs. Serve plain for a low calorie meal or topped with the following:

- Barbecue sauce, chili sauce, or catsup.
- Dairy sour cream, parsley, and crumbled bacon.

Handle ground beef lightly to prevent it from toughening. We have included a technique for a Basic Browning Sauce, but ground beef will brown slightly as it stands and you may prefer not to use a browner.

Always use lean ground beef or chuck for microwaving. Ground beef patties can be cooked on a microwave plastic roasting rack, which allows most of the drippings to drain away. Meat loaf can be shaped into a flat circle or pressed into a glass or microwave plastic baking ring.

When microwaving ground beef, select HIGH power for the fastest cooking or MEDIUM-HIGH or even MEDIUM if slower cooking is preferred.

Follow the same techniques for ground pork and ham. Top with sweet-and-sour or other preferred sauces. Either MEDIUM-HIGH or MEDIUM power settings can be used to cook ground pork and ham. The amount of sugar in the curing process will help you determine which setting to use.

BEEF MICROWAVING CHART

Desired Doneness	Temperature at End of Cooking Time	After 10 to 15 Minutes Standing Time	Approximate Minutes at MEDIUM Per Pound
Rare	125° to 130°	140°	10 to 12
Medium	145° to 150°	155°	13 to 15
Well Done	155° to 160°	165°	14 to 16

CARROT MEAT LOAF
(Conventional Recipe)

> 3 **pounds ground beef**
> 1 **large onion, grated**
> 3 **carrots, grated**
> 12 **saltines, finely crushed**
> 1 **large potato, grated**
> 2 **eggs**
> **Soy sauce**
> **Salt and pepper to taste**
> 2 **tablespoons honey**

Combine the first 6 ingredients; then add ½ cup soy sauce and season with salt and pepper. Mix well, and pack into a large loaf pan. Unmold onto a shallow baking pan. Brush top with soy sauce. Bake at 350° for 1 hour and 15 minutes; then brush with the honey. Bake for 15 minutes longer.
Yield: 6 to 8 servings.

To Microwave Carrot Meat Loaf

- Substitute ground chuck for ground beef.
- Use only 1½ pounds of beef.
- Adjust other ingredients to about half of the original.
- Substitute grated carrot for the grated potato.
- Combine soy sauce and catsup as a glaze.
- Shape into a rounded flat loaf and cook in a 12- x 8-inch baking dish, rather than a loaf pan.

CARROT MEAT LOAF

Power: HIGH
Microwave Time: 15 to 20 Minutes

> 1½ **pounds ground chuck**
> 1 **small onion, grated**
> 2 **carrots, grated**
> 6 **saltines, finely crushed**
> 1 **egg**
> 1 **teaspoon salt**
> ⅛ **teaspoon pepper**
> 1 **tablespoon soy sauce**
> 1 **tablespoon catsup**

Combine first 7 ingredients. Blend well. Place the mixture in a 12- x 8-inch baking dish and shape into a rounded loaf. Mix soy sauce and catsup. Brush meat loaf with soy-catsup mixture. Cover with waxed paper.
Microwave at HIGH 15 to 20 minutes. Check for doneness at the minimum time. Let stand, covered, about 6 to 8 minutes before slicing.
Yield: 6 servings.

BASIC MEAT LOAF

Power: MEDIUM
Microwave Time: 12 Minutes

> 1 **pound ground chuck**
> 2 **eggs, lightly beaten**
> ½ **cup cracker crumbs**
> 2 **tablespoons minced onion**
> ¾ **teaspoon salt**
> ¼ **teaspoon pepper**
> ⅓ **cup catsup**
> ½ **cup grated Cheddar cheese**

Combine all ingredients except cheese in a bowl. Arrange this mixture in a doughnut shape in a 9-inch glass pie plate.
Cover with waxed paper. Microwave at MEDIUM 10 minutes. Rotate dish ½ turn after 5 minutes. Remove drippings and sprinkle with cheese. Microwave at MEDIUM 2 minutes.
Let stand, covered, 6 to 8 minutes before serving.
Yield: 4 servings.

MACHO MEAT LOAF

Power: MEDIUM-HIGH
Microwave Time: 14 to 16 Minutes

- 1½ pounds ground chuck
- 1 (1½-ounce) envelope dry onion soup mix
- 1 egg, beaten
- ½ cup cracker meal
- ½ teaspoon salt
- ⅛ teaspoon pepper
- ⅛ teaspoon garlic salt
- 1 (8-ounce) can tomato sauce
- 1 (2½-ounce) can sliced mushrooms, drained

Combine ground beef, soup mix, egg, cracker meal, salt, pepper, and garlic salt. Press into a microwave baking ring or place meat in a flat casserole and form into a doughnut shape.

Cover with waxed paper. Microwave at MEDIUM-HIGH 12 to 13 minutes. Remove any excess drippings.

Pour tomato sauce over the meat and top with mushroom slices. Microwave at MEDIUM-HIGH 2 to 3 minutes. Let stand, covered, 3 to 5 minutes.

Yield: 6 servings.

TANGY MEAT LOAF

Power: MEDIUM
Microwave Time: 15 to 16 Minutes

- 1½ pounds ground chuck
- 1 egg, slightly beaten
- ¼ cup dry bread crumbs
- ¼ cup finely chopped onion
- ¼ cup milk
- ¼ cup chopped green pepper
- ½ teaspoon salt
- ¼ teaspoon garlic powder
- ¼ teaspoon pepper
- 1 tablespoon Worcestershire sauce Basic Glaze

Combine all ingredients in a large bowl. Shape into a flat round loaf or press into a microwave ring mold.

Cover with waxed paper. Microwave at MEDIUM 15 to 16 minutes or until done. Let stand, covered, in the baking dish 5 minutes.

To serve, remove excess drippings. Reserve 1 tablespoon of meat drippings for glaze. Turn out on a serving platter. Spoon hot Basic Glaze over meat loaf to serve.

Yield: 6 servings.

Basic Glaze:

Power: HIGH
Microwave Time: 1 Minute

- 1 tablespoon brown sugar
- 1 tablespoon Worcestershire sauce
- ¼ teaspoon prepared mustard
- 1 tablespoon meat loaf drippings

Combine all ingredients in a glass custard cup. Microwave at HIGH 1 minute. Spoon over Tangy Meat Loaf when ready to serve.

Yield: ⅓ cup.

SOMETHING SPECIAL MEAT LOAF

Power: HIGH
Microwave Time: 14 to 15 Minutes

- ¾ pound fresh mushrooms, divided
- 1½ pounds ground chuck
- ½ cup soft bread crumbs
- ½ cup catsup
- 2 eggs, lightly beaten
- 1½ teaspoons salt
- ¼ teaspoon pepper
- 2 tablespoons butter or margarine Meat Loaf Topping

Wipe mushrooms with a damp paper towel and trim stem ends. Reserve 10 whole mushrooms. Finely chop remaining mushrooms. Place in a large bowl and stir in ground beef, crumbs, catsup, eggs, salt, and pepper. Stir lightly.

Shape half the meat mixture into an oval about 1-inch thick in a flat baking dish. Press 5 of the reserved mushrooms down in the center of the meat. Cover with remaining meat and pat into an oval shape. Cover with waxed paper.

Microwave at HIGH 7 minutes. Rotate dish ¼ turn. Microwave at HIGH 6 to 8 minutes. Let stand, covered, while preparing Topping.

Slice remaining mushrooms. Place in a 2-cup glass measure with butter. Microwave at HIGH 1 to 2 minutes.

To serve, place meat loaf on serving platter. Spoon Topping over meat loaf and garnish with mushroom slices that have been cooked in butter.

Yield: 6 servings.

Meat Loaf Topping:

Power: HIGH
Microwave Time: 2 to 3 Minutes

⅓   cup catsup
¼   cup pineapple preserves
2   teaspoons Worcestershire sauce

Combine all ingredients in a 2-cup glass measure. Microwave at HIGH 2 to 3 minutes or until thoroughly heated.

Yield: ¾ cup.

CABBAGE ROLLS

Power: HIGH
Microwave Time: 22 to 27 Minutes

8   whole, fresh cabbage leaves
½   cup water
1   pound lean ground chuck
1½   teaspoons salt, divided
⅛   teaspoon pepper
½   cup instant rice, uncooked
3   tablespoons finely chopped onion
1   (15-ounce) can tomato sauce
2   tablespoons firmly packed brown sugar
2   tablespoons lemon juice

Place cabbage leaves and water in a 3-quart casserole. Cover with plastic wrap. Microwave at HIGH 7 to 9 minutes, or until leaves are soft and pliable.

Stir together ground beef, 1 teaspoon salt, pepper, rice, and onion. Divide into 8 portions and place one portion on each of the partially cooked cabbage leaves. Roll leaf around meat mixture. Place rolls, seam-side down, in a 3-quart casserole.

Blend remaining ½ teaspoon salt and other ingredients. Pour over cabbage rolls. Cover with plastic wrap. Microwave at HIGH 15 to 18 minutes. Rotate dish ½ turn and baste rolls with sauce after 7 to 9 minutes of microwaving. Let stand, covered, for 5 minutes before serving.

Yield: 4 servings.

CHILI BEEF CASSEROLE

Power: HIGH/MEDIUM-HIGH
Microwave Time: 13 to 16 Minutes

1   pound ground chuck
1   medium-sized onion, sliced
½   cup chopped celery
2   teaspoons seasoned salt
½   teaspoon pepper
1½   teaspoons chili powder
1   (12-ounce) can whole kernel corn, drained
1   (15½-ounce) can red kidney beans, drained
1   (3¼-ounce) can pitted and halved ripe olives, drained
1   (8-ounce) can tomato sauce
1   cup coarsely crushed corn chips
½   cup shredded Cheddar cheese

Combine ground beef, onion, and celery in a 2½-quart casserole. Microwave at HIGH 6 to 7 minutes.

Add remaining ingredients except corn chips and cheese. Stir to combine. Microwave at HIGH 5 to 6 minutes.

Top with corn chips. Sprinkle with cheese. Microwave at MEDIUM-HIGH 2 to 3 minutes to melt cheese.

Let stand, covered with waxed paper, 3 to 5 minutes before serving.

Yield: 6 to 8 servings.

SPICY BURGERS WITH MUSHROOM SAUCE

Power: HIGH/MEDIUM-HIGH
Microwave Time: 12 to 15 Minutes

1½	pounds ground chuck
1	(1½-ounce) envelope dry onion soup mix
1	egg, beaten
1	tablespoon Worcestershire sauce
1	(10¾-ounce) can cream of mushroom soup, undiluted
⅓	cup water
	Toast or cooked rice

Combine ground beef, soup mix, egg, and Worcestershire sauce. Shape mixture into 6 patties. Arrange patties on a microwave roasting rack placed in a 12- x 8-inch glass baking dish. Cover with waxed paper. Microwave at HIGH 7 to 8 minutes.

Remove patties. Pour off meat drippings from dish. Return patties to the baking dish.

Combine soup and ⅓ cup water. Pour over the patties. Cover with plastic wrap. Microwave at MEDIUM-HIGH 5 to 7 minutes or until sauce is bubbly hot. Serve over toast or hot cooked rice.

Yield: 4 servings.

BEEF AND RICE DINNER

Power: HIGH/MEDIUM
Microwave Time: 23 to 24 Minutes

1	pound ground chuck
3	cups cooked rice
1	(12-ounce) can whole kernel corn, drained
½	teaspoon salt
¼	teaspoon pepper
2	(8-ounce) cans tomato sauce, divided
½	cup finely chopped onion
¼	cup chopped green pepper
½	teaspoon ground oregano

Place ground beef in 1½-quart casserole. Microwave at HIGH 3 to 4 minutes. Stir once or twice during microwaving to break the meat apart. Drain to remove excess drippings, if necessary.

Arrange rice in a single layer in a 2-quart casserole. Spread corn over the rice. Sprinkle with salt and pepper. Pour 1 can tomato sauce over corn and spread with chopped onion. Spread cooked beef in a layer over the onions. Combine remaining tomato sauce, green pepper, and oregano. Pour over other layers.

Cover with plastic wrap. Microwave at MEDIUM 20 minutes, rotating dish after 10 minutes of microwaving. Let stand, covered, 5 minutes before serving.

Yield: 4 to 6 servings.

BEEF RING

Power: MEDIUM-HIGH
Microwave Time: 12 to 14 Minutes

1½	pounds ground chuck
1	cup stuffing mix
¼	cup milk
2	eggs
1	small onion, minced
1½	teaspoons salt
1¼	teaspoons hot sauce
	Cooked Spanish rice or mashed potatoes

Combine all ingredients except Spanish rice in a large glass bowl. Press into a microwave ring mold.

Cover with waxed paper. Microwave at MEDIUM-HIGH 12 to 14 minutes. Let stand, covered, 5 to 6 minutes before removing from mold.

To serve, unmold onto serving platter. Fill center with Spanish rice or mashed potatoes.

Yield: 6 servings.

Any hungry gang will love Chuckwagon Stew (p.126) cooked in the microwave oven and served in a casserole. Bake bread conventionally.

CHEESEBURGER-VEGETABLE CASSEROLE

Power: HIGH
Microwave Time: 20 to 21 Minutes

1	pound ground chuck
½	cup chopped onion
¼	cup butter or margarine
¼	cup all-purpose flour
1	teaspoon salt
	Dash of pepper
1½	cups milk
1¼	cups (6-ounces) shredded sharp American cheese, divided
1	teaspoon Worcestershire sauce
1	(10-ounce) package frozen mixed vegetables
¼	cup chopped pimiento
	Packaged instant mashed potatoes (enough for 4 servings)

Crumble the ground beef in a 2-quart casserole. Stir in the chopped onion. Cover with waxed paper. Microwave at HIGH 5 minutes. Stir several times during cooking to break up meat. Drain off excess drippings.

Place the butter in a 4-cup glass measure. Microwave at HIGH 30 seconds. Stir in the flour, salt, and pepper. Gradually stir in the milk. Microwave at HIGH, uncovered, 1 minute; stir. Microwave at HIGH until thickened and bubbly, about 3 minutes more, stirring at 30 second intervals. Stir in 1 cup of the cheese and the Worcestershire sauce. Add to meat mixture.

Break up frozen vegetables. Stir vegetables and pimiento into meat mixture. Turn mixture into an 8-inch glass baking dish. Cover with waxed paper. Microwave at HIGH 10 minutes. Rotate dish ½ turn after 5 minutes.

Prepare the packaged, instant mashed potatoes according to package directions,

except decrease water by ¼ cup. Spoon the prepared potatoes around edge of casserole. Sprinkle remaining shredded cheese over potatoes. Microwave, uncovered, at HIGH 1 minute or until cheese is melted.
Yield: 4 to 6 servings.

HAMBURGER CASSEROLE WITH ZUCCHINI

Power: HIGH
Microwave Time: 23 to 25 Minutes

1½	pounds ground chuck
1	medium-sized onion, chopped
1	(16-ounce) can tomatoes with juice
1	(15-ounce) can tomato sauce
	Garlic salt to taste
1	teaspoon salt
¼	teaspoon pepper
2	(16-ounce) cans whole kernel corn and juice
3	medium-size zucchini, sliced

Combine beef and onion in a 3-quart casserole. Microwave, uncovered, at HIGH 4 to 5 minutes. Drain off excess drippings. Add tomatoes and tomato sauce. Microwave at HIGH, covered, 4 to 5 minutes.

Add garlic salt, salt, pepper, corn, and zucchini. Stir well. Cover with plastic wrap. Microwave at HIGH 15 minutes. Rotate dish ½ turn after 8 minutes. Let stand, covered, 2 minutes before serving.
Yield: 6 to 8 servings.

Juicy and tender, Pork Roast (p.135) is fast and easy to serve. When accompanied by Fresh Asparagus (p.176) and Gingered Carrots (p.180), it is special enough for a company dinner.

BEEF STUFFED GREEN PEPPERS

Power: HIGH
Microwave Time: 15 to 18 Minutes

- 6 medium green peppers
- 1 teaspoon salt
- ⅛ teaspoon pepper
- 1 tablespoon Worcestershire sauce
- ⅓ cup precooked rice, uncooked
- 1 egg, beaten
- 1 (10¾-ounce) can tomato soup, undiluted and divided
- ¼ cup finely chopped onion
- 1½ pounds ground chuck, browned
- ½ cup shredded sharp Cheddar cheese

Cut a slice from stem end of each pepper. Remove seeds and membrane.

Combine salt, pepper, Worcestershire sauce, rice, egg, ¾ cup soup, onion, and ground beef. Stir lightly.

Pack each pepper with approximately ½ cup of the mixture. Place filled peppers in a round microwave casserole. (Peppers should fit tightly.) Pour remaining soup over filled peppers. Cover with plastic wrap. Microwave at HIGH 15 to 18 minutes. Sprinkle with cheese. Let stand, covered, 2 to 3 minutes.
Yield: 6 servings.

BAKED STUFFED GREEN PEPPERS

Power: HIGH
Microwave Time: 22 to 25 Minutes

- 6 small green peppers
- 1½ pounds ground chuck
- ¼ cup finely chopped onion
- ⅓ cup oats, uncooked
- 1 teaspoon salt
- ⅛ teaspoon pepper
- 1 egg, slightly beaten
- 1 cup spaghetti sauce, divided

Cut top off each pepper. Remove seeds and membrane. Combine ground beef, onion, oats, salt, pepper, egg, and ⅓ cup spaghetti sauce. Fill peppers with meat mixture.

Place the peppers in a 2½- or 3-quart casserole. (They should fit snugly.) Spread remaining spaghetti sauce over peppers. Cover with plastic wrap.

Microwave at HIGH 22 to 25 minutes. Let stand, covered, 5 minutes before serving.
Yield: 6 servings.

CHEESY MACARONI AND MEATBALLS

Power: HIGH
Microwave Time: 20 to 22 Minutes

- 2 eggs, slightly beaten
- 1 slice bread, crumbled
- 2 tablespoons finely chopped onion
- 2 tablespoons finely chopped green pepper
- 2 tablespoons finely chopped parsley
- ½ teaspoon oregano
- ¼ teaspoon garlic salt
- 1 pound ground chuck
- 1 (7¼-ounce) package macaroni and cheese dinner
- 4 cups hot water
- ½ teaspoon salt
- 1 (2½-ounce) envelope sour cream sauce mix
- 2 cups milk

Combine eggs, bread, onion, green pepper, parsley, oregano, and garlic salt. Blend well; then add the ground beef. Shape into 24 meatballs. Arrange the meatballs on a microwave roasting rack placed in a 12- x 8-inch baking dish. Microwave at HIGH 5 minutes. Turn each meatball after 2 minutes. Remove meatballs and drain drippings from dish.

Place macaroni from the dinner in a 2-quart casserole. Add 4 cups hot water and ½ teaspoon salt. Cover with plastic wrap. Microwave at HIGH 5 minutes. Stir well. Microwave at HIGH 5 minutes. Drain.

Add dry cheese mix from the dinner and sour cream sauce mix to the macaroni. Stir well. Add milk. Pour the macaroni mixture in the 12- x 8-inch baking dish. Top with meatballs. Microwave, uncovered, at HIGH 5 to 7 minutes. Rotate dish ½ turn after 3 minutes. Let stand 2 to 3 minutes before serving.
Yield: 6 servings.

EASY MEATBALLS

Power: HIGH/MEDIUM
Microwave Time: 21 to 22 Minutes

> 1 **pound ground chuck**
> 2 **tablespoons quick-cooking oats, uncooked**
> 1 **cup bread crumbs**
> 1 **onion, sliced**
> 1 **teaspoon salt**
> 1 **(1-pound) can whole tomatoes, drained**

Combine beef, oats, and bread crumbs. Shape into 12 balls. Arrange on microwave roasting rack placed in a 12- x 8-inch baking dish. Microwave at HIGH 6 minutes. Rotate dish after 3 minutes.

Remove drippings from dish. Place cooked meatballs directly in dish. Spread onion slices over meatballs. Stir salt into tomatoes and spread over onions and meatballs.

Cover with waxed paper. Microwave at MEDIUM 15 to 16 minutes. Stir after 8 minutes. Let stand, covered, 3 to 5 minutes before serving.

Yield: 4 servings.

TACOS IN A BOWL

Power: HIGH
Microwave Time: 15 to 18 Minutes

> 1 **pound ground chuck**
> ½ **teaspoon chili powder**
> 1 **(10¾-ounce) can cream of celery soup, undiluted**
> 1 **(4-ounce) can diced green chili peppers, drained**
> ¼ **teaspoon instant minced onion**
> ½ **cup water**
> 1 **(6-ounce) package corn chips**
> 2 **large firm ripe tomatoes, sliced and peeled**
> 1 **cup shredded mild Cheddar cheese**

Preheat browning dish according to manufacturer's directions 4½ minutes. Place ground beef in preheated browning dish.

Stir in chili powder. Microwave at HIGH 3 minutes, stirring at 1 minute intervals. Drain off excess drippings, if necessary.

Combine soup, chili peppers, onion, and water in a small bowl. Stir until well blended.

Layer ½ of corn chips in a 2-quart casserole. Arrange half each of ground beef and tomatoes in layers over the chips. Pour over tomato layer half of soup mixture and sprinkle on half the cheese. Repeat the layers in same order, except reserve remaining cheese. Microwave, uncovered, at HIGH 12 to 15 minutes. Sprinkle cheese on top at end of cooking time.

Yield: 6 to 8 servings.

HASTY HASH

Power: HIGH
Microwave Time: 22 to 25 Minutes

> ¼ **cup butter or margarine**
> 1 **cup chopped onion**
> ¾ **cup water**
> 1 **(¾-ounce) envelope brown gravy mix**
> 3 **cups chopped cooked beef**
> 2 **(12-ounce) packages frozen hash brown potatoes, thawed slightly**
> 1½ **teaspoons salt**
> ⅛ **teaspoon pepper**
> **Paprika**

Place butter in a 1½-quart casserole. Microwave at HIGH 1 minute. Stir in onion. Cover with waxed paper. Microwave at HIGH 5 minutes, stirring once.

Combine water and gravy mix in a 2-cup glass measure. Microwave at HIGH 2 to 3 minutes. Stir well at 1 minute intervals.

Combine beef and potatoes in a large mixing bowl. Add onion, gravy, salt, pepper, and blend well.

Spread mixture in a 12- x 8-inch glass baking dish. Sprinkle with paprika. Cover with waxed paper. Microwave at HIGH 14 to 16 minutes. Rotate dish ½ turn after 7 to 8 minutes. Let stand, covered, 2 to 3 minutes before serving.

Yield: 6 to 8 servings.

SPECIAL SIRLOIN STEAK

Power: HIGH
Microwave Time: 3 to 4 Minutes per
pound

  6 to 8 scallions, chopped
  2 cloves garlic, minced
  1 cup salad oil
  ½ cup soy sauce
  1 cup dry red wine
  1 teaspoon hot sauce
  4 pounds sirloin steak, cut into
     ⅛-inch thick slices

Combine scallions, garlic, oil, soy sauce,
wine, and hot sauce in a 4-quart casserole.
Stir steak into marinade. Turn to coat all
steak pieces well. Cover and marinate several hours or overnight in the refrigerator.
  Use either of the following methods to
microwave:
• Preheat browning skillet according to
  manufacturer's directions (4 to 6 minutes). Microwave at HIGH 5 to 6 pieces at
  a time, 1 minute per side. Repeat until all
  steak pieces are cooked.
• Place steak pieces on a microwave roasting rack. Microwave at HIGH 1 to 2 minutes per side. Repeat until all steak pieces
  are cooked.
  Yield: 8 to 10 servings.

Micronote: Package one or two servings of
leftovers for the freezer in either sealable
freezer bags or plastic wrap. They can be
thawed and heated for individual servings
or to serve as part of "make your own" TV
dinners.

CHUCKWAGON STEW

Power: HIGH/MEDIUM
Microwave Time: 1 to 1½ hours

  1½ pounds lean beef stew meat, cut
       in 1-inch cubes
  1   tablespoon commercial brown
      bouquet sauce
  1   cup beef broth
  1½ teaspoons salt
  ⅛   teaspoon pepper
  ½   to 1 teaspoon chili powder
  ¼   teaspoon ground thyme
  1   bay leaf, crushed
  4   small potatoes, peeled and
      halved
  3   small carrots, peeled and cut in
      1½-inch pieces
  3   stalks celery, cut in 1½-inch
      pieces
  1   cup frozen peas
  1   (16-ounce) jar boiled whole,
      onions, drained
  2   tablespoons cornstarch
  2   tablespoons water

Combine the first 8 ingredients in a 3-quart
casserole. Stir well. Cover with plastic
wrap. Microwave at HIGH for 10 minutes.
  Add potatoes, carrots, and celery; stir to
coat with meat juices. Cover and microwave at MEDIUM for 45 to 50 minutes.
  Add peas and onions, cover, and microwave at MEDIUM for 8 to 10 minutes.
  Combine cornstarch and water. Stir into
stew. Microwave at HIGH for 2 to 3 minutes
or until thickened. Let stand, covered, 10
minutes before serving.
  Yield: 6 to 8 servings.

SWISS POT ROAST

Power: HIGH/MEDIUM/LOW
Microwave Time: 1⅔ to 2 Hours

  1 (3½-pound) boneless roast
     (chuck, English cut, or rump)
  1 (1½-ounce) envelope dry onion
     soup mix
  1 (10¾-ounce) can tomato soup,
     undiluted
  2 tablespoons soy sauce

Trim excess fat from meat. Place in a 3-quart casserole. Combine soup mix, soup, and soy sauce in a bowl. Pour over the meat. Cover with plastic wrap.

Microwave at HIGH 10 minutes. Rotate dish ½ turn. Microwave at MEDIUM 45 to 50 minutes. Remove cover and baste the roast well with its juices. Cover with plastic wrap. Microwave at LOW 45 to 50 minutes.

Yield: 6 servings.

POT ROAST AND VEGETABLES

Power: HIGH/MEDIUM-LOW/
MEDIUM-HIGH
Microwave Time: 1½ to 2 Hours

    1 (3- to 4-pound) chuck roast
    2 teaspoons salt
    1 teaspoon pepper
    1 beef bouillon cube
    ¼ cup hot water
    1 large onion, sliced
    1 (1-pound) package carrots, cut in
        1-inch pieces
    6 medium potatoes, peeled and
        quartered

Trim away excess fat and place roast in a 4-quart casserole. Rub with salt and pepper. Dissolve bouillon in hot water. Pour over the roast. Add sliced onion.

Cover with plastic wrap. Microwave at HIGH 10 to 15 minutes. Rotate dish ½ turn. Microwave at MEDIUM-LOW 45 to 48 minutes.

Add carrots and potatoes. Cover with plastic wrap. Microwave at MEDIUM-HIGH 45 to 48 minutes. Let stand, covered, 3 to 5 minutes.

Yield: 6 to 8 servings.

STEAMED CORNED BEEF

Power: HIGH/MEDIUM
Microwave Time: 1½ to 2 Hours

    1 (3-to 4-pound) corned beef
        round or brisket
    2 cups water
    1 onion, thinly sliced
    1 bay leaf
    8 whole ginger cloves

Place beef, fat side up, in a 3-quart casserole. Add water, onion, bay leaf, and cloves. Cover with plastic wrap. Microwave at HIGH 30 to 35 minutes.

Turn beef over and baste with the juice. Cover with plastic wrap. Microwave at MEDIUM 30 minutes. Turn beef over, baste with juice, and cover again. Microwave at MEDIUM 30 to 35 minutes or until the beef is tender, when pierced with a meat fork.

Serve thinly sliced surrounded with vegetables.

Yield: 2 to 3 servings per pound.

NEW ENGLAND BOILED DINNER

Power: HIGH
Microwave Time: 25 to 35 Minutes plus
    Corned Beef cooking time

    1 steamed corned beef
    6 medium potatoes, peeled
    6 medium carrots, peeled and cut
        in pieces
    6 cabbage wedges

Microwave corned beef according to directions above. Remove beef from juice and wrap in foil to keep warm.

Add potatoes and carrots to broth. Place cabbage on top of the other vegetables. Cover with plastic wrap. Microwave at HIGH 25 to 35 minutes or until vegetables are tender.

To serve, slice corned beef very thin and serve with vegetables.

Yield: 6 servings.

BEANS AND KRAUT SUPPER

Power: MEDIUM-HIGH
Microwave Time: 17 to 18 Minutes

- 1 **pound wieners**
- 1 **(31-ounce) can pork and beans**
- ⅔ **cup chili sauce**
- 1 **(16-ounce) can shredded sauerkraut, drained**
- 1 **cup shredded mild Cheddar cheese**

Cut wieners into ¼-inch pieces. Combine with pork and beans and chili sauce in a 2-quart casserole. Spread sauerkraut over top. Cover with glass lid or plastic wrap.
Microwave at MEDIUM-HIGH 15 to 16 minutes. Sprinkle cheese on top. Microwave at MEDIUM-HIGH 2 minutes or until cheese is melted.
Yield: 4 servings.

COUNTRY STYLE FRANKS

Power: HIGH
Microwave Time: 10 to 11 Minutes

- 1 **medium-sized green pepper, chopped**
- 1 **medium-sized onion, chopped**
- 2 **tablespoons butter or margarine**
- 1 **(1-pound) package beef frankfurters, cut in 1-inch pieces**
- 1 **(12-ounce) can whole kernel corn, drained**
- 1 **(16-ounce) can tomatoes, drained**

Combine green pepper, onion, and butter in a 13- x 9-inch baking dish. Cover with plastic wrap. Microwave at HIGH 3 minutes. Add frankfurters to onion and pepper. Microwave at HIGH 2 minutes or until frankfurters are hot. Stir in corn and tomatoes. Blend well. Cover with plastic wrap. Microwave at HIGH 5 to 6 minutes. Let stand, covered, 3 minutes.
Yield: 4 to 6 servings.

CRUSTED VEAL ROAST

Power: MEDIUM
Microwave Time: 15 to 28 Minutes per pound

- 1 **(3- to 5-pound) veal roast**
- ⅓ **cup prepared mustard**
- ½ **teaspoon garlic powder**
- 1 **onion chopped**
- ½ **teaspoon oregano**
- 1 **teaspoon commercial brown bouquet sauce**

Place veal roast, fat side up, on a microwave roasting rack placed in a flat glass baking dish.
Combine remaining ingredients. Brush roast to coat with the sauce. Cover loosely with waxed paper. Microwave at MEDIUM half the total estimated time. Rotate dish ½ turn. Microwave at MEDIUM the remaining half of time. Check for doneness by inserting standard meat thermometer in meat at side. It should read 160° and will rise to 170° after standing. Remove thermometer and return to oven if more cooking is desired.
Let stand, covered, 10 to 20 minutes before slicing. Brush roast with remaining sauce and slice thinly to serve.
Yield: 2 to 3 servings per pound.

GLAZED VEAL

Power: HIGH/MEDIUM
Microwave Time: 55 Minutes to 1 Hour

- 2 **pounds boneless veal, cut in 1-inch cubes**
- ¼ **cup molasses**
- ¼ **cup soy sauce**
- 2 **scallions, chopped**
- 1 **clove garlic, crushed**
- ¼ **cup lemon juice**
- ½ **teaspoon salt**
- ¼ **teaspoon ground ginger**
- 1 **cup water**
  Hot rice

Combine all ingredients in a 3-quart casserole. Stir to coat all the veal pieces. Cover with plastic wrap. Chill and marinate several hours.

Microwave, covered, at HIGH 20 minutes. Stir well. Microwave at MEDIUM 25 to 30 minutes or until veal is tender. Stir well.

Microwave at MEDIUM, uncovered, 10 to 15 minutes. Let stand 5 minutes before serving. Serve over hot rice.

Yield: 6 to 8 servings.

LAMB RIBLETS CREOLE

Power: HIGH/MEDIUM-HIGH
Microwave Time: 35 to 40 Minutes

  2 pounds lamb riblets
  1 (¾-ounce) envelope brown gravy
     mix
  ¼ teaspoon salt
  ¼ teaspoon pepper
  1 clove garlic, minced
  1 teaspoon dried marjoram
  ¼ teaspoon hot sauce
  ⅛ teaspoon each dried basil,
     ground thyme, crushed bay
     leaf
  1 (8-ounce) can tomato sauce
  ⅓ cup water

Combine lamb and gravy mix in a 2- or 2½-quart casserole. Microwave, uncovered, at HIGH 5 minutes. Add remaining ingredients. Stir until well blended. Cover with waxed paper. Microwave at MEDIUM-HIGH 30 to 35 minutes or until tender, stirring occasionally.

Yield: 4 servings.

ROASTED LAMB

Power: MEDIUM
Microwave Time: 10 to 12 Minutes per
  pound

  1 (5-pound) leg of lamb
     Basic Browning Sauce (see
     p.117)

Brush lamb with Basic Browning Sauce. Place fat side down on a microwave roasting rack in a 13- x 9-inch baking dish. Cover with waxed paper. Microwave at MEDIUM half the estimated time.

Turn fat side up, brush with Basic Browning Sauce, and cover with waxed paper. Microwave at MEDIUM remaining half of time. Check for doneness by inserting standard meat thermometer into meat at side. It should be 140° for medium, 170° for well done. Remove thermometer and return to microwave if more cooking is desired.

Let stand, covered, 10 minutes before slicing.

Yield: 6 to 8 servings.

LAMB STEW

Power: HIGH
Microwave Time: 52 to 58 Minutes

  2 pounds boned lamb shoulder,
     cut in 1-inch pieces
  2 teaspoons commercial brown
     bouquet sauce
  2 teaspoons salt
  1¾ cups water, divided
  6 medium-sized carrots, cut in
     1-inch pieces
  2 onions, sliced
  3 celery stalks, cut in 1-inch
     pieces
  1 tablespoon Worcestershire sauce
  3 tablespoons all-purpose flour
  ¾ cup water

Combine lamb, brown bouquet sauce, salt, and 1 cup water in a 3-quart casserole. Cover with plastic wrap. Microwave at HIGH 5 to 6 minutes.

Stir in carrots, onions, celery, and Worcestershire sauce. Cover with plastic wrap. Microwave at HIGH 45 to 50 minutes or until meat and vegetables are tender. Stir several times during cooking.

Combine flour and remaining water. Stir into stew. Microwave at HIGH 2 to 3 minutes or until thickened.

Yield: 8 servings.

BAKED HAM WITH GLAZE

Power: HIGH
Microwave Time: 10 to 12 Minutes per pound

1 (3- to 5-pound) fully cooked ham

Place ham in a 12- x 8-inch baking dish. *Do not use a trivet.* Cover with plastic wrap. Microwave at HIGH 10 to 12 minutes per pound or until temperature reaches 120° to 130°. To serve, spread with desired glaze before slicing or serve with glaze to spoon over slices.
Yield: 2 to 3 servings per pound.

Cherry Ginger Glaze:

Power: HIGH
Microwave Time: 5 to 7 Minutes

1 (12-ounce) jar cherry preserves
¼ cup red wine vinegar
¼ cup firmly packed brown sugar
1 teaspoon ground ginger
1 tablespoon butter or margarine

Combine preserves, vinegar, brown sugar, and ginger in a 1-quart glass bowl. Microwave at HIGH 5 to 7 minutes. Stir once or twice during cooking. Stir in butter.
Spoon over ham as a glaze or serve as a topping.
Yield: 1½ cups.

Strawberry Glaze:

Power: HIGH
Microwave Time: 5 to 6 Minutes

1 (12-ounce) jar strawberry jelly
½ teaspoon dry mustard
¼ teaspoon ground allspice
1½ tablespoons red wine vinegar

Combine jelly, mustard, allspice, and vinegar in a 1½-quart casserole. Microwave at HIGH 5 to 6 minutes or until slightly thickened. Spoon over ham to glaze or serve as a topping with ham slices.
Yield: 1½ cups.

BAKED HAM

Power: MEDIUM-HIGH
Microwave Time: 16 to 20 Minutes

1 (3- to 4-pound) pre-cooked ham

Place ham, fat side down, in a flat glass baking dish. Cover with plastic wrap. Microwave at MEDIUM-HIGH 8 to 10 minutes.
Turn fat side up. Cover with plastic wrap. Microwave at MEDIUM-HIGH 8 to 10 minutes. Let stand, covered, 15 minutes before slicing.
Yield: 6 to 8 servings.

HAM AND SPICED FRUIT

Power: HIGH/MEDIUM
Microwave Time: 14 to 16 Minutes

1 (3-pound) canned ham
2 (23-ounce) cans sweet potatoes, drained
1 cup firmly packed brown sugar
1 teaspoon dry mustard
1 (16-ounce) can peach halves, drain and reserve juice
1 (16-ounce) can pear halves, drain and reserve juice
1 cup white seedless grapes
½ teaspoon pumpkin pie spice

Place ham in a 12- x 8-inch baking dish. Arrange sweet potatoes around ham.

Combine brown sugar, mustard, and ½ cup of the reserved fruit juices. Pour over ham and sweet potatoes.

Microwave at HIGH 5 minutes. Rotate dish ½ turn. Microwave at MEDIUM 5 minutes.

While ham is cooking, combine the drained peach and pear halves, grapes, and pumpkin pie spice. Arrange the fruits over the ham and sweet potatoes. Microwave at HIGH 4 to 6 minutes or until fruits are heated. Let stand 2 minutes before serving.

Yield: 8 servings.

HAM STEAK AND CRANBERRY-ORANGE SAUCE

Power: HIGH
Microwave Time: 3 to 5 Minutes

- 1 (10-inch thick) ham steak
- 1 cup whole-berry cranberry sauce
- 1 tablespoon orange juice
- 1 teaspoon prepared horseradish

Preheat browning dish according to manufacturer's directions. Place ham steak on preheated dish. Cover with a paper towel. Microwave at HIGH 1 to 2 minutes.

Combine cranberry sauce, orange juice, and horseradish. Turn ham slice over and top with cranberry sauce mixture. Microwave at HIGH 2 to 3 minutes or until cranberry mixture is hot.

Yield: 2 to 4 servings.

HAM LOAF

Power: MEDIUM
Microwave Time: 20 to 24 Minutes

- ¾ pound ground ham
- ¾ pound ground fresh pork
- 2 eggs, beaten
- 1 cup evaporated milk
- ½ (10¾-ounce) can tomato soup, undiluted
- ½ cup cracker crumbs
- 1 teaspoon salt
  Epicurean Sauce

Combine all ingredients except Sauce. Blend well. Pack in a 2½-quart casserole. Cover with waxed paper. Microwave at MEDIUM 20 to 24 minutes. Remove loaf from microwave. Insert a standard meat thermometer into center of loaf. Temperature should be 180°. Remove thermometer and return to microwave for more cooking, if necessary.

Let stand, covered, 5 minutes before serving with Epicurean Sauce.

Yield: 8 to 10 servings.

Micronote: If the microwave has a temperature probe, select MEDIUM power and 180°.

Epicurean Sauce:

- ½ pint whipping cream
- ⅓ cup mayonnaise
- ¼ cup horseradish
- 2 teaspoons prepared mustard
- ½ teaspoon salt
- 2 tablespoons finely chopped parsley

Whip cream until stiff. Fold in other ingredients. Chill well and serve with Ham Loaf.

Yield: 2 cups.

NUTTY HAM 'N YAM BAKE

Power: HIGH
Microwave Time: 12½ to 15½ Minutes

2 tablespoons butter or margarine
3 cups cooked cubed ham
⅓ cup chopped onion
½ teaspoon ground cinnamon
¼ cup sugar
¾ cup pineapple juice
2 tablespoons cornstarch
1 (17-ounce) can yams, diced and
    drained, juice reserved
1 cup dry roasted peanuts,
    crushed and divided
½ cup firmly packed brown sugar

Place butter in a 2-quart casserole. Microwave at HIGH 30 seconds. Add ham and onion. Combine cinnamon, sugar, pineapple juice, cornstarch, and juice from yams. Stir into the ham and onion mixture. Stir well.

Cover with plastic wrap. Microwave at HIGH 6 to 8 minutes, stirring at 2 minute intervals.

Mix diced yams and ⅔ cup peanuts. Stir into the ham mixture. Spread brown sugar over top of ham mixture and sprinkle with reserved peanuts.

Microwave, uncovered, at HIGH 6 to 7 minutes, or until firm and thickened. Let stand 2 to 3 minutes before serving.

Yield: 8 servings.

COUNTRY CASSEROLE

Power: HIGH/MEDIUM
Microwave Time: 10½ to 11 Minutes

¼ cup butter or margarine
1 medium-size onion, chopped
1 cup water
1 chicken bouillon cube
3 cups cubed ham
1 (1-pound) can applesauce
1 (8-ounce) package herb-seasoned
    stuffing mix

Microwave butter in a 1-quart glass casserole at HIGH 1 minute. Add onion. Cover dish with plastic wrap. Microwave at HIGH 2 minutes to soften onion.

Microwave 1 cup water in a 1-cup glass measure at HIGH 2½ minutes. Add chicken bouillon cube.

Combine onion, ham, chicken broth, applesauce, and herb stuffing mix. Pour into a greased 2-quart glass casserole. Cover with waxed paper. Microwave at MEDIUM 5 minutes. Serve warm.

Yield: 6 to 8 servings.

ALL-IN-ONE PORK CHOP MEAL

Power: HIGH/MEDIUM-HIGH
Microwave Time: 26 to 29 Minutes

1 onion, chopped
¼ cup butter or margarine
6 loin-cut pork chops
1 (1-pound) bag frozen nugget
    potatoes
1 teaspoon salt
¼ teaspoon pepper
1 (10¾-ounce) can cream of
    mushroom soup, undiluted
1 (8-ounce) carton commercial sour
    cream
½ cup chopped green pepper

Place onion and butter in a 1-cup glass measure. Microwave at HIGH 1 minute. Set aside.

Place pork chops in 12- x 8-inch baking dish. Spread potatoes over chops. Sprinkle with salt and pepper. Cover with waxed paper. Microwave at MEDIUM-HIGH 10 minutes.

Combine onion, soup, and sour cream in a bowl. Spread over potatoes. Sprinkle green pepper over the soup mixture.

Cover with plastic wrap. Microwave at MEDIUM-HIGH 15 to 18 minutes.

Yield: 6 servings.

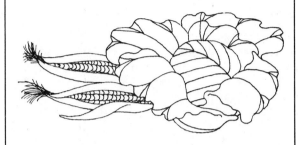

BARBECUED PORK CHOPS AND RICE

Power: HIGH/MEDIUM
Microwave Time: 22 to 27 Minutes

⅓	cup chopped onion
⅓	cup chopped celery
⅓	cup chopped green pepper
1½	cups quick-cooking long grain rice, uncooked
1	(½- to 1-ounce) envelope instant tomato soup mix
1	(16-ounce) can tomatoes
1½	teaspoons salt
½	teaspoon pepper
6	loin pork chops
1½	teaspoons barbecue seasoning spice

Combine onion, celery, and green pepper in a 3-quart casserole. Cover with waxed paper. Microwave at HIGH 2 minutes.

Add rice, soup mix, tomatoes, salt, and pepper. Stir well. Spread evenly in casserole with onion mixture. Sprinkle each pork chop with barbecue seasoning spice. Place on top of rice-tomato mixture.

Cover with plastic wrap. Microwave at HIGH 5 minutes. Rotate dish ¼ turn. Microwave at MEDIUM 15 to 20 minutes. Let stand, covered, 3 to 5 minutes.

Yield: 6 servings.

STUFFED PORK CHOPS

Power: MEDIUM
Microwave Time: 25 to 32 Minutes

1	tablespoon commercial brown bouquet sauce
1	tablespoon dry red wine
4	(1-inch thick) pork chops, with pocket cut for stuffing
1¼	cups stuffing mix
1	tablespoon butter or margarine, melted
½	teaspoon salt
⅛	teaspoon pepper
⅛	teaspoon poultry seasoning
⅓	cup hot water
4	(½-inch thick) apple slices
¼	cup firmly packed brown sugar

Combine brown bouquet sauce and wine. Brush on chops to coat well.

Combine stuffing mix, butter, seasonings, and hot water. Stir to moisten and mix. Fill the pocket of each chop with stuffing.

Place chops in a flat glass baking dish. Arrange with the thin end piece toward the center of the dish. Brush with sauce. Top each chop with an apple slice. Cover with waxed paper.

Microwave at MEDIUM 10 to 12 minutes. Rotate dish and brush with any remaining sauce. Sprinkle apples with brown sugar. Cover with waxed paper. Microwave at MEDIUM 15 to 20 minutes, or until tender.

Yield: 4 servings.

PORK MICROWAVING TIMES AND TECHNIQUES

Roast	Size	Power	Microwave Time
Loin (either bone-in or boneless)	4 pounds	MEDIUM-HIGH/ MEDIUM-LOW	30 to 40 Minutes

Technique: Tie roast with string to hold in shape. Place roast, bone side up, on microwave roasting rack in flat casserole. Cover with waxed paper. Microwave at MEDIUM-HIGH a little less than half the cooking time (about 15 minutes). Rotate dish ½ turn once. Turn roast bone side down. Microwave, covered, at MEDIUM-HIGH about 15 minutes more. Reduce power to MEDIUM-LOW and microwave covered until temperature reaches 165°.

Remove from oven. Cover with foil, shiny side in, and let stand 5 to 10 minutes. Temperature should rise about 5°.

Shoulder	4 pounds	MEDIUM-HIGH/ MEDIUM-LOW	60 to 65 Minutes

Technique: Prepare roast the same as the loin. Start with lean side up and cover with waxed paper. Microwave at MEDIUM-HIGH ½ the cooking time (about 30 minutes). Rotate dish ½ turn once. Turn lean side down. Microwave, covered, at MEDIUM-HIGH about 25 minutes more or until temperature reaches 160°. Reduce power to MEDIUM-LOW and microwave, covered, until temperature reaches 165°. Cover with foil, shiny side in, and let stand 5 to 10 minutes. Temperature should rise about 5°.

TAWNY PORK ROAST

Power: MEDIUM-HIGH/
    MEDIUM-LOW
Microwave Time: 10 to 12 Minutes per
    pound

> 1 **(5- to 6-pound) tied double loin
>   pork roast
>   Brush-On-Browner**

Place roast, fat side down, on a microwave plastic roasting rack in a 12- x 8-inch baking dish. Cover roast with waxed paper.

Microwave at MEDIUM-HIGH half the estimated time. Rotate dish halfway through first half of microwaving time.

Remove roast from oven. Pat dry and coat thoroughly with Brush-On-Browner. Microwave at MEDIUM-HIGH remaining half of time or until temperature reaches 165°. Check for doneness by inserting standard meat thermometer into lean part of roast. Remove thermometer. If more cooking is desired, microwave at MEDIUM-LOW until temperature reaches 165°.

Let stand, covered with waxed paper, while making Tawny Gravy.

Yield: 3 servings per pound.

Brush-On-Browner:

> 1 **egg, slightly beaten**
> 1 **teaspoon commercial brown
>   bouquet sauce**
> ¾ **teaspoon ground sage**
> ½ **teaspoon pepper**
> ¼ **teaspoon ground cinnamon**
> ¼ **teaspoon paprika**

Combine all ingredients in a small bowl. Blend well and brush on ground beef, pork, lamb, veal, and beef roasts to give a rich brown color and glaze.

Brush the browner on a dry roast. Cover any unused browner with plastic wrap. Can be stored in refrigerator up to 7 days.

Tawny Gravy:

Power: HIGH
Microwave Time: 6½ to 7½ Minutes

  6 tablespoons butter or margarine
  4 tablespoons all-purpose flour
     Chicken broth, as needed
  ½ cup milk
  ½ cup water
  ½ teaspoon commercial brown
        bouquet sauce

Microwave butter at HIGH 30 seconds to melt in a 2-quart casserole. Stir in flour. Microwave at HIGH 1 minute.

Strain juices from pork roast. Skim off fat and discard. Add chicken broth to meat juice to equal 2 cups. Slowly stir into flour-butter mixture. Stir well to remove lumps. Stir in milk, water, and bouquet sauce. Microwave at HIGH 5 to 6 minutes or until thick and bubbly.

Yield: 3 cups.

PORK ROAST

Power: MEDIUM-LOW/MEDIUM-
   HIGH
Microwave Time: 10 to 12 Minutes per
   pound

  1 (5-pound) pork loin, trimmed of
        excess fat
     Basic Browning Sauce (see
        p.117)

Oven Roasting Bag Method:

Place roast in oven roasting bag. Add ½ cup water. Tie bag securely with strip cut from end of roasting bag. (*Do not use enclosed metal tie.*) Make an X-shaped cut near the tied end. Place pork in the bag in a 13- x 9-inch baking dish.

Microwave at MEDIUM-LOW half the estimated time. Rotate dish ½ turn.

Microwave the remaining time at ME-DIUM-LOW. Test for 170° by inserting a standard meat thermometer into cut end of meat. Remove thermometer and return to microwave. If more cooking is needed,

microwave at MEDIUM-LOW until temperature is 170°. Let stand in bag 10 to 12 minutes before slicing.

Waxed Paper Method:

Brush pork loin with Basic Browning Sauce. Place the loin bone side up in a 13- x 9-inch baking dish without a rack. Cover with waxed paper. Microwave at MEDIUM-HIGH half the estimated time.

Turn fat side up, brush with sauce, and microwave at MEDIUM-HIGH about 15 minutes more. Test for 165° by inserting a standard meat thermometer into cut end of meat. Remove thermometer. If more cooking is needed, microwave at MEDIUM-LOW until temperature is 170°. Let stand, covered, 10 to 12 minutes before slicing.

Yield: 6 to 8 servings.

PEACHY SAUSAGE RING ★

Power: HIGH
Microwave Time: 14 to 17 Minutes

  1   egg
  ⅔   cup milk
  ¾   cup quick-cooking oats,
          uncooked
  1½   pounds pork sausage
  ⅔   cup chopped apple
  ¾   teaspoon salt
  ¾   teaspoon crushed basil
  ½   teaspoon ground sage
  ½   teaspoon pepper
  6   canned peach halves, drained

Combine egg, milk, and oats in a bowl. Let stand 5 minutes. Add remaining ingredients, except peaches.

Arrange peach halves, cut side up, in a microwave ring pan. Spoon the sausage mixture over the peaches and pack uniformly. Cover with paper towel. Microwave at HIGH 14 to 17 minutes, rotating dish ¼ turn at 5 minute intervals.

Drain drippings and let stand, covered, 5 to 8 minutes.

Yield: 6 servings.

SAUSAGE CASSEROLE

Power: HIGH
Microwave Time: 15 to 21 Minutes

- 1 pound mild pork sausage
- 1 medium-sized onion, chopped
- 1 medium-sized green pepper, chopped
- ½ cup chopped celery
- 1 cup cooked rice
- 1 (10¾-ounce) can cream of chicken soup, undiluted
- 1 (10¾-ounce) can cream of mushroom soup, undiluted
- 1 (2-ounce) can mushrooms, drained
- 1 (2-ounce) jar pimiento, chopped and drained
- 1 cup shredded sharp Cheddar cheese

Place sausage in 12- x 8-inch baking dish. Microwave at HIGH 6 to 7 minutes. Stir well after 3 minutes. Add onion, green pepper, and celery. Microwave at HIGH 3 to 5 minutes. Drain off excess drippings.

Stir rice into sausage mixture. Add soups, mushrooms, and pimiento. Cover with waxed paper. Microwave at HIGH 5 to 7 minutes. Sprinkle cheese on top. Microwave at HIGH, covered, 1 to 2 minutes.

Yield: 8 servings.

PIZZA SUPPER PIE

Power: HIGH/MEDIUM-HIGH
Microwave Time: 11 to 12 Minutes

- 1 pound fresh pork sausage
- ¾ cup chopped onion
- 4 eggs, slightly beaten
- ½ cup milk
- 1 cup shredded Cheddar cheese
- ½ teaspoon oregano
- 1 baked 9-inch pastry shell (in a glass pie plate)
- ½ cup pizza sauce
- 6 triangles processed American cheese slices

Crumble sausage in a 9-inch glass pie plate. Add onion. Microwave at HIGH 4 minutes or until sausage turns gray. Stir well. Drain excess drippings.

Combine eggs, milk, cheese, and oregano in another bowl. Stir in sausage and onion. Pour into baked pastry shell.

Microwave at MEDIUM-HIGH 5 to 6 minutes. Test for doneness by inserting a knife near center. Knife comes out clean when done.

Spread pizza sauce over top and arrange cheese in spoke fashion. Microwave at MEDIUM-HIGH 2 minutes.

Yield: 6 servings.

BACON MICROWAVING TIMES AND TECHNIQUES

Bacon	Power	Amount	Microwave Time
Thin Sliced	HIGH	2 slices	2 minutes
		4 slices	3½ minutes
		6 slices	5 minutes
Thick Sliced	HIGH	2 slices	3 minutes
		4 slices	4½ minutes
		6 slices	6½ minutes

Technique: Arrange bacon slices on a paper plate between paper towels or on a microwave roasting rack in a flat casserole. Microwave at HIGH until browned and crisp.

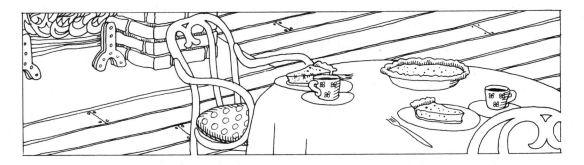

PIES AND PASTRY

Microwaved pie fillings can be as varied as a cooked pudding poured into a baked crust or a fluffy marshmallow-type liqueur- or fruit-flavored filling. Make pie crusts from crumbs, pastry mix, or your own never-fail recipe for pie crusts.

To achieve a browner crust or pastry-type shell, add cocoa to the flour before mixing, add a few drops of yellow food coloring to pastry dough when mixing, brush with beaten egg yolk or vanilla, or spread a light coating of honey over the crust before cooking it in the microwave oven. Bake pastry shells in an 8- or 9-inch glass pie plate *before* filling, and prick well with a fork, just as you do for a conventionally baked crust.

For crumb crusts combine crushed crumbs and melted butter. Press to shape in an 8- or 9-inch glass pie plate. Microwave at HIGH or MEDIUM-HIGH depending on the ingredients used. Cool and fill with your preferred filling.

PUMPKIN-WHIPPED CREAM PIE
(Conventional Recipe)

- 32 large marshmallows
- ½ cup milk
- 1 cup cooked mashed pumpkin
- ½ teaspoon ground cinnamon
- ½ teaspoon ground allspice
- 1 tablespoon melted butter
- 1 cup whipping cream, whipped
- 1 (9-inch) Pecan Crunch Crust

Combine the marshmallows and milk in a sauce pan and place over low heat until marshmallows are melted. Remove from heat and stir in pumpkin, cinnamon, allspice, and butter. Fold in the whipped cream and pour into Pecan Crunch Crust. Chill for 3 hours.

Yield: one 9-inch pie.

PECAN CRUNCH CRUST
(Conventional Recipe)

   1½   cups graham cracker crumbs
   1   tablespoon sugar
   ⅛   teaspoon ground cinnamon
   ½   cup melted butter
   ½   cup chopped pecans

Combine the graham cracker crumbs, sugar, cinnamon, and butter in a bowl and mix well. Press into bottom and sides of pie plate. Bake at 350° for 8 minutes, then cool. Sprinkle pecans over crust.
   Yield: one 9-inch crumb crust.

To Microwave Pumpkin-Whipped Cream Pie

• Melt butter first; set aside.
• Combine marshmallows and milk in a 2-quart casserole.
• Add other ingredients; then fold in whipped cream.

To Microwave Pecan Crunch Crust

• Place butter in glass pie plate.
• Microwave to melt, then add other ingredients.
• Press to shape.

PUMPKIN-WHIPPED CREAM PIE

Power: HIGH/MEDIUM
Microwave Time: 2 to 2½ Minutes

   1   tablespoon butter or margarine
   32   large marshmallows
   ½   cup milk
   1   cup cooked mashed pumpkin
   ½   teaspoon ground cinnamon
   ¼   teaspoon ground nutmeg
   ¼   teaspoon ground allspice
   1   cup whipping cream, whipped
   1   baked 9-inch pastry shell or
        graham cracker crust

Microwave butter in a small glass dish at HIGH 15 seconds.
   Combine marshmallows and milk in a 2-quart glass casserole. Microwave at MEDIUM 1½ to 2 minutes. Stir mixture after 1 minute. Stir in pumpkin, cinnamon, nutmeg, allspice, and melted butter. Fold in whipped cream. Pour into baked crust. Chill for 3 hours.
   Yield: one 9-inch pie.

PECAN CRUNCH CRUST

Power: HIGH
Microwave Time: 1½ to 2¼ Minutes

   ½   cup butter or margarine
   1½   cups graham cracker crumbs
   1   tablespoon sugar
   ⅛   teaspoon ground cinnamon
   ½   cup chopped pecans

Microwave butter in a 9-inch glass pie plate at HIGH 20 seconds. Combine graham cracker crumbs, sugar, cinnamon, and pecans with melted butter. Press evenly into bottom of pie plate. Place an 8-inch pie plate inside the 9-inch plate to hold crust in place. Microwave at HIGH 1 to 2 minutes. Cool before filling.
   Yield: one 9-inch crumb crust.

CRUMB PIE SHELL

Power: HIGH
Microwave Time: 2½ to 4 Minutes

   ⅓   cup butter or margarine
   1¼   cups finely crushed cookie
        crumbs
   ¼   cup sugar
   ½   cup chopped pecans (optional)

Place butter in a 9-inch glass pie plate. Microwave at HIGH 30 to 45 seconds. Add crumbs, sugar, and pecans, if desired, and blend well. Press to shape evenly in the pie plate.

Microwave at HIGH 2 to 3 minutes. Let stand to cool before filling.

Yield: one 9-inch cookie shell.

Micronote: Crumbs may be either vanilla wafer, chocolate wafer, graham cracker, or ginger snap.

FLAKY PASTRY

Power: HIGH
Microwave Time: 5 to 7 Minutes for 1
   pastry shell

   2   **cups all-purpose flour**
   1   **teaspoon salt**
   ⅔   **cup shortening (at room**
         temperature)
   2   **to 4 tablespoons ice water**

Combine flour and salt in a bowl. Add shortening and cut in with pastry blender until crumbly in texture. Sprinkle water on mixture and stir with a fork to form a ball.

Divide pastry in half and wrap each half in plastic wrap. Chill several minutes before rolling out.

When ready to shape, roll each pastry on a floured surface to ⅛ inch thick. Place in 9-inch glass pie plate. Prick sides and bottom evenly with a fork. Microwave at HIGH 5 to 7 minutes or until dry-looking and not doughy. Cool before filling.

Yield: two 9-inch pastry shells.

FROZEN PIE SHELL

Power: HIGH
Microwave Time: 5 to 6 Minutes

   1   **frozen pastry shell**

Allow frozen shell to thaw slightly. Transfer it to a 9-inch glass pie plate. Press into the pie plate to shape. Prick bottom and sides of shell evenly with a fork. Microwave at HIGH 5 to 6 minutes. Rotate dish ½ turn after 3 minutes. Cool before filling.

Yield: one 9-inch pastry shell.

PIE CRUST MIX

Power: HIGH
Microwave Time: 5 to 6 Minutes

   1   **(11½-ounce) package pie crust**
         mix

Prepare mix according to package instructions. Roll out and place one pastry shell in a 9-inch glass pie plate. Flute or decorate edge as desired. Prick bottom and sides of shell evenly.

Microwave at HIGH 5 to 6 minutes. Rotate dish ½ turn after 3 minutes. Cool before filling.

Yield: one 9-inch pastry shell.

ALMOND PASTRY

Power: HIGH
Microwave Time: 5 to 7 Minutes

   1¼   **cups all-purpose flour**
   ¼   **cup ground almonds**
   ¼   **cup sugar**
   ¼   **teaspoon salt**
   ½   **cup shortening**
   1   **egg, beaten**
   1   **to 4 tablespoons chilled water**
         All-purpose flour

Combine the flour, almonds, sugar, and salt. Cut in shortening with a pastry blender until crumbly and coarse. Add beaten egg and enough cold water to make a stiff dough.

Wrap dough in plastic wrap. Chill thoroughly. Place on floured rolling surface. Roll out to ⅛ inch thick. Place in a 9-inch glass pie plate. Prick sides and bottom evenly with a fork.

Microwave at HIGH 5 to 7 minutes or until pastry is dry-looking and not doughy. Cool before filling.

Yield: one 9-inch pastry shell.

CHOCOLATE WAFER CRUST

Power: HIGH
Microwave Time: 1 Minute

6 tablespoons butter or margarine
1½ cups chocolate wafer crumbs

Microwave butter in 9-inch glass pie plate at HIGH 1 minute. Stir in wafer crumbs. Press mixture evenly in pie plate. Chill.
Yield: one 9-inch wafer crust.

COCONUT CRUST

Power: HIGH
Microwave Time: 2½ to 3 Minutes

¼ cup butter or margarine
2 cups flaked coconut

Microwave butter in a 9-inch glass pie plate at HIGH ½ to 1 minute. Mix coconut and melted butter. Press mixture evenly in pie plate to form crust. Microwave at HIGH 2 minutes. Cool before filling.
Yield: one 9-inch coconut shell.

PEANUT-PRETZEL CRUST

Power: HIGH
Microwave Time: ½ to 1 Minute

½ cup butter or margarine
1 (8 ¼-ounce) jar unsalted dry roasted nuts, crushed
½ cup crushed pretzels
½ cup powdered sugar

Microwave butter in a 9-inch glass pie plate at HIGH ½ to 1 minute. Combine nuts, pretzels, and sugar with melted butter. Press evenly in pie plate to form a crust. Chill before filling.
Yield: one 9-inch pretzel crust.

MICROWAVED MERINGUE

Power: HIGH
Microwaving Time: 2½ to 3 Minutes

3 egg whites
Dash of salt
¼ teaspoon cream of tartar
6 tablespoons sugar

Beat egg whites until foamy. Add salt and cream of tartar. When soft whites reach peak stage, slowly beat in sugar. Beat until whites are stiff and glossy, not dry. Spread meringue over pie or pudding. Microwave at HIGH 2½ to 3 minutes. Rotate dish ¼ turn after 1 minute.
Yield: meringue for one 9-inch pie or 6 servings.

QUICK BANANA PIE

Power: HIGH
Microwave Time: 6 to 7 Minutes

1 (4½-ounce) package vanilla pudding mix
2 cups milk
1 baked 9-inch pastry shell
2 bananas, sliced
Whipped cream

Combine pudding mix and milk in 4-cup glass measure. Microwave at HIGH 3 minutes. Stir. Microwave at HIGH an additional 3 to 4 minutes. Stir and cool.
Pour half the pudding mixture into the pastry shell. Cover mixture with sliced bananas. Add remaining filling. Chill.
Garnish with whipped cream before serving.
Yield: one 9-inch pie.

CHOCOLATE PIE

Power: MEDIUM
Microwave Time: 3 to 4 Minutes

- 1 (6-ounce) package semisweet chocolate morsels
- 2 tablespoons sugar
- 3 tablespoons milk
- 3 eggs, separated
- 1 baked 9-inch pastry shell
  Whipped cream
  Grated chocolate

Combine chocolate morsels, sugar, and milk in a 1½-quart glass bowl. Microwave at MEDIUM 3 to 4 minutes or until heated thoroughly. Stir well after 1 or 1½ minutes.

Beat egg yolks in a small bowl. Stir a small amount of the chocolate mixture into the beaten yolks, then add to the remaining chocolate mixture.

Beat whites until stiff peaks form. Fold egg whites into chocolate mixture. Pour filling into the baked pastry shell. Chill until firm.

To serve, garnish with whipped cream and grated chocolate.

Yield: one 9-inch pie.

FANTASTIC CHOCOLATE PIE

Power: MEDIUM
Microwave Time: 3 to 4 Minutes

- 24 large marshmallows
- ½ cup milk
- 1 (6-ounce) package semisweet chocolate morsels
- 2 tablespoons crème de cacao
- 2 tablespoons coffee liqueur
- 1 cup whipping cream
- 1 (9-inch) Chocolate Wafer Crust (see p. 140)
  Grated chocolate
  Whipped cream

Microwave marshmallows, milk, and chocolate morsels in a 3-quart casserole at MEDIUM 3 to 4 minutes. Stir. Cool slightly.

Add crème de cacao and coffee liqueur to milk mixture. Chill 20 to 30 minutes.

Whip cream until stiff. Fold into chocolate mixture. Pour filling into Chocolate Wafer Crust. Garnish with grated chocolate and whipped cream. Freeze.

Remove from freezer 5 to 10 minutes before serving.

Yield: one 9-inch pie.

CHOCOLATE PEANUT PIE

Power: HIGH/MEDIUM
Microwave Time: 10 Minutes

- ¼ cup butter or margarine
- 2 (1-ounce) squares unsweetened chocolate
- ¾ cup sugar
- ½ cup firmly packed light brown sugar
- ½ cup milk
- ¼ cup light corn syrup
- 1½ teaspoons vanilla extract
- 3 eggs
- 1 cup chopped salted peanuts
- 1 baked 9-inch pastry shell (in a glass pie plate)
  Whipped cream or ice cream

Microwave butter and chocolate in a 2-cup glass measure at HIGH 1½ to 2 minutes. Stir after 1 minute.

Combine sugar, brown sugar, milk, corn syrup, vanilla, and eggs in a mixing bowl. Stir well. Beat chocolate mixture into sugar mixture. Stir in peanuts.

Pour filling mixture into baked pastry shell. Microwave at MEDIUM 4 minutes. Edges will begin to set. Stir filling. Microwave at MEDIUM 4 additional minutes, or until a knife comes out clean when inserted into center of pie.

Serve with whipped cream or ice cream.
Yield: one 9-inch pie.

FUDGE NUT PIE

Power: HIGH/MEDIUM
Microwave Time: 9 Minutes

- ½ cup butter or margarine
- 1 (6-ounce) package semisweet chocolate morsels
- ½ cup chopped pecans
- ½ cup shredded coconut
- 1 cup sugar
- 2 eggs, beaten
- 1 baked 9-inch pastry shell (in a glass pie plate)

Microwave butter and chocolate morsels in a 2-quart glass bowl at HIGH 1 minute. Mix in pecans, coconut, and sugar. Stir in eggs.

Pour filling into baked pastry shell. Microwave at MEDIUM 8 minutes. Rotate dish ¼ turn at 2 minute intervals. Stir once after 4 minutes. Cool before serving.

Yield: one 9-inch pie.

CRÈME DE MENTHE PIE

Power: HIGH
Microwave Time: 2 Minutes

- 3 cups miniature marshmallows
- ¼ cup milk
- ¼ cup crème de cacao
- ¼ cup green crème de menthe
- 2 cups whipping cream, divided
- 1 prepared 9-inch chocolate crumb crust
  Pistachio nuts, chopped
  Maraschino cherries, chopped

Combine marshmallows and milk in a large glass mixing bowl. Microwave at HIGH about 2 minutes or until marshmallows begin to puff. Stir to blend well. Add crème de cacao and crème de menthe. Stir well. Cool until the consistency of unbeaten egg whites.

Whip cream until thick. Fold the cooled marshmallow mixture into half the whipped cream. Pour into the crust. Chill at least 4 hours.

Garnish with remaining whipped cream, pistachio nuts, and cherries.

Yield: one 9-inch pie.

HAWAIIAN COCONUT ICEBOX PIE

Power: HIGH/MEDIUM
Microwave Time: 8½ to 10½ Minutes

- 2 cups milk
- 3 tablespoons cornstarch
- 1 cup sugar
- 2 tablespoons butter or margarine
- 3 eggs, separated
- 1 teaspoon vanilla extract
- 1 teaspoon coconut extract
- 1 teaspoon plain gelatin
- 6 tablespoons sugar
  Dash of salt
- 1 (3½-ounce) can shredded coconut
- 1 baked 9-inch pastry shell

Microwave milk in a 4-cup glass measure at HIGH 3 to 4 minutes. Combine cornstarch and sugar. Stir into scalded milk. Microwave mixture at MEDIUM 3 minutes. Stir. Add butter. Microwave at MEDIUM 30 seconds. Stir.

Beat egg yolks. Slowly add egg yolks to hot mixture. Microwave at MEDIUM 2 to 3 minutes. Add vanilla and coconut extracts.

Pour plain gelatin in a small amount of water to dissolve. Add to warm custard mixture. Cool slightly.

Beat egg whites until soft peaks form. Gradually beat in sugar and salt until egg whites form stiff peaks. Fold egg whites and coconut into cooled custard mixture.

Pour filling into baked pastry shell. Chill until firm.

Yield: one 9-inch pie.

OLD-FASHIONED
COCONUT CUSTARD PIE

Power: HIGH/MEDIUM
Microwave Time: 10 to 12 Minutes

       2 **cups milk**
      ¾ **cup sugar**
      ½ **cup commercial biscuit mix**
       4 **eggs**
      ¼ **cup butter or margarine**
     1½ **teaspoons vanilla extract**
       1 **cup flaked coconut**

Combine milk, sugar, biscuit mix, eggs, butter, and vanilla in jar of an electric blender. Blend at Low 3 minutes. Add coconut and blend at Low 30 seconds. Pour mixture into greased 9-inch glass pie plate. Let mixture stand 5 minutes.

Microwave at HIGH 2 minutes. Rotate dish ½ turn. Microwave at MEDIUM 8 to 10 minutes.

Allow pie to stand, uncovered, 5 minutes before serving. Pie filling makes a crust.
Yield: one 9-inch pie.

COFFEE PIE

Power: MEDIUM
Microwave Time: 6 to 7 Minutes

      ½ **cup water**
       2 **tablespoons instant coffee granules**
      18 **to 20 large marshmallows**
       2 **egg yolks, slightly beaten**
       1 **teaspoon vanilla extract**
          Dash of salt
      ¼ **teaspoon ground nutmeg**
       1 **cup finely chopped pecans**
       1 **cup whipping cream**
       1 **baked 9-inch graham cracker crust**
      ½ **cup pecan halves**

Combine water, coffee, and marshmallows in a 4-cup glass measure. Microwave at MEDIUM 5 minutes. Stir mixture after 2 minutes. Slowly stir egg yolks into marshmallow mixture. Microwave at MEDIUM 1 to 2 minutes. Stir mixture after 1 minute. Stir in vanilla, salt, and nutmeg. Chill mixture until partially set. Beat until smooth. Fold in chopped nuts.

Whip cream until stiff. Reserve a portion for garnish. Fold remaining whipped cream into coffee mixture. Pour into graham cracker crust.

Garnish with pecan halves and reserved whipped cream.
Yield: one 9-inch pie.

LEMON PIE

Power: HIGH
Microwave Time: 5 to 7 Minutes

       1 **cup sugar**
      ⅓ **cup cornstarch**
     1½ **cups hot water**
       3 **eggs, separated**
       4 **to 5 tablespoons fresh lemon juice**
     1⅓ **tablespoons finely grated lemon rind**
       3 **tablespoons butter**
       1 **baked 9-inch pastry shell Microwaved Meringue (See p. 140)**

Combine sugar and cornstarch in a 4-cup glass measure. Stir in hot water. Microwave at HIGH 3 to 4 minutes or until thick. Stir well after 2 minutes.

Beat egg yolks and slowly stir in part of the hot pudding. Then beat the egg yolk mixture into the hot pudding mixture in the cup. Add lemon juice and rind.

Microwave at HIGH 2 to 3 minutes or until thick. Add butter and stir until melted. Pour the hot mixture into the baked pie shell. Top with Meringue and microwave according to directions.
Yield: one 9-inch pie.

LIME CHIFFON BANANA PIE

Power: MEDIUM
Microwave Time: 3½ to 4 Minutes

      4 cups miniature marshmallows
      ⅓ cup fresh lime juice
      4 eggs, separated
      3 to 4 drops green food coloring
      1 tablespoon grated lime rind
      ¼ cup sugar
      1 banana, peeled
      1 9-inch graham cracker crust
         Whipped cream
         Lime slices

Microwave marshmallows and lime juice in a 3-quart glass mixing bowl at MEDIUM 3 minutes. Stir mixture at 1 minute intervals.

Beat egg yolks in a small bowl. Stir a small amount of hot marshmallow mixture into egg yolks. Stir egg yolks into remaining marshmallow mixture. Microwave at MEDIUM ½ to 1 minute. Stir at 15 second intervals until mixture thickens.

Stir in food coloring and lime rind. Cool.

Beat egg whites until soft peaks are formed. Slowly add sugar. Fold egg whites into lime mixture.

Slice banana into graham cracker crust. Pour lime filling over banana slices. Chill.

Garnish with whipped cream and lime slices.

Yield: one 9-inch pie.

EASY FRUIT PIE

Power: HIGH
Microwave Time: 11 to 14 Minutes

      ¼ cup butter or margarine
      ¾ cup sugar
      ½ cup firmly packed brown sugar
      ½ cup water
     2½ cups sliced fresh peaches or
            apples
     1½ cups self-rising flour
      2 teaspoons ground cinnamon
      ½ cup shortening
     1¼ cups milk
         Brown sugar

Microwave butter in a 2-quart casserole at HIGH 1 minute. Stir in sugars, water, and fruit. Microwave at HIGH 3 minutes. Sift flour and cinnamon in a bowl together. Cut in shortening. Add milk. Stir well. Spoon batter over fruit mixture. Sprinkle with brown sugar. Microwave at HIGH 3 to 5 minutes. Rotate dish ½ turn. Microwave at HIGH 4 to 5 minutes or until done.

Yield: 6 to 8 servings.

EASY PEACH CHEESE PIE

Power: MEDIUM/HIGH
Microwave Time: 3½ to 5 Minutes

      ¾ cup all-purpose flour
      6 tablespoons firmly packed dark
            brown sugar
      ⅓ cup margarine
      2 teaspoons grated orange rind
      2 to 3 tablespoons cold water
      1 (8-ounce) package cream cheese
      ½ cup powdered sugar
      1 teaspoon vanilla extract
      1 (9-ounce) container non-dairy
            whipped topping, divided
      1 (16-ounce) can peaches, drained
            or 2 cups fresh sliced peaches

Blend together flour and brown sugar. Cut margarine and orange rind into flour mixture. Stir in enough cold water to form mixture into a ball. Pat dough into a 9-inch glass pie plate. Microwave at MEDIUM 3 to 4 minutes. Crust will puff up and settle down. Cool before filling.

Microwave cream cheese in a 2-cup glass measuring cup at HIGH ½ to 1 minute. Cream together softened cream cheese, powdered sugar, and vanilla. Fold in half of whipped topping. Spread mixture evenly in cool pie shell. Top with remaining whipped topping and peaches.

Yield: one 9-inch pie.

GEORGIA PEACH COBBLER

Power: HIGH
Microwave Time: 10½ to 12½ Minutes

- 1 (29-ounce) can peach slices or 5 cups sliced fresh peaches
- 1 (3½-ounce) package butterscotch pudding and pie filling mix
- ¼ cup butter or margarine
- ⅔ cup quick-cooking oats, uncooked
- ½ cup unsifted all-purpose flour
- ½ cup firmly packed brown sugar
- ½ cup chopped nuts
- 1 teaspoon ground cinnamon
- 1 teaspoon ground nutmeg

Drain peach slices, reserving ¼ cup liquid. Place peach slices and reserved liquid in 9-inch round glass cake dish. Sprinkle with 2 tablespoons dry pudding mix.

Microwave butter in a 1-quart glass bowl at HIGH 30 seconds or until softened. Stir in remaining ingredients, including remaining pudding mix, until crumbly. Spoon onto peach mixture. Microwave, covered with a paper towel, at HIGH 10 to 12 minutes or until bubbly near center, rotating dish once or twice. Let stand, covered, 3 to 5 minutes before serving.

Yield: 8 servings.

Micronote: Omit the liquid if using fresh peaches.

PRESIDENTIAL PIE

Power: HIGH/MEDIUM
Microwave Time: 7 to 8 Minutes

Crust:

- ¼ cup butter or margarine
- 1¼ cups crushed graham crackers
- ¼ cup powdered sugar
- ½ cup peanut butter

Microwave butter in a 9-inch glass pie plate at HIGH 1 minute. Combine graham crackers, powdered sugar, and peanut butter with melted margarine. Press evenly into bottom of pie plate.

Filling:

- 2 cups milk
- ¼ cup cornstarch
- ⅔ cup sugar
- ¼ teaspoon salt
- 3 egg yolks, beaten
- ½ teaspoon vanilla extract
- 2 tablespoons butter or margarine
- 1 (3-ounce) can flaked coconut
  Whipped topping
  Coconut
  Peanuts, crushed

Microwave milk in a 4-cup glass measure at MEDIUM 3 to 4 minutes. Combine cornstarch, sugar, and salt. Stir mixture into hot milk. Microwave at HIGH 3 minutes. Stir mixture at 1 minute intervals. Slowly mix in beaten egg yolks. Microwave at MEDIUM ½ minute. Stir. Add vanilla, butter, and coconut. Pour filling into crust. Cool 10 minutes.

Garnish with whipped topping, coconut, and crushed peanuts.

Yield: one 9-inch pie.

PEANUT BUTTERSCOTCH PIE

Power: MEDIUM/HIGH
Microwave Time: 5½ to 6½ Minutes

  1 **cup firmly packed brown sugar**
  2 **tablespoons cornstarch**
  2 **egg yolks**
  ¼ **cup cold water**
  2 **cups milk**
  3 **tablespoons peanut butter**
  1 **tablespoon butter or margarine**
  1 **baked 9-inch pastry shell**

Combine brown sugar, cornstarch, egg yolks, and water. Beat well.

Microwave milk in a 4-cup glass measure at MEDIUM 2½ minutes. Stir in cornstarch mixture, peanut butter, and butter. Microwave filling mixture at HIGH 3 to 4 minutes. Stir filling at 1 minute intervals until thickened.

Cool filling. Pour into baked pastry shell.
Yield: one 9-inch pie.

PECAN PIE

Power: HIGH/MEDIUM-
  HIGH/MEDIUM
Microwave Time: 18½ to 24 Minutes

  3 **tablespoons butter or margarine**
  3 **eggs, beaten**
  1 **cup dark corn syrup**
  ¼ **cup firmly packed brown sugar**
  1½ **teaspoons all-purpose flour**
  1 **teaspoon vanilla extract**
  1½ **cups pecan halves**
  1 **baked 9-inch pastry shell (in a glass pie plate)**

Microwave butter in a 2-cup glass measuring cup at HIGH 1½ to 2 minutes. Add eggs, corn syrup, brown sugar, flour, and vanilla to melted butter. Microwave at MEDIUM-HIGH 2 minutes. Stir in pecans. Pour filling into pastry shell. Microwave at MEDIUM 15 to 20 minutes, or until sides are firm. Center will be soft but will firm while standing. Cool.

Yield: one 9-inch pie.

CRUNCH TOP
SWEET POTATO PIE

Power: HIGH
Microwave Time: 10 to 12 Minutes

  1 **(3½-ounce) can flaked coconut**
  6 **tablespoons butter or margarine, divided**
  ½ **(8-ounce) package cream cheese**
  1¾ **cups cooked mashed sweet potato**
  1 **egg**
  ½ **cup powdered sugar**
  1 **teaspoon vanilla extract**
  ¼ **cup chopped pecans**
  ¼ **cup all-purpose flour**
  ¼ **cup firmly packed brown sugar**
  ½ **teaspoon ground cinnamon**
  Dash of ground nutmeg

Spread coconut for crust in a 9-inch glass pie plate. Microwave at HIGH 2 minutes.

Microwave 2 tablespoons butter in a small glass custard cup at HIGH 1 minute. Mix melted butter into coconut. Spread crust evenly in pie plate. Microwave at HIGH 2 minutes.

Microwave cream cheese in a 2½-quart glass mixing bowl at HIGH ½ to 1 minute. Add sweet potato, egg, powdered sugar, and vanilla. Beat until smooth. Pour mixture into coconut crust.

Microwave 4 tablespoons butter in small glass mixing bowl at HIGH ½ to 1 minute. Stir in pecans, flour, brown sugar, cinnamon, and nutmeg. Sprinkle topping over sweet potato filling.

Microwave at HIGH 4 to 5 minutes. Chill before serving.

Yield: one 9-inch pie.

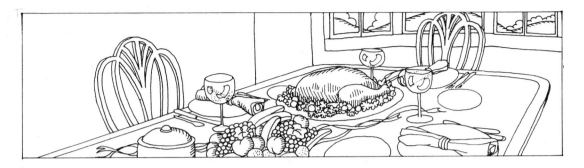

POULTRY

Because poultry is high in natural moisture, all the varieties microwave with exceptional quality. And, because whole turkey and chicken are hollow in the center, they cook quickly.

Proper arrangement is the key to successful microwaving of chicken pieces. Place thicker, meatier parts toward the outside of the dish and thin bony parts in the center. A single layer of chicken pieces will cook more evenly. Use a flat casserole or a round glass baking tray.

WHAT IS NEEDED FOR MICROWAVING POULTRY

There are some pieces of equipment needed for microwaving poultry. Most of them are the same as needed for meat roasting.

- A flat casserole, probably 12- x 8-inches
- A roasting rack, either microwave plastic or a glass lid or saucer to turn down in the casserole
- Aluminum foil for shielding
- A quality thermometer either conventional or microwave
- Waxed paper
- A waxed paper cover or an oven cooking bag to hold in the heat and create steam for poultry requiring steam for cooking

All poultry should be completely *defrosted* before cooking. If stuffing is being used, add it just before cooking.

Protect the bony parts of whole poultry with small pieces of light-weight foil to prevent overcooking.

Whole turkey, chicken, Cornish hens, and other whole poultry should be turned once during cooking. Start with breast-side-down. Complete cooking with breast-side-up.

CLASSIC CHICKEN DIVAN
(Conventional Recipe)

- 2   bunches fresh broccoli
- ¼   cup butter or margarine
- ¼   cup all-purpose flour
- 2   cups chicken broth
- ½   cup half-and-half
- 3   tablespoons sherry
- ½   teaspoon salt
    Dash of pepper
- 3   cups cooked chicken, sliced
- ½   cup grated Parmesan cheese, divided

Cook the broccoli in boiling, salted water until tender and drain. Melt the butter in a saucepan and blend in flour. Add the chicken broth and cook until thick, stirring constantly. Stir in the cream, sherry, salt, and pepper. Place broccoli in 13- x 9-x 2-inch baking dish and pour half the sauce over broccoli. Add the chicken. Add half the Parmesan cheese to remaining sauce and pour over the chicken. Sprinkle with remaining Parmesan cheese. Bake at 350° for 20 minutes or until heated through. Broil until golden brown.

Yield: 6 serving.

To Microwave Chicken Divan

- Substitute frozen broccoli for fresh.
- Use soup and granules for a quick sauce.
- Add wine and curry powder to achieve extra flavor.
- Sprinkle cheese over the food close to the end of microwaving time.

CLASSIC CHICKEN DIVAN

Power: HIGH/MEDIUM
Microwave Time: 25 to 29 Minutes

- 2   (10-ounce) packages broccoli flowerettes
- 3   cups cooked chicken, sliced
- 2   (10¾-ounce) cans cream of chicken soup, undiluted
- 2   tablespoons seasoned chicken broth granules
- ½   teaspoon curry powder
- ½   cup dry white wine
- 2   tablespoons butter or margarine, melted
- ¾   cup shredded mild white cheese

Pierce broccoli packages with a fork. Place in large flat microwave baking dish or on paper plates.

Microwave at HIGH 8 minutes. Set aside to cool.

Spread cooked chicken slices in 13- x 9-inch glass casserole.

Combine soup, broth granules, curry, wine, and butter in a bowl. Pour ⅔ of the soup mixture over chicken; spread broccoli over soup. Pour remaining soup mixture over broccoli.

Cover with waxed paper. Microwave at MEDIUM 15 to 18 minutes. Sprinkle cheese over top. Microwave at MEDIUM 2 to 3 minutes.

Yield: 6 servings.

BARBECUE CHICKEN

Power: HIGH
Microwave Time: 20 to 22 Minutes

- 1   (2½- to 3-pound) broiler-fryer chicken, cut up
- 3   tablespoons catsup
- 2   tablespoons vinegar
- 1   tablespoon lemon juice
- 2   tablespoons Worcestershire sauce
- 2   tablespoons firmly packed dark brown sugar
- 2   tablespoons butter or margarine
- 1   teaspoon salt
- 1   teaspoon cornstarch

Wash and dry chicken pieces. Combine remaining ingredients, except cornstarch, in a 8- to 9-inch glass pie plate. Microwave at HIGH 1 minute or until butter is melted. Mix well.

Dip chicken pieces in sauce. Arrange sauce-coated chicken pieces in a 13- x 9-inch flat baking dish.

Cover with plastic wrap. Microwave at HIGH 18 to 20 minutes or until tender. Let stand, covered, 4 to 5 minutes.

Combine cornstarch and remaining sauce. Microwave at HIGH 1 minute and drizzle over chicken to serve.

Yield: 4 servings.

BEEF BAKED CHICKEN

Power: HIGH
Microwave Time: 14 to 17 Minutes

- 2 whole chicken breasts, halved and boned
- 1 (3-ounce) package dried beef, chopped
- 4 slices bacon
- 1 (8-ounce) carton commercial sour cream
- 1 (10¾-ounce) can cream of mushroom soup, undiluted
  Paprika

Place chicken breast pieces between two pieces of waxed paper. Pound to flatten. Place dried beef on top of each chicken piece. Roll up each chicken-beef portion. Wrap one bacon slice around each. Secure with a wooden toothpick. Place rolled chicken in a microwave baking dish.

Cover with plastic wrap. Microwave at HIGH 12 to 14 minutes. Remove excess bacon drippings.

Combine sour cream and soup. Spoon over chicken. Microwave at HIGH 2 to 3 minutes or until bubbly. Sprinkle lightly with paprika to serve. Let stand 3 to 5 minutes.

Yield: 4 servings.

CHICKEN CACCIATORE

Power: HIGH/MEDIUM
Microwave Time: 30 to 32 Minutes

- 1 (3-pound) broiler-fryer chicken, cut up
- 1 teaspoon salt
- ½ teaspoon garlic powder
- ¼ teaspoon powdered thyme
- 2 (8-ounce) cans tomato sauce
- 2 tablespoons instant minced onion
- 1 teaspoon oregano
- ¼ teaspoon pepper
  Cooked spaghetti

Cut larger pieces of chicken in half. Wash and wipe dry. Place chicken in a 4-quart casserole.

Combine remaining ingredients. Pour over chicken pieces. Be sure chicken pieces are coated well. Cover with plastic wrap.

Microwave at HIGH 10 minutes. Stir well. Microwave at MEDIUM 20 to 22 minutes or until chicken is cooked. Stir once or twice during microwaving. Let stand, covered, 3 to 5 minutes. Serve over cooked spaghetti.

Yield: 4 to 6 servings.

CHEEZY CHICKEN

Power: HIGH
Microwave Time: 12 to 15 Minutes

- 4 chicken breast halves, skinned
- ¼ cup butter or margarine, melted
- 3 cups cheese crackers, crushed

Brush chicken pieces with butter. Roll in cracker crumbs. Arrange pieces in a flat microwave baking dish. Cover with waxed paper.

Microwave at HIGH 12 to 15 minutes. Rotate dish ½ turn halfway through microwaving time. Let stand, covered, 2 to 3 minutes.

Yield: 4 servings.

CHICKEN AND DRESSING DINNER

Power: HIGH
Microwave Time: 8 to 10 Minutes per pound

- 2 cups sliced onion
- 2 teaspoons poultry seasoning
- 1 teaspoon salt
  Dash of pepper
- 2 to 2½ cups water
- 2 quarts bread crumbs
- 1 (3- to 4-pound) broiler-fryer chicken, cut up
- ½ cup butter or margarine, melted
  Paprika

Combine onion, poultry seasoning, salt, pepper, and water in a large glass mixing bowl. Mix thoroughly. Microwave at HIGH 1 minute.

Place bread crumbs in a 4-quart casserole. Add the water mixture and stir to combine. Arrange chicken pieces over the bread mixture.

Drizzle the melted butter over chicken and stuffing. Sprinkle with paprika. Cover with waxed paper. Microwave at HIGH 8 to 10 minutes per pound. Rotate dish ½ turn after 4 to 5 minutes, also turning each of the chicken pieces over.

Yield: 4 to 6 servings.

EASY CORDON BLEU

Power: HIGH/MEDIUM
Microwave Time: 11½ to 12½ Minutes

- 2 large chicken breasts, boned and halved
- 4 thin slices ham
- 4 pieces cheese (1- x 1- x ½-inch)
- 4 tablespoons butter or margarine
- 1 teaspoon lemon herb-seasoned salt
- ½ cup grated Swiss cheese

Place each boned and halved chicken breast between two sheets of waxed paper. Flatten by pounding with a mallet. On each piece place a slice of ham and piece of cheese. Pull up sides of chicken and cover ham and cheese. Secure with a wooden toothpick.

Place butter in a 9-inch round glass baking dish. Microwave at HIGH 30 seconds or to melt. Add seasoned salt. Carefully place chicken pieces in the seasoned butter. Spoon butter over chicken. Cover with waxed paper.

Microwave at HIGH 2 minutes. Spoon liquid over chicken. Cover with waxed paper. Microwave at MEDIUM 7 to 8 minutes.

Sprinkle grated cheese over chicken. Microwave at MEDIUM 2 minutes or until cheese is melted. Let stand, covered, 3 to 5 minutes. Serve with liquid.

Yield: 4 servings.

DIVINE CHICKEN

Power: MEDIUM-HIGH
Microwave Time: 12 to 15 Minutes

- ¾ cup fine dry bread crumbs
- ⅔ cup grated Parmesan cheese
- 4 tablespoons minced parsley
- ¼ teaspoon pepper
- 1 cup melted butter or margarine
- 1 clove garlic, crushed
- 2 teaspoons salt
- 4 chicken breast halves, boned
- 6 tablespoons lemon juice
  Dash of paprika

Blend bread crumbs, Parmesan cheese, parsley, and pepper. Combine melted butter and garlic with salt. Dip chicken into butter then into crumb mixture, coating thoroughly. Roll each piece into firm roll and skewer with wooden toothpick. Arrange in a 12- x 8-inch casserole. Sprinkle with lemon juice and drizzle remaining butter over chicken.

Cover with waxed paper. Microwave at MEDIUM-HIGH 12 to 15 minutes. Let stand 3 to 4 minutes before serving. Sprinkle with paprika to serve.

Yield: 2 to 4 servings.

14-CARAT GOLD CHICKEN ★

Power: HIGH
Microwave Time: 11 to 13 Minutes

- 10 large chicken thighs, boned
- ½ cup butter or margarine
- ¼ teaspoon salt
- 1 teaspoon poultry seasoning
- ½ teaspoon garlic powder
- 1½ teaspoons dried tarragon
- ½ cup commercial sour cream
- 4 to 6 drops yellow food coloring
- ¼ cup grated Parmesan cheese
  Pimiento

Wash and dry chicken pieces. Place butter in a glass bowl. Microwave at HIGH 30 seconds to soften. Rub each chicken piece with the softened butter.

Combine salt, poultry seasoning, and garlic powder. Sprinkle each piece with seasoning mixture. Set aside for 10 minutes before cooking.

Preheat browning skillet according to manufacturer's directions. Place chicken pieces in the preheated browning dish. Cover with a paper towel. Microwave at HIGH 2½ minutes. Turn chicken pieces over, and microwave at HIGH 2½ minutes.

Sprinkle with tarragon. Cover with glass lid. Microwave at HIGH 5 to 7 minutes. Place cooked chicken on serving platter suitable for microwave. Cover with waxed paper. Set aside.

Combine sour cream, food coloring, ¼ cup pan drippings, and Parmesan cheese in a small bowl. Spoon sauce evenly over chicken pieces. Microwave at HIGH 30 seconds.

To serve, garnish each piece with a thin strip of pimiento.

Yield: 4 to 6 servings.

FOSTER'S CHICKEN PARMESAN ★

Power: HIGH
Microwave Time: 10 to 12 Minutes

- ½ cup dry white wine
- 1 teaspoon dried tarragon
- ½ teaspoon ground thyme
- 4 chicken breast halves, skinned
- ½ cup grated Parmesan cheese
- ½ cup chopped parsley

Blend wine with tarragon and thyme. Pour into shallow baking dish. Place chicken breasts in marinade. Chill and marinate for 1 hour, turning breasts once during hour.

Remove breasts from marinade and spoon marinade over both sides of breasts so that they are wet. Sprinkle Parmesan cheese on both sides to coat well. Arrange in a baking dish or place on a microwave plastic roasting rack in a 12- by 8-inch baking dish.

Microwave at HIGH 5 minutes. Remove from oven, turn each breast over, and rotate dish ½ turn. Microwave at HIGH 5 to 7 minutes. Chicken should be lightly browned on thin edges.

Let stand, covered, with waxed paper, 3 to 5 minutes. To serve, garnish with chopped parsley.

Yield: 4 servings.

STUFFED CHICKEN BREAST

Power: HIGH/MEDIUM
Microwave Time: 10½ to 11½ Minutes

½	**cup butter or margarine**
¼	**teaspoon white pepper**
¼	**teaspoon lemon herb-seasoned salt**
¼	**cup grated Parmesan cheese**
6	**chicken breast halves, boned and flattened**
2	**tablespoons dry white wine**
1½	**cups soft bread crumbs**
3	**tablespoons chopped green onion**

Place butter in a 9-inch glass pie plate. Microwave at HIGH 30 seconds. Add pepper, seasoned salt, and cheese. Dip each side of chicken breasts in butter mixture. Place three halves in a round casserole.

Combine wine, bread crumbs, and green onion. Spread bread crumb mixture over chicken halves in casserole and top with remaining halves.

Cover with plastic wrap. Microwave at HIGH 2 minutes. Rotate dish ½ turn. Microwave at MEDIUM 8 to 9 minutes. Let stand, covered, 2 minutes before serving.

Yield: 4 to 6 servings.

PIQUANT STUFFED CHICKEN BREASTS

Power: HIGH
Microwave Time: 14 to 16 Minutes

½	**cup ground walnuts**
3	**shallots, chopped**
2	**tablespoons butter or margarine**
½	**teaspoon salt**
2	**tablespoons chopped parsley**
½	**teaspoon dry mustard**
¼	**teaspoon hot sauce**
2	**whole chicken breasts, halved**
⅓	**cup melted butter or margarine**
½	**teaspoon paprika**

Blend the walnuts, shallots, butter, salt, parsley, mustard, and hot sauce to a smooth paste. Loosen the skin on the chicken breasts. Stuff the paste under the skin. Brush the pieces with a combination of ⅓ cup melted butter and ½ teaspoon paprika. Arrange breasts in a 2-quart glass dish skin side down.

Cover with waxed paper. Microwave at HIGH 8 minutes. Turn and rearrange pieces; baste with butter. Microwave at HIGH 6 to 8 minutes. Let stand, covered, 2 to 3 minutes. Excellent served hot or cold.

Yield: 4 servings.

CHICKEN L'ORANGE

Power: HIGH
Microwave Time: 22 to 26 Minutes

1	**(3-pound) broiler-fryer chicken, cut up**
¼	**cup butter or margarine, melted**
¼	**teaspoon paprika**
3	**oranges**
	Water
2	**tablespoons finely slivered orange rind**
4	**tablespoons all-purpose flour**
½	**teaspoon salt**
⅛	**teaspoon pepper**
1	**tablespoon firmly packed brown sugar**
¼	**teaspoon ground ginger**

Wash and dry chicken. Brush chicken pieces with melted butter. Sprinkle lightly with paprika. Arrange chicken pieces, meatier parts toward edge of dish, skin side up, in a 12- x 8-inch baking dish.

Cover with waxed paper. Microwave at HIGH 18 to 20 minutes. Rotate dish ½ turn after 10 minutes.

While chicken is cooking, juice oranges. Add water to make 1¼ cups. Blend with slivered rind and set juice and rind aside.

Remove cooked chicken from dish. Add remaining ingredients to drippings in dish. Stir to make a smooth paste. Add reserved juice and rind.

Microwave at HIGH 3 to 4 minutes or until thick. Stir well at 1 minute intervals.

Return chicken pieces to dish. Spoon thickened sauce over pieces to coat well. Microwave at HIGH 1 to 2 minutes. Let stand, covered, 2 minutes.

Yield: 4 to 6 servings.

EASY TOMATO CHICKEN BAKE

Power: MEDIUM-HIGH
Microwave Time: 21 to 25 Minutes

    2 pounds chicken pieces
    1 cup tomato juice
    ½ teaspoon garlic powder
    ½ teaspoon oregano
    1 teaspoon salt
    ¼ teaspoon pepper

Wash and dry chicken pieces. Combine remaining ingredients in a flat glass baking dish. Roll chicken pieces to coat well.

Cover with plastic wrap. Microwave at MEDIUM-HIGH 15 minutes. Spoon sauce over chicken. Cover and microwave at MEDIUM-HIGH 6 to 10 minutes. Let stand, covered, 5 to 6 minutes before serving.

Yield: 4 servings.

PEANUT-CHICKEN CURRY

Power: HIGH
Microwave Time: 9½ to 12½ Minutes

    4 chicken breast halves
    ¼ cup all-purpose flour
    4 tablespoons butter or margarine
    1 egg
    ⅓ cup crunchy peanut butter
    1 teaspoon curry powder
    ½ teaspoon salt
    ⅛ teaspoon black pepper
    ⅛ teaspoon cayenne pepper
    ⅓ cup buttermilk
    2 teaspoons fresh lemon juice
    ½ cup seasoned dry bread crumbs
       Chutney
       Hot cooked rice

Bone and skin chicken pieces. Wash and dry. Dip in flour. Set aside.

Microwave butter in a flat baking dish at HIGH 30 seconds to melt. Set aside.

Combine remaining ingredients except bread crumbs, chutney, and rice. Mixture will be somewhat thick and should be well mixed.

Dip floured chicken pieces in peanut butter mixture, then in bread crumbs.

Place chicken pieces in dish containing butter. Turn to coat well. Microwave, uncovered, at HIGH 9 to 12 minutes. Rotate dish ½ turn after 5 to 6 minutes of microwaving. Cover with waxed paper and let stand 2 to 3 minutes before serving. Serve with chutney and hot cooked rice.

Yield: 4 servings.

PINEAPPLE CHICKEN ITALIENNE

Power: HIGH/MEDIUM-HIGH
Microwave Time: 25 to 28 Minutes

    1 (3-pound) broiler-fryer chicken,
       cut up
    ½ green pepper, cut in strips
    1 small onion, thinly sliced
    1 tablespoon cornstarch
    1 teaspoon salt
    ⅛ teaspoon pepper
    1 (8-ounce) can tomato sauce
    ½ (8-ounce) can crushed pineapple,
       drained
    1 teaspoon firmly packed brown
       sugar
    ⅛ teaspoon ground ginger
    ¼ teaspoon salt

Arrange chicken pieces, meatier parts toward edge, in a 12- x 8-inch baking dish. Place pepper strips and onion slices over chicken.

Combine cornstarch, salt, and pepper. Blend well with a small amount of tomato sauce. Stir until smooth, then add remaining tomato sauce and other ingredients. Pour over chicken.

Cover with plastic wrap. Microwave at HIGH 10 minutes. Rotate dish ½ turn. Microwave at MEDIUM-HIGH 15 to 18 minutes or until done.

Yield: 4 to 6 servings.

HONEY CHICKEN

Power: HIGH
Microwave Time: 19 to 23 Minutes

- ½   **teaspoon garlic powder**
- 2   **teaspoons salt**
- ¼   **teaspoon pepper**
- 6   **chicken breast halves**
- 1   **egg yolk**
- 2   **tablespoons honey**
- ¼   **cup butter or margarine, divided**
- 1   **(20-ounce) can crushed pineapple, drained**
- ⅓   **cup orange juice**
- ¾   **cup toasted, chopped almonds**

Combine garlic powder, salt, and pepper. Rub chicken with mixture. Beat egg yolk and honey with half of the butter; brush over chicken.

Place chicken pieces in a greased 10-inch baking dish; add crushed pineapple and orange juice. Cover with waxed paper. Microwave at HIGH 16 to 18 minutes. Rotate dish ½ turn after 8 or 9 minutes of microwaving. Baste with remaining butter. Sprinkle almonds over chicken. Microwave at HIGH 3 to 5 minutes. Let stand, covered, 2 to 3 minutes before serving.

Yield: 6 servings.

LEMON CHICKEN

Power: HIGH/MEDIUM-HIGH
Microwave Time: 15 to 20 Minutes

- ¼   **cup butter or margarine**
- 2   **lemons, divided**
- ¼   **teaspoon garlic powder**
- ¼   **teaspoon pepper**
- ⅛   **teaspoon oregano**
- 1   **teaspoon salt**
- ¼   **cup dry white wine**
- 4   **whole chicken breasts, boned and halved**
  Paprika

Place butter in 12- x 8-inch baking dish. Microwave at HIGH 30 seconds to melt. Remove juice from 1½ lemons. Slice the remaining half of lemon into very thin

slices. Add lemon juice, garlic powder, pepper, oregano, salt, and wine to the melted butter.

Dip the chicken in the butter mixture being sure to coat all sides. Arrange the chicken pieces with meatier part to the edge of the dish. Place lemon slices over chicken pieces.

Cover with waxed paper. Microwave at MEDIUM-HIGH 15 to 20 minutes or until chicken is done. Let stand, covered, 2 to 3 minutes before serving. Spoon drippings over each piece and sprinkle with paprika to serve.

Yield: 4 to 8 servings.

CHICKEN MOUTARDE

Power: HIGH
Microwave Time: 18 to 20 Minutes

- 4   **whole chicken breasts, halved**
- 3   **tablespoons Dijon mustard**
- 2   **tablespoons butter or margarine, melted**
  Paprika

Remove skin from chicken pieces and dry thoroughly. Mix mustard and butter. Brush on chicken.

Place chicken pieces in a 12- x 8- baking dish, meatier parts toward edge of dish. Cover with waxed paper. Microwave at HIGH 18 to 20 minutes or until chicken is tender.

Rotate dish ½ turn after 9 to 10 minutes of microwaving. Let stand, covered, 5 minutes. Sprinkle with paprika before serving.

Yield: 4 servings.

Crushed cheese wafers are used as a coating to add color and flavor to Cheezy Chicken (p.149). Herbed Rice (p.115) is a perfect side dish.

DILLY MUSTARD CHICKEN

Power: HIGH
Microwave Time: 16 to 19 Minutes

- ⅔ **cup dry bread crumbs**
- 1 **teaspoon salt**
- 6 **chicken breast halves**
- 1 **(8-ounce) carton commercial sour cream**
- 2 **tablespoons prepared mustard**
- 1 **tablespoon dillseed**

Combine bread crumbs and salt. Roll chicken pieces in crumbs to coat. Place chicken in a baking dish.

Blend sour cream, mustard, and dillseed. Spread over chicken pieces.

Cover with waxed paper. Microwave at HIGH 16 to 19 minutes. Rotate dish ½ turn at 6 minute intervals. Let stand, covered, 3 to 5 minutes.

Yield: 6 servings.

SHENANDOAH CHICKEN

Power: HIGH/MEDIUM
Microwave Time: 26 Minutes

- 1 **(1-pound) can applesauce**
- ½ **teaspoon ground allspice**
- 1 **teaspoon salt**
- 1 **tablespoon all-purpose flour**
- 1 **tablespoon tomato paste**
- 1 **cup chopped celery**
- 1 **tablespoon lemon juice**
- ¼ **cup chopped onion**
- ½ **cup rye cracker crumbs**
- ½ **teaspoon paprika**
- ½ **teaspoon salt**
- 3 **whole chicken breasts split, or other chicken pieces**
- ½ **cup evaporated milk**

The sauce and bacon for a Hot Brown Sandwich (p.48) are easy to microwave. Serve this traditional sandwich for lunch . . . or anytime as a special treat.

Combine applesauce, allspice, salt, flour, tomato paste, celery, lemon juice, and onion. Pour mixture into a greased 12- x 8-inch glass baking dish. Microwave at HIGH 1 minute.

Combine cracker crumbs, paprika, and salt. Dip chicken pieces in evaporated milk. Roll chicken in cracker mixture to coat chicken.

For microwaving, arrange chicken pieces on top of applesauce mixture with meatier parts to the edge of dish. Cover dish with waxed paper. Microwave chicken at MEDIUM 25 minutes. Rotate dish ½ turn at 10 minute intervals. Let chicken stand, covered, 5 minutes before serving.

Yield: 6 servings.

CHICKEN AND SHRIMP SUPREME

Power: HIGH/MEDIUM-HIGH
Microwave Time: 19 to 22 Minutes

- 4 **whole chicken breasts, halved**
- 2 **cups Basic White Sauce (see p.164)**
- 1 **(8-ounce) package frozen cooked shrimp, thawed and drained**
- 1 **cup fresh or canned mushrooms, sliced**
- ¼ **pound mild Cheddar cheese, shredded**

Arrange chicken breasts, meatier portion toward outer edge, in 12- x 8-inch baking dish. Microwave at HIGH 10 to 12 minutes, rotating dish ½ turn after 5 to 6 minutes of microwaving. Cool and remove meat from bone in large pieces. Return meat to dish.

Pour white sauce over chicken pieces. Top with shrimp, mushrooms, and cheese. Cover with waxed paper. Microwave at MEDIUM-HIGH 9 to 10 minutes, rotating ½ turn after 5 minutes microwaving. Let stand, covered, 2 to 3 minutes before serving.

Yield: 4 to 6 servings.

SWEET-AND-SOUR CHICKEN

Power: HIGH
Microwave Time: 22 to 26 Minutes

- 4 **chicken legs and thighs**
- 1 **onion, chopped**
- 2 **teaspoons water**
- 1 **(10-ounce) bottle chili sauce**
- 4 **tablespoons lemon juice**
- ¼ **cup firmly packed brown sugar**
- ⅓ **cup sugar**
- 1 **tablespoon Worcestershire sauce**
- 2 **tablespoons cider vinegar**
- 1 **teaspoon salt**
  Dash of pepper

Wash and dry chicken. Place chicken pieces skin side down in an 8-inch square baking dish.

Combine onion and water in a 4-cup glass measure. Cover with plastic wrap. Microwave at HIGH 2 to 3 minutes. Add all other ingredients. Cover. Microwave at HIGH 4 to 5 minutes.

Pour hot sauce over chicken. Cover with waxed paper. Microwave at HIGH 16 to 18 minutes, rotating dish ¼ turn at 5 minute intervals. Let stand, covered, 3 to 4 minutes.
Yield: 4 servings.

CHICKEN TERIYAKI

Power: HIGH
Microwave Time: 14 to 16 Minutes

- 1½ **pounds chicken pieces**
- ⅔ **cup soy sauce**
- ½ **cup dry white wine**
- 2 **tablespoons sugar**
- ½ **teaspoon ground ginger**
- 1 **clove garlic, minced**

Place chicken pieces, skin side up, in 12- x 8-inch baking dish. Blend all ingredients in small bowl. Stir to dissolve sugar. Pour over chicken. Cover with plastic wrap. Marinate 1 to 2 hours at room temperature, turning chicken pieces once.

Cover with plastic wrap. Microwave at HIGH 14 to 16 minutes, rotating dish ½

turn after 7 to 8 minutes of microwaving. Let stand, covered, 4 to 5 minutes before serving.
Yield: 4 servings.

CHICKEN ZUCCHINI CASSEROLE

Power: HIGH
Microwave Time: 31 to 38 Minutes

- 1 **(2½- to 3-pound) broiler-fryer chicken, cut up.**
- 6 **cups sliced zucchini**
- ¼ **cup chopped onion**
- 2 **tablespoons water**
- 1 **(8-ounce) carton commercial sour cream**
- 1 **(10¾-ounce) can of cream of chicken soup, undiluted**
- 1 **cup grated carrots**
- 1 **(8-ounce) package herb-seasoned stuffing mix**
- ½ **cup butter or margarine, melted**

Wash and dry chicken pieces. Place in flat microwave baking dish. Cover with waxed paper. Microwave at HIGH 8 to 9 minutes. Rearrange chicken pieces, if necessary. Cover and microwave at HIGH 8 to 10 minutes. When cool, remove meat from bones and cut into small pieces.

Combine zucchini, onion, and water in a 2-quart casserole. Cover with plastic wrap. Microwave at HIGH 5 to 7 minutes. Let stand, covered. Drain if necessary.

Combine sour cream and soup in a bowl. Add carrot, chicken, and cooked vegetables. Combine stuffing and melted butter. Divide half the stuffing mix between two 8-inch baking dishes. Spread half of the chicken mixture over stuffing in each dish. Top each with remaining stuffing mix.

Microwave at HIGH 10 to 12 minutes or until heated through. Let stand, covered with waxed paper, 2 to 3 minutes before serving.
Yield: 8 to 12 servings.
Micronote: This can also be prepared in a 13- x 9-inch dish for 8 to 12 servings. For 4 to 6 servings wrap, label, and freeze one 8-inch casserole for use later.

CHICKEN SUMMER VEGETABLE DUO

Power: HIGH
Microwave Time: 25 to 26 Minutes

¼ cup butter
6 chicken breast halves, skinned and boned
1 (10¾-ounce) can cream of onion soup, undiluted
¾ cup commercial sour cream
3 tomatoes, finely chopped
1 teaspoon salt
3 zucchini, sliced
Hot cooked rice

Preheat large browning skillet according to manufacturer's directions. Add butter to dish to melt. Place chicken breasts in dish. Microwave at HIGH 3 minutes. Turn chicken pieces over; microwave at HIGH 2 to 3 minutes more.

Combine soup, sour cream, tomatoes, and salt in a bowl. Spread zucchini slices over chicken and pour soup mixture over zucchini slices.

Cover with plastic wrap. Microwave at HIGH 20 minutes. Rotate dish ½ turn after 10 minutes of microwaving.

Let stand, covered, 2 to 3 minutes. Serve over hot cooked rice.
Yield: 6 servings.

CHICKEN À LA KING

Power: HIGH
Microwave Time: 9 to 10 Minutes

¼ cup butter or margarine
½ cup chopped green pepper
½ cup fresh sliced mushrooms
1 (10¾-ounce) can cream of celery soup, undiluted
2 tablespoons chopped pimiento
1 teaspoon sugar
½ teaspoon salt
1 teaspoon Worcestershire sauce
2 cups cooked, cubed chicken
Hot rice, toast, or biscuits

Microwave butter in a 4-cup glass measure at HIGH 45 seconds. Add green pepper and mushrooms. Microwave at HIGH 2 minutes, stirring once. Add soup, pimiento, sugar, salt, and Worcestershire sauce. Microwave at HIGH 2 minutes.

Stir in chicken. Microwave at HIGH 5 minutes, rotating ¼ turn after 2½ minutes of microwaving. Serve over hot rice, toast or biscuits.
Yield: 4 to 6 servings.

CURRIED TWO-IN-ONE DINNER

Power: HIGH/MEDIUM-HIGH
Microwave Time: 15 to 16 Minutes

2 (10-ounce) packages frozen broccoli
1 cup cornbread crumbs
1 (10½-ounce) can cream of mushroom soup, undiluted
⅓ cup mayonnaise
1 tablespoon lemon juice
1 teaspoon curry powder
2 cups cooked chopped chicken or turkey
¼ cup commercial sour cream
½ cup shredded Cheddar cheese

Pierce broccoli packages with a fork. Place on paper plates side by side in oven. Microwave at HIGH 3 to 4 minutes. Set aside.

Place cornbread crumbs in bottom of a 2½-quart casserole. Combine soup, mayonnaise, lemon juice, curry powder, chicken, and sour cream. Pour over the bread crumbs. Microwave, covered, at HIGH 10 minutes.

Sprinkle cheese over top. Microwave at MEDIUM-HIGH 2 minutes. Let stand, covered, 2 or 3 minutes before serving.
Yield: 6 servings.

CHICKEN CRÊPES

Power: HIGH
Microwave Time: 3 to 5 Minutes

> 2 cups finely chopped cooked chicken
> 1 cup chopped nuts
> ½ cup finely chopped ripe olives
> ½ teaspoon salt
> ⅛ teaspoon pepper
> 1 teaspoon Worcestershire sauce
> 1 tablespoon lemon juice
> 2 tablespoons sherry
> 12 cooked crêpes
> 1 cup Cheese Sauce (see p.165)

Combine all ingredients except the crêpes and Cheese Sauce. Divide the chicken mixture among the crêpes. Roll and arrange the crêpes in a 13- x 9-inch baking dish. Pour Cheese Sauce over filled crêpes.

Cover with waxed paper. Microwave at HIGH 3 to 5 minutes or until hot. Let stand, covered, 2 to 3 minutes before serving.

Yield: 6 to 8 servings.

CHICKEN LOAF WITH MUSHROOM SAUCE

Power: HIGH
Microwave Time: 18 to 20 Minutes

> 5 cups cooked diced chicken
> 2 cups fresh bread crumbs
> 1 cup cooked rice
> 1½ teaspoons salt
> ⅛ cup chopped pimiento
> 3 cups chicken broth
> 4 eggs, well beaten
> Mushroom Sauce (see p.165)

Combine first 7 ingredients in a large bowl adding eggs last. Spread mixture in 12- x 8-inch baking dish.

Microwave at HIGH 18 to 20 minutes. Rotate dish ½ turn after 9 minutes of microwaving. To serve, cut in squares and top with Mushroom Sauce.

Yield: 8 servings.

HOT CHICKEN SALAD

Power: HIGH
Microwave Time: 7 to 9 Minutes

> 3 cups cooked chicken or turkey, cubed
> 2 cups celery, chopped
> ½ cup chopped green pepper
> ¼ cup chopped green onion
> 1 teaspoon salt
> ⅛ teaspoon pepper
> ¼ cup lemon juice
> 1 cup mayonnaise
> ¼ cup chopped pimiento
> 1 cup almonds
> 1½ cups crushed potato chips
> ½ cup shredded Cheddar cheese

Place cubed chicken in a 10-inch casserole. Combine celery, green pepper, and onion in a 2-cup glass measure. Cover with plastic wrap. Microwave at HIGH 2 to 3 minutes or until tender-crisp. Drain, if necessary.

Stir cooked celery mixture, salt, pepper, lemon juice, mayonnaise, pimiento, and almonds into the chicken. Top with potato chips and Cheddar cheese. Microwave at HIGH 5 to 6 minutes. Let stand 2 to 3 minutes before serving.

Yield: 4 to 6 servings.

CHICKEN SOUFFLÉ

Power: HIGH/MEDIUM
Microwave Time: 20 to 23 Minutes

> 12 slices of white bread
> Butter or margarine
> 2 cups cooked chicken, chopped
> 1 cup shredded sharp Cheddar cheese
> 1½ teaspoons salt
> ½ teaspoon pepper
> 4 eggs, beaten
> 3 cups milk
> 1 hard-cooked egg
> Pimiento

Remove crusts from bread and spread each slice with butter. Place 6 slices of bread in a flat glass baking dish. Top with chicken and cheese. Cover with remaining bread slices. Blend remaining ingredients except the egg and pimiento and pour over bread and chicken. Cover with plastic wrap and chill several hours or overnight.

When ready to serve, microwave, covered, at HIGH 10 to 12 minutes. Rotate dish ½ turn. Microwave at MEDIUM 10 to 11 minutes. When done, the outside edges will be firm and center slightly soft. Let stand, covered, directly on counter 3 to 5 minutes before serving. Garnish with sieved or finely chopped egg and pimiento strips.

Yield: 6 servings.

CHICKEN TETRAZZINI

Power: HIGH
Microwave Time: 13 to 14 Minutes

- 1 (7-ounce) package thin spaghetti, cooked and drained
- ¼ pound fresh mushrooms
- ½ cup butter or margarine
- 2 cups cooked, diced chicken
- 2 (10½-ounce) cans cream of chicken soup, undiluted
- 2 (8-ounce) cartons commercial sour cream
- 1 cup shredded Cheddar cheese, divided
- 1 teaspoon monosodium glutamate

Combine spaghetti, mushrooms, butter, chicken, soup, sour cream, ½ cup cheese, and monosodium glutamate in a 3-quart casserole. Microwave, uncovered, at HIGH 11 to 12 minutes. Stir well after 6 minutes.

Sprinkle remaining cheese over top of mixture. Microwave at HIGH 2 minutes. Let stand, covered, with waxed paper 2 to 3 minutes.

Yield: 4 to 6 servings.

ROAST CHICKEN

Power: MEDIUM-HIGH
Microwave Time: 8 to 10 Minutes per pound

- 1 (3- to 4-pound) broiler-fryer chicken
- 3 tablespoons Basic Browning Sauce (see p. 117)
  Green grapes
  Whole filberts

Wash and thoroughly dry chicken. Cross wings in back of chicken and tie legs together with heavy string. Brush all areas of the chicken with the Browning Sauce. Place chicken, breast side down, on microwave roasting rack inside 12- x 8-baking dish. Cover with waxed paper.

Microwave at MEDIUM-HIGH half the estimated time.

Turn breast side up; brush with any remaining sauce. Microwave remaining time or until done. Chicken is done when juices run clear and no pink shows when cut at inner thigh. Let stand, covered, 10 to 12 minutes before carving to serve. Garnish with green grapes and filberts.

Yield: 2 to 4 servings.

Micronote: Chicken pieces can be quickly cooked for use in salads, sandwiches, or casseroles. Arrange skin side down with meatier parts toward the edge in a flat baking dish. Cover with waxed paper. Microwave at HIGH 6 to 8 minutes per pound. Cool and cut the meat off the bones.

HERB-ROASTED CHICKEN

Power: HIGH/MEDIUM
Microwave Time: 8 to 10 Minutes per
  pound

    1 **(3- to 5-pound) chicken**
    ⅓ **cup butter or margarine,**
        softened
    2 **teaspoons lemon juice**
    1 **tablespoon finely chopped**
        parsley
    1 **tablespoons finely chopped**
        green onion
    1 **teaspoon commercial brown**
        bouquet sauce

Wash chicken under cold running water. Pat with a paper towel until thoroughly dry.

Combine butter, lemon juice, parsley, and green onion. With a rubber spatula, loosen the skin at the sides of the breast and around the legs. Carefully push the butter mixture between the skin and the meat. Reserve 1 teaspoon of butter mixture and stir in the brown bouquet sauce.

Tie wings and legs to the body of the chicken with heavy string. Brush the exterior with butter-bouquet sauce mixture.

Place chicken, breast side down, on a microwave roasting rack in a 12- x 8-inch baking dish. Cover loosely with waxed paper. Microwave at HIGH for the first half of total time. Turn breast up and microwave, covered, at MEDIUM the remaining half of time or until done.

Check for doneness by inserting a standard meat thermometer into the thick part of thigh at inside. It should register 180°. Remove the thermometer and return to the oven at MEDIUM if more cooking is required.

Let stand, covered with a tent of foil, 5 to 10 minutes before serving.

Yield: 1 to 2 servings per pound.
Micronote: If you don't use a thermometer, remove the chicken when the following occur:
• Legs move freely.
• Juices run clear and no pink shows when the flesh between the leg and body is cut.

HONEY-GLAZED ROAST CHICKEN

Power: MEDIUM-HIGH
Microwave Time: 8 to 10 Minutes per
  pound

    1 **(3- to 4-pound) broiler-fryer**
        chicken
    ⅓ **cup honey**
    2 **tablespoons soy sauce**
    1 **teaspoon grated orange rind**
    1 **tablespoon orange juice**

Wash and dry chicken well. Cross wings in back of chicken and tie legs together with heavy string.

Combine the remaining ingredients. Brush the chicken thoroughly with the honey mixture. Place chicken, breast side down, on microwave roasting rack inside a 12- x 8-inch baking dish. Cover with waxed paper.

Microwave at MEDIUM-HIGH 4 to 5 minutes. Turn breast side up. Brush with remaining sauce. Microwave at MEDIUM-HIGH remaining time or until done. Chicken is done when juices run clear and no pink shows when cut at inner thigh. Let stand, covered, 10 to 12 minutes before carving.

Yield: 2 to 4 servings.
Micronote: Frozen chicken must be completely thawed before you begin microwaving.

TURKEY

Power: HIGH
Microwaving Time: 8 to 9 Minutes per
  pound

    1 **(6- to 12-pound) turkey, thawed**
    2 **tablespoons butter or margarine,**
        melted
    2 **tablespoons commercial brown**
        bouquet sauce

88

Turkey should be completely thawed before microwaving. If using the microwave to thaw, follow manufacturer's directions for placement in the oven. Use thin strips of foil to shield parts which may begin to cook during the thawing process. When almost thawed, place the turkey under cold running water to complete thawing.

The quality of the finished microwaved turkey will be better if the turkey is completely thawed before cooking.

When ready to roast, remove the giblets and any metal clamps. Dry the turkey thoroughly. Combine the butter and bouquet sauce. Brush all surfaces of the dry turkey with the sauce. Then roast by either of the following methods.

Oven Cooking Bag Method:

This method requires less handling and produces a moist surface.

Cut a 2-inch strip from open end of oven cooking bag. Place prepared turkey in bag and put in a large flat baking dish. Pour ½ to ¾ cup water over turkey. Use the cut strip to tie the bag closed. (*Do not use enclosed metal tie.*) Cut slits in oven bag.

Microwave at HIGH minimum time. Check for doneness by inserting a standard oven thermometer into the meatiest part of the thigh. Temperature should be 170° to 175° when the turkey is first removed from the microwave, and should reach 185° after standing 10 minutes. Remove thermometer and return turkey to microwave at HIGH if more cooking time is required. Let stand, covered with foil, 15 to 20 minutes before carving.

Waxed Paper Method:

This method produces a drier surface and requires more attention.

Place prepared turkey, breast side down, in a large flat baking dish. Cover with waxed paper. Microwave at HIGH ½ the estimated time. Turn breast side up; cover again with waxed paper. Microwave at HIGH remaining minimum time. Check for doneness by inserting a standard oven thermometer into the meatiest part of the thigh. Temperature should be 170° to 175° when the turkey is first removed from the microwave, and should reach 185° after standing 10 minutes. Remove the thermometer and return turkey to microwave at HIGH if more cooking is required. Let stand, covered with foil, 15 to 20 minutes or longer before carving.

Yield: 2 to 3 servings per pound.

AFTER THANKSGIVING DINNER

Power: HIGH
Microwaving Time: 11 to 14 Minutes

½	cup butter or margarine
3	cups crumbled cornbread
1	cup dry bread crumbs
3	cups chopped cooked turkey
1¼	cups turkey or chicken broth
1	(10½-ounce) can cream of mushroom soup, undiluted
1	cup chopped celery
1	cup chopped onion
1	teaspoon poultry seasoning
1	teaspoon salt
1	teaspoon pepper

Place butter in a large glass mixing bowl. Microwave at HIGH 1 to 2 minutes or until melted. Add cornbread and bread crumbs. Stir to coat. Add other ingredients and combine thoroughly.

Spread mixture into a buttered 2-quart casserole. Cover with waxed paper. Microwave at HIGH 10 to 12 minutes. Let stand, covered, 2 minutes before serving.

Yield: 4 to 8 servings.

BRAISED TURKEY BREAST

Power: MEDIUM/HIGH
Microwaving Time: 11 to 13 Minutes per
   pound plus 4½ to 5½ Minutes for
   sauce

   1 (6- to 7-pound) whole turkey
      breast
   ½ cup water
      Basic Browning Sauce (see p.
      117)
   ¼ cup butter or margarine
   2 teaspoons all-purpose flour
   ½ teaspoon salt
   ½ teaspoon onion salt
   ⅛ teaspoon pepper
   1 cup tomato juice
   1 cup turkey broth

Follow manufacturer's directions to completely thaw the turkey breast before cooking it.

   Place thawed turkey breast, skin side
down, on microwave roasting rack in a 12- x
8-inch baking dish. Pour water in dish.
Cover with plastic wrap.

   Microwave at MEDIUM half the estimated time. Remove plastic wrap. Carefully drain excess liquid into a 2-cup glass
measure. Reserve. Brush entire turkey
breast with Browning Sauce.

   Turn turkey so that skin side is up. Cover
with plastic wrap and rotate dish ½ turn.
Microwave remaining half of estimated
time. Test for doneness by inserting standard meat thermometer into thick part of
breast meat. Avoid the bone. It should be
175°. Remove thermometer and return to
microwave if more cooking is required.
Transfer turkey to a warm platter and keep
hot.

   To prepare sauce, pour rest of juice from
turkey into 2-cup measure to total 1 cup
broth. Place butter in a 4-cup glass measure. Microwave at HIGH 30 seconds to
melt. Stir in flour and seasonings. Microwave at HIGH 1 minute. Gradually stir in
tomato juice and broth. Microwave at
HIGH 3 to 4 minutes, stirring at 30 to 45
second intervals until thickened. Serve
with sliced turkey.

   Yield: 2 to 3 servings per pound.

BROWN GAME HENS

Power: HIGH
Microwave Time: 20 to 25 Minutes

   2 (14-ounce) Rock Cornish game
      hens, thawed
      Salt
      Pepper
   ¼ cup finely chopped onion
   1 tablespoon butter or margarine
   ¼ cup golden seedless raisins
   1 (11-ounce) can mandarin
      oranges, drained and syrup
      reserved
   1 teaspoon dry sherry
   ¾ cup cooked long grain rice
   ¼ cup slivered almonds
   1 tablespoon minced parsley
   1 teaspoon finely grated orange
      rind
   2 tablespoons butter or margarine,
      melted
   1 teaspoon commercial brown
      bouquet sauce

Completely thaw hens; then rinse under
cold running water. Pat dry. Season inside
with salt and pepper.

   Combine onion and 1 tablespoon butter
in a 2-cup glass measure. Microwave at
HIGH 1 to 2 minutes. Stir in raisins, 2
tablespoons mandarin orange syrup, and
sherry. Microwave at HIGH 1 to 2 minutes
to plump raisins.

   Add rice, ¼ cup orange sections, almonds, parsley, and orange rind. Toss
lightly to mix.

   Stuff each hen cavity loosely with the rice
mixture. Close with wooden toothpicks.
Tie legs together and wings to body with
kitchen string.

   Place stuffed hens, breast side down, on
microwave roasting rack in 12- x 8-inch
baking dish. Brush evenly and completely
with sauce made from 2 tablespoons melted
butter and brown bouquet sauce.

Cover with waxed paper. Microwave at HIGH 10 minutes. Turn breast side up. Brush with remaining sauce. Cover with waxed paper. Microwave at HIGH 8 to 11 minutes or until meat thermometer inserted into inside of thigh registers 185°. Let stand, covered, 5 minutes.

To serve, arrange on platter and garnish with remaining orange sections.

Yield: 2 servings.

SUCCULENT CORNISH HEN

Power: HIGH
Microwaving Time: 29 to 32 Minutes

- ½ cup butter or margarine, divided
- ⅓ cup water
- 2 (1-pound) Cornish hens
- ¼ cup chopped green pepper
- ½ cup chopped green onion
- 1 cup packaged herb-seasoned stuffing mix
- 2 tablespoons commercial brown bouquet sauce
- ½ cup orange marmalade

Combine 3 tablespoons of the butter, water, and giblets removed from hens in a 1-quart casserole. Cover with plastic wrap. Microwave at HIGH 6 to 7 minutes.

Remove giblets and reserve liquid. Chop giblets. Add giblets, green pepper, onion, and stuffing mix to liquid. Mix well. Stuff each of the hens with half of the stuffing mixture. Place the hens, breast side down, in a 12- x 8-inch buttered baking dish.

Microwave remaining butter at HIGH 1 minute in a small bowl to melt. Add brown boquet sauce and marmalade. Stir well. Baste hens thoroughly with the butter-marmalade mixture. Cover with waxed paper. Microwave at HIGH 8 minutes. Baste well and turn hens breast side up.

Rotate dish ½ turn. Microwave at HIGH 8 minutes. Baste well. Microwave at HIGH 4 minutes. Check for doneness. Leg will move easily and juice will not show any pink. Microwave at HIGH 2 to 4 minutes more if necessary. Let stand, covered with a tent of foil, 3 to 5 minutes before serving. To serve, place all remaining sauce in the baking dish. Microwave at HIGH 30 seconds to heat. Spoon over the cornish hen or serve the sauce separately.

Yield: 2 servings.

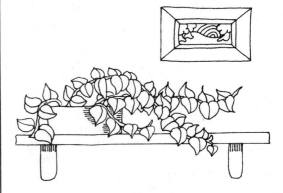

STEAMED QUAIL

Power: HIGH/MEDIUM-HIGH
Microwaving Time: 9 to 13 Minutes

- 4 whole quail
- ¼ cup all-purpose flour
- ½ teaspoon salt
- ⅛ teaspoon pepper
- ¼ cup butter

Following manufacturer's directions, preheat browning skillet 4 to 5 minutes.

Split quail down back and flatten. Combine flour, salt, and pepper. Lightly flour quail. Place butter in browning skillet. Arrange quail in preheated browning skillet. Microwave at HIGH 1 minute per side. Cover with lid. Microwave at MEDIUM-HIGH 8 to 12 minutes or until juices run clear. Let stand, covered, 5 minutes before serving.

Yield: 2 to 4 servings.

SAUCES

If you have ever tried to make a sauce while cooking several other foods and been un-happy with the results (lumpy or scorched), the microwave oven may just give you the help you need—and everyone agrees that there is no better way to perk up a meal than with a sauce.

CONTAINER FOR SAUCES

When planning sauces, choose a bowl or dish for serving which can also be used as a microwaving container, if possible. For an easy-to-use container, measure, mix, and microwave in a 2- or 4-cup glass measure. Its handle makes it easy to use and pour from, and it will be large enough for most sauces, which expand when microwaved.

Stirring is required when microwaving sauces, but usually one or two times, thoroughly, will prevent lumps.

Use HIGH power for most sauces, but microwave sauces with eggs or sweet sauces at MEDIUM or MEDIUM-LOW to achieve a smoother consistency.

Almost any of your favorite sauce recipes will convert to a microwave recipe. It may be necessary to either increase the thick-ener or decrease the liquid. You may find that less spice and seasoning is needed for microwaved sauces.

EASY SAUCE IDEA

- Combine 1 package (6-ounce) semisweet chocolate morsels and ½ cup of evap-orated milk in a 2-cup glass measure.
- Microwave at MEDIUM 2 minutes or until chocolate morsels are melted and milk is hot. Stir well with a wire whip until the milk and chocolate are blended.
- Makes 1 cup of delicious chocolate top-ping.

HEATING PREPARED SAUCES

Buy ice cream toppings and sauces in glass jars. They will be ready to heat when the lid is removed. Remove prepared sauces from their can to a glass measure or casserole. Cover with waxed paper and microwave at HIGH 2 to 3 minutes to heat. Stir well before serving.

BASIC WHITE SAUCE

Power: HIGH
Microwave Time: 6½ to 7½ Minutes

4	tablespoons butter or margarine
4	tablespoons all-purpose flour
¾	teaspoon salt
2	cups milk

Place butter in a 4-cup glass measure. Microwave at HIGH 30 seconds. Blend in flour and salt until smooth. Gradually add milk.

Microwave at HIGH 6 to 7 minutes, stirring at 1 minute intervals. Sauce should be thick and smooth.

Yield: 2 cups.

RICH WHITE SAUCE

Power: HIGH
Microwave Time: 6 to 7 Minutes

- 4 tablespoons butter or margarine
- 4 tablespoons all-purpose flour
- 1 teaspoon salt
- 2 cups milk
- 1 egg yolk, beaten

Microwave butter in a 1-quart casserole at HIGH 30 seconds or until melted. Stir in flour and salt. Stir well and gradually add milk. Blend thoroughly.

Microwave at HIGH 5 to 6 minutes, stirring several times. Add some of the hot sauce to beaten egg yolk. Return the egg mixture to the sauce. Stir well. Microwave at HIGH 30 seconds.

Yield: 2½ cups.

CHEESE SAUCE

Power: HIGH
Microwave Time: 5 to 5½ Minutes

- ¼ cup butter or margarine
- ¼ cup all-purpose flour
- 2 cups milk
- ½ teaspoon salt
- ⅛ teaspoon dry mustard
- ⅛ teaspoon pepper
  Dash of paprika
- 2 tablespoons sherry
- 1 cup shredded Cheddar cheese

Microwave butter in a 4-cup glass measure at HIGH 30 seconds to melt. Blend in flour. Stir in milk.

Microwave at HIGH 3 minutes, stirring once or twice, or until thick and smooth.

Stir in seasonings, sherry, and grated cheese. Microwave at HIGH 1½ to 2 minutes. Stir well to blend cheese into sauce.

Use as a topping for crêpes or stir into hot cooked macaroni or noodles.

Yield: 2½ cups.

HOLLANDAISE SAUCE

Power: HIGH/MEDIUM
Microwave Time: 2 to 2½ Minutes

- ½ cup butter or margarine
- ½ cup half-and-half
- 2 egg yolks
- 2 tablespoons lemon juice
- ½ teaspoon dry mustard
- ½ teaspoon salt
  Dash of hot sauce

Place butter in a 4-cup glass measure. Microwave at HIGH 1 minute to melt.

Stir in the remaining ingredients with a wire whisk. Microwave at MEDIUM 1 to 1½ minutes. Stir at 20 second intervals. Beat thoroughly at end of cooking time. Serve with fish or vegetables.

Yield: 1 cup.

MUSHROOM SAUCE

Power: HIGH
Microwave Time: 4½ to 6½ Minutes

- ¼ cup butter or margarine
- ¼ cup all-purpose flour
- 2 cups chicken broth
- ½ teaspoon lemon juice
- ½ teaspoon chopped parsley
- 1 (8-ounce) can mushroom pieces, drained

Microwave butter in a 4-cup glass measure at HIGH 30 seconds to melt. Blend in flour. Gradually stir in broth until well blended. Microwave at HIGH 2 to 3 minutes, stirring at 1 minute intervals.

Add lemon juice, parsley, and mushroom pieces. Microwave at HIGH 2 to 3 minutes. Serve over baked chicken, chicken loaf, or other foods.

Yield: 2½ cups.

SWEET MUSTARD SAUCE

Power: HIGH
Microwave Time: 4½ to 5½ Minutes

- 6 **tablespoons butter or margarine**
- 6 **tablespoons all-purpose flour**
- 2 **cups milk**
- 1 **tablespoon dry mustard**
- 1 **tablespoon sugar**
- 1 **tablespoon lemon juice**

Place butter in a 4-cup glass measure. Microwave at HIGH 30 seconds to melt. Blend in flour. Stir in milk. Microwave at HIGH 4 to 5 minutes. Stir once or twice during cooking.

Combine mustard, sugar, and lemon juice. Stir into the hot thickened sauce. Serve hot with cooked ham.

Yield: 2 cups.

BLUEBERRY SAUCE

Power: HIGH
Microwave Time: 2 to 3 Minutes

- 1 **(16-ounce) can blueberry pie filling**
- ¼ **cup honey**
- ¼ **cup butter**
- 3 **tablespoons lemon juice**

Combine all ingredients in a 4-cup glass measure. Stir to mix well. Microwave at HIGH 2 to 3 minutes. Serve warm.

Yield: 2½ cups.

Micronote: To store the sauce, place it in a glass jar and refrigerate. When ready to serve, remove the lid and reheat in the jar, or pour into a safe-for-microwave serving dish. Reheat in the serving dish.

CHERRY SAUCE

Power: HIGH
Microwave Time: 3 to 4 Minutes

- ½ **cup cherry preserves**
- ¼ **cup dark corn syrup**
- 2 **tablespoons vinegar**
- ⅓ **teaspoon salt**
- ⅛ **teaspoon ground nutmeg**
- ⅛ **teaspoon ground cinnamon**
- ⅛ **teaspoon ground cloves**

Combine all ingredients in a 2-cup glass measure. Microwave at HIGH 3 to 4 minutes or until bubbly hot.

Yield: ¾ cup.

MELBA SAUCE

Power: LOW/HIGH
Microwave Time: 5 to 8 Minutes

- 1 **(10-ounce) package frozen raspberries**
- ½ **cup sugar**
- 2 **tablespoons cornstarch**
- ½ **cup currant jelly**
- 1 **teaspoon lemon juice**

Remove raspberries from package and place in a 1-quart casserole. Microwave at LOW 2 to 3 minutes. Blend sugar and cornstarch. Stir into raspberries. Add jelly and lemon juice. Microwave at HIGH 3 to 5 minutes. Stir well after 3 minutes. Cool before serving over cheesecake, ice cream, fruit, or cake.

Yield: 1½ cups.

FRESH PEACH SAUCE

Power: HIGH/MEDIUM
Microwave Time: 6 to 9 Minutes

4 fresh peaches, peeled and
crushed
½ cup sugar
½ cup orange juice
2 teaspoons lemon juice
1 teaspoon vanilla extract

Combine peaches, sugar, and orange juice
in a 1½-quart casserole. Stir to dissolve
sugar. Cover with waxed paper. Microwave at HIGH 2 to 3 minutes. Stir well.
  Microwave, covered, at MEDIUM 4 to 6
minutes. Stir at 1 minute intervals.
  Stir in lemon juice and vanilla. Cool to
room temperature. Cover tightly and store
in the refrigerator. Use as a dessert topping
with fresh peaches, ice cream, or cake.
  Yield: 2 cups.

RUM RAISIN SAUCE

Power: HIGH
Microwave Time: 3 to 5 Minutes

⅓ cup seedless raisins
½ cup water
1 tablespoon cornstarch
½ cup orange juice
⅓ cup currant jelly
½ teaspoon grated orange rind
2 tablespoons firmly packed
brown sugar
½ teaspoon rum flavoring
Dash of salt

Combine raisins, water, cornstarch, and
juice in a 4-cup glass measure. Stir well.
Microwave at HIGH 1 to 2 minutes.
  Combine remaining ingredients. Stir into
raisin mixture. Microwave at HIGH 2 to 3
minutes or until thickened. Stir thoroughly
after 1 minute.
  Serve warm over ham or pound cake, or
chilled as a topping for ice cream.
  Yield: 1½ cups.

SHERRY CUSTARD SAUCE

Power: HIGH/MEDIUM
Microwave Time: 3 to 5 Minutes

1 tablespoon cornstarch
¼ cup orange juice
3 egg yolks
½ cup sugar
½ cup sherry

Combine cornstarch and orange juice in a
4-cup glass measure. Microwave at HIGH 1
to 2 minutes or until thick. Stir well. Cool.
  Beat egg yolks until lemon colored. Beat
in sugar. Gradually add sherry. Stir into the
cooled orange juice mixture. Microwave at
MEDIUM 2 to 3 minutes, stirring at 45
second intervals.
  Cool and store in refrigerator until ready
to use. Serve with fresh fruit and whipped
cream.
  Yield: 1½ cups.

STRAWBERRY TOPPING

Power: HIGH
Microwave Time: 4 to 5 Minutes

1 (10-ounce) package frozen
strawberries
3 tablespoons cornstarch
⅓ cup sugar
¼ cup water

Remove the frozen strawberries from
package and place in a 2-cup measure.
Microwave at HIGH 2 minutes. Stir in
cornstarch, sugar, and water. Microwave at
HIGH 2 to 3 minutes or until thickened.
  Serve as a topping for cheesecake or pour
over other desserts.
  Yield: 1½ cups.

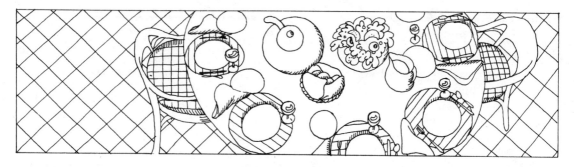

SOUPS

Soups requiring only heating are ideal for microwaving. Choose canned or dehydrated soup, and heat in single or multiple servings.

When preparing soups from scratch, choose quick-cooking recipes or combine cooked vegetables and meat with a microwaved cream sauce. Partially cooked foods will speed preparation. Use canned broth or stock as a base for meat and vegetables. Start the dish cooking at HIGH, then lower the power to MEDIUM-LOW which will keep it simmering to develop flavors.

CONTAINERS FOR THESE FOODS

Generally, large heat-proof mixing bowls and casseroles or safe-for-microwave soup tureens are excellent choices for soups. They also can be used for serving, which cuts down on clean-up.

Use dinnerware cups, plates or bowls, a paper cup with a handle, or a pottery mug for individual portions. (Before using, be sure to test all glassware with the Microwave Dish Test explained in Step 7.) Before serving, stir all soups well to combine heated and unheated portions.

Store any leftover soups or stew in safe-for-microwave bowls covered with plastic wrap. These bowls can then go back to the microwave oven as a cooking and serving container.

BLACK BEAN SOUP

Power: HIGH
Microwave Time: 13 to 16 Minutes

       4 slices bacon, cut in 1-inch pieces
       1 cup coarsely chopped onion
      ¾ teaspoon chili powder
      ¾ teaspoon commercial brown
          bouquet sauce
       2 (10- to 12-ounce) cans black
          bean soup, undiluted
       2 (12-ounce) cans vegetable juice
      ⅛ teaspoon cumin

Combine bacon, onion, chili powder, and brown bouquet sauce in a 2-quart casserole. Microwave, uncovered, at HIGH 5 to 7 minutes or until onion is tender. Remove bacon and onion with a slotted spoon and set aside. Leave 1 tablespoon drippings in casserole.

Stir in soup, vegetable juice, and cumin. Blend by hand or with mixer until smooth. Cover with plastic wrap. Microwave at HIGH 8 to 9 minutes or until hot and bubbly. Stir after 4 minutes.

To serve, ladle soup into serving bowls and top each with a tablespoon of bacon-onion mixture (reheated, if necessary).

Yield: 4 to 6 servings.

CREAM OF BROCCOLI SOUP

Power: HIGH
Microwave Time: 19 to 11 Minutes

- 1 (10-ounce) package frozen chopped broccoli
- 1 onion, finely chopped
- 1 carrot, thinly sliced
- 2 stalks celery, chopped
- 2 potatoes, peeled and chopped
- 1 teaspoon salt
- 3 cups chicken broth
- 1 cup half-and-half
- ½ cup thinly sliced boiled ham, diced
- ½ cup commercial sour cream
- ¼ cup chopped chives

Place frozen broccoli in a box on a paper plate. Pierce box several times with a fork. Microwave at HIGH 6 to 7 minutes. Set aside. Combine onion, carrot, celery, potatoes, salt, and chicken broth in a 2-quart glass casserole. Cover with plastic wrap. Microwave at HIGH 8 minutes.

Drain the broccoli and add to soup mixture. Puree the soup a portion at a time in the blender. Return the puree to the casserole. Add half-and-half and ham. Microwave at HIGH 5 to 6 minutes or until hot.

To serve, ladle into bowls. Place a spoonful of sour cream on top and garnish with chopped chives.

Yield: 6 servings.

HOT BROCCOLI SOUP

Power: HIGH
Microwave Time: 8 to 10 Minutes

- 1 (10-ounce) package frozen chopped broccoli
- 1 (10¾-ounce) can cream of onion soup, undiluted
- 1⅓ cups milk
- ¼ cup dry white wine
- 3 tablespoons butter
- ½ teaspoon dried basil, crushed
- ⅛ teaspoon white pepper

Take broccoli from package and place in a 2-quart casserole. Cover with plastic wrap. Microwave at HIGH 4 to 5 minutes. Stir to break apart and drain, if necessary. Add soup, milk, wine, butter, basil, and pepper. Microwave at HIGH 4 to 5 minutes. Stir after 3 minutes. To serve, ladle soup into serving bowls.

Yield: 4 servings.

CLAM CHOWDER

Power: HIGH
Microwave Time: 10 to 12 Minutes

- 4 slices bacon, cut in 1-inch pieces
- ⅓ cup chopped onion
- 1 (10¾-ounce) can cream of potato soup, undiluted
- 1 cup milk
- ¼ teaspoon celery seed
- 1 (7- to 8-ounce) can minced clams Paprika

Place bacon pieces in a 2-quart casserole. Cover with paper towel. Microwave at HIGH 4 minutes. With a slotted spoon, remove bacon. Place on paper towel to drain. Crumble.

Remove bacon drippings and return 2 tablespoons to casserole. Stir in onion. Cover with waxed paper. Microwave at HIGH 2 minutes. Stir in potato soup, milk, celery seed, and undrained clams. Cover with waxed paper and microwave at HIGH 4 to 6 minutes. Stir well after 3 minutes.

Let stand, covered, 3 minutes. To serve, ladle the chowder into soup bowls. Sprinkle with crumbled bacon and paprika.

Yield: 2 to 4 servings.

CRAB BISQUE

Power: HIGH/MEDIUM
Microwave Time: 14 to 16 Minutes

2 (10¾-ounce) cans cream of celery
    soup, undiluted
2 (10¾-ounce) cans green pea
    soup, undiluted
4 cups milk
1 (7½-ounce) can crabmeat,
    drained
1 teaspoon salt
¼ cup chopped parsley
   Paprika

Combine soups and blend in a 3-quart casserole. Gradually add milk. Add drained crabmeat and salt. Cover with waxed paper. Microwave at HIGH 4 minutes. Stir well. Microwave at MEDIUM 10 to 12 minutes or until heated thoroughly. Garnish with parsley and paprika.
   Yield: 6 to 8 servings.

CREAM OF PEANUT SOUP

Power: HIGH/MEDIUM
Microwave Time: 14 to 18½ Minutes

1 small onion, chopped
1 rib of celery, chopped
2 tablespoons butter
1½ tablespoons all-purpose flour
1 quart chicken stock or canned
    chicken broth
1 cup smooth peanut butter
1 cup half-and-half
   Chopped peanuts

Combine onion, celery, and butter in a 2-quart casserole. Microwave, covered, at HIGH 3 to 3½ minutes. Stir in flour. Add chicken stock. Cover. Microwave at HIGH 5 to 7 minutes. Stir at 2 minute intervals.
   Add peanut butter and half-and-half. Stir to blend well. Microwave at MEDIUM 6 to 8 minutes. Do not allow to boil.
   To serve, ladle into serving bowls and garnish with chopped peanuts.
   Yield: 6 servings.

RICE CONSOMMÉ

Power: HIGH/MEDIUM-HIGH
Microwave Time: 22 to 26 Minutes

1 cup long grain rice, uncooked
½ cup butter or margarine
2 medium-size onions, chopped
2 cans beef consommé

Heat large browning dish 6 minutes. Add rice and butter. Cover with lid. Microwave at HIGH 2 to 4 minutes or until rice is brown. Stir once or twice. Add onions and consommé. Microwave, covered, at MEDIUM-HIGH 14 to 16 minutes. Stir after 7 or 8 minutes. Ladle into serving bowls to serve.
   Yield: 4 servings.

QUICK SHRIMP GUMBO

Power: HIGH/LOW
Microwave Time: 43 Minutes

1 (32-ounce) can whole tomatoes
2 garlic cloves, crushed
1 medium-sized onion, chopped
1 small pepper, chopped
1 (10-ounce) package frozen cut
    okra
½ cup celery, chopped
1½ teaspoons salt
¼ teaspoon pepper
1 bay leaf
2 tablespoons bacon drippings
1½ pounds medium-sized shrimp,
    shelled and deveined
   Hot cooked rice
   Parsley sprigs

Combine first 10 ingredients in a 2-quart casserole dish. Cover with plastic wrap. Microwave at HIGH 20 minutes. Stir well. Microwave at LOW 20 minutes.
   Stir in shrimp. Microwave at HIGH 3 minutes. Let stand, covered, 10 minutes. Serve over rice and garnish with parsley sprigs.
   Yield: 8 servings.
   Micronote: Gumbo may be prepared ahead of time and heated when ready to serve.

CURRIED TOMATO BISQUE

Power: HIGH
Microwave Time: 8 to 9 Minutes

> 2 **tablespoons melted butter or margarine**
> ¼ **cup finely sliced green onions**
> 2 **(10¾-ounce) cans tomato soup, undiluted**
> 2½ **cups water**
> ½ **to ¾ teaspoon curry powder**
> 2 **hard-cooked egg yolks, grated**

Place butter in 2-quart casserole or soup tureen. Add onion. Cover with waxed paper. Microwave at HIGH 2 minutes.

Stir in tomato soup, water, and curry powder. Cover loosely with paper towel. Microwave at HIGH 6 to 7 minutes or until thoroughly heated. Serve, hot or cold, garnished with egg yolk.

Yield: 4 to 6 servings.

Micronote: If using a microwave thermometer, heat bisque to 150° to 160°. Soup may also be heated in single portions. One cup heats at HIGH in about 1½ minutes.

HOT SUMMER VEGETABLE SOUP

Power: HIGH
Microwave Time: 8 to 10 Minutes

> 4 **fresh ripe tomatoes, peeled**
> 1 **(16-ounce) can whole tomatoes**
> 1¼ **cups beef broth**
> 1 **small cucumber, peeled and cut in chunks**
> ½ **medium-sized green pepper, finely chopped**
> 1 **stalk celery, thinly sliced**
> 4 **sprigs parsley, finely chopped**
> ¼ **cup chopped green onion**
> ¼ **teaspoon garlic salt**
> ¼ **teaspoon pepper**
> ⅛ **teaspoon hot sauce**
> **Seasoned croutons**

Combine ½ each of the tomatoes, broth, and cucumber in blender container. Cover and process just to chop. Repeat with remaining tomatoes, broth, and cucumber.

Combine blended ingredients in a 2-quart casserole. Add other ingredients except croutons. Stir well to combine. Cover with plastic wrap.

Microwave at HIGH 8 to 10 minutes or until vegetables are just barely tender. Let stand, covered, 3 to 5 minutes.

To serve, ladle into soup bowls and garnish with croutons.

Yield: 4 to 6 servings.

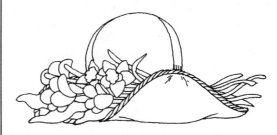

CREAMED VEGETABLE SOUP

Power: HIGH
Microwave Time: 11 to 15 Minutes

> 4 **slices bacon, cut in 2-inch pieces**
> ¼ **cup all-purpose flour**
> 1 **teaspoon salt**
> 3 **cups milk**
> 4 **cups cooked mixed vegetables**

Place the bacon pieces in a 2½-quart casserole. Cover with paper towel. Microwave at HIGH 4 to 5 minutes. Remove bacon and the drippings. Return ⅓ cup bacon drippings to casserole. Stir in flour and salt; blend well. Slowly add milk. Microwave at HIGH, uncovered, 3 to 4 minutes or until thickened.

Stir in cooked vegetables and bacon pieces. Microwave at HIGH 4 to 6 minutes or until heated through. Stir once or twice during cooking. Ladle into serving bowls.

Yield: 6 servings.

Micronote: Use leftover cooked vegetables for this hearty soup, or cook 2 packages of your choice of frozen vegetables.

VEGETABLES

Versatility is the word which best describes vegetables cooked in the microwave oven. They can be cooked any number of ways and retain their color and flavor. They can be cooked to tender-crisp stage or to a more done stage if preferred. Vegetables should be cooked, tightly covered, in a small amount of water.

CONTAINERS

There are several choices of containers which work well depending on the type and quantity of vegetable being cooked.

Whole vegetables such as fresh broccoli and asparagus can be arranged with the tougher stem ends toward the outside of a flat shallow casserole. A plastic wrap covering will hold in the steam. Be sure to turn back a corner of the plastic wrap to form a vent.

Choose a flat serving tray or a large glass pie plate for corn-on-the-cob, cauliflower, and other fresh vegetables. Again, plastic wrap works as an easy-to-use cover.

Small, shallow casseroles can be used for frozen vegetables. They can also be microwaved in their package if the package meets the following requirements:
• It has no metal parts.
• It is pierced or slit to allow some steam to escape.
• It is placed on a paper or glass plate.

Individual servings of fresh or canned vegetables can be microwaved in small bowls or casseroles, custard cups, saucers, or serving plates. Plastic wrap can be used for one or two whole vegetables such as corn-on-the-cob, zucchini, yellow squash, or whole apples.

TECHNIQUES FOR MICROWAVING FRESH VEGETABLES

• Vegetables with thick skins like acorn squash and potatoes can be placed on a paper plate or a flat, shallow casserole to microwave. Pierce the skins of these vegetables to prevent them from bursting while cooking.
• Prepare other fresh vegetables for cooking just as you would for conventional cooking. Choose a container and add a small amount (1 to 2 tablespoons) of water.

- Cover with casserole lid or plastic wrap.
- Microwave at HIGH to cook. Stir well once.
- Season and serve.
- Vegetables like broccoli and asparagus should be arranged with the stalk portion toward the outside of the dish. This will help even out the cooking and prevent the tender flower ends from overcooking.

TECHNIQUES FOR MICROWAVING STARCHY VEGETABLES

- Potatoes and carrots require more liquid (cream, juice, or broth) than other fresh vegetables. Add ¼ cup to the cut-up vegetables.
- Cover with casserole lid or plastic wrap.
- Microwave at HIGH or MEDIUM-HIGH to cook.
- Season and serve.

TECHNIQUES FOR MICROWAVING FROZEN VEGETABLES

- Choose a small casserole or use the vegetable pouch or box. Pierce or slit the box.
- Place the vegetables and 1 tablespoon of water in the casserole. *(Do not add salt.)*
- Cover with plastic wrap.
- Microwave at HIGH to cook. (Follow the times given in the oven manual.)
- Season and serve.

TECHNIQUES FOR MICROWAVING CANNED VEGETABLES

- Drain most of the liquid off vegetables.
- Place in the appropriate size container.
- Cover and microwave at HIGH to heat.
- Season and serve.

GERMAN POTATO SALAD
(Conventional Recipe)

6	to 8 slices bacon, cooked and diced
6	medium-sized potatoes, unpared
⅓	cup chopped celery
1	teaspoon salt
⅛	teaspoon pepper
1	teaspoon dry mustard
¼	cup sugar
½	cup water
¼	to ½ cup red wine vinegar
1	egg, slightly beaten
	Onion rings (optional)
	Crisp bacon (optional)

Cook bacon until crisp, reserving drippings. Cook the potatoes until tender; remove the skins while hot and slice. Combine the bacon, potatoes, and celery. To the bacon drippings add salt, pepper, dry mustard, sugar, water, vinegar, and beaten egg. Cook the mixture only until the egg thickens; pour it over the bacon-potato mixture and heat until the liquid is absorbed. Garnish, if desired, with onion rings and additional pieces of crisp bacon.
Yield: 6 to 8 servings.

To Microwave German Potato Salad

- Cook potatoes, celery, and parsley.
- Cook bacon.
- Combine salad dressing ingredients in bacon drippings. Omit egg.
- Pour over the hot cooked potatoes and bacon.

GERMAN POTATO SALAD

Power: HIGH
Microwave Time: 19 to 22 Minutes

    4   to 6 medium-sized potatoes,
          peeled and sliced
    ⅓   cup chopped celery
    1   tablespoon finely chopped
          parsley
    3   tablespoons water
    5   slices bacon, cut in ½-inch
          pieces
    1½ tablespoons all-purpose flour
    2   tablespoons sugar
    1   teaspoon salt
    ½   teaspoon celery seed
    ⅛   teaspoon pepper
    ¾   cup water
    ⅓   cup red wine vinegar

Combine potatoes, celery, parsley, and water in a 2½-quart casserole. Cover with plastic wrap. Microwave at HIGH 10 to 12 minutes. Stir after 5 minutes. Let stand, covered, while cooking bacon.

Place bacon in a 1½-quart casserole. Cover with paper towel. Microwave at HIGH 4 minutes. Stir after 2 minutes to separate the pieces. Remove bacon with a slotted spoon. Place on paper towel to drain.

Stir flour, sugar, salt, celery seed, and pepper into bacon drippings until smooth. Microwave at HIGH 2 minutes or until hot. Stir well after 1 minute. Add water and vinegar. Microwave at HIGH 3 to 4 minutes or until mixture becomes thick. Stir well after 1 minute.

When thick, stir until smooth and pour over the hot cooked potatoes. Add crumbled bacon and toss gently to combine. Cover and let stand 2 to 3 minutes or until ready to serve.

Yield: 4 to 6 servings.

Micronote: Remove metal caps from syrup bottles and microwave to heat.

ARTICHOKES

Power: HIGH
Microwave Time: 12 to 15 Minutes

    4   whole fresh artichokes
    ½   cup water
        Hot Lemon Butter (see p. 49)

Wash the artichokes and trim stem at bottom. Cut sharp points off each leaf and remove tough or hard lower leaves.

Place the prepared artichokes upright in a casserole. Add water. Cover with plastic wrap. Microwave at HIGH 12 to 15 minutes. Rotate dish ½ turn after 7 minutes. Let stand, covered, 3 to 4 minutes.

Serve whole while hot with Hot Lemon Butter or chill and serve as a salad.

Yield: 4 servings.

ARTICHOKE HEARTS
AND PECANS

Power: HIGH/MEDIUM
Microwave Time: 7 to 8 Minutes

    1   (16-ounce) can artichoke hearts,
          drained
    2   tablespoons butter
    2   tablespoons all-purpose flour
    1   cup half-and-half
    ½   teaspoon salt
    ⅛   teaspoon pepper
    ⅛   teaspoon hot sauce
    ½   cup chopped pecans
    ¼   cup dry bread crumbs
    2   tablespoons Parmesan cheese

Stand the artichoke hearts in a flat, round, glass casserole.

Place butter in a 4-cup glass measure. Microwave at HIGH 30 seconds. Add flour and blend thoroughly. Gradually stir in half-and-half, salt, pepper, and hot sauce. Microwave at HIGH 2 minutes, stirring once or twice.

Pour heated sauce over artichoke hearts. Sprinkle with pecans, bread crumbs, and cheese. Microwave at MEDIUM 5 minutes to heat.

Let stand, covered with waxed paper, 2 minutes before serving.

Yield: 6 servings.

SHRIMP-STUFFED ARTICHOKES

Power: HIGH
Microwave Time: 2 to 2½ Minutes

- 2 slices bacon
- 1 (6½-ounce) can shrimp, drained
- 2 hard-cooked eggs, chopped
- ¼ cup finely chopped celery
- ½ teaspoon horseradish
- ¼ cup commercial sour cream
- 4 fresh artichokes, cooked, drained, and chilled
  Fresh zucchini slices

Place bacon on microwave roasting rack. Cover with paper towel. Microwave at HIGH 2 to 2½ minutes. Cool slightly.

Crumble bacon into a small mixing bowl. Add shrimp, chopped eggs, celery, horseradish, and sour cream.

Spread artichoke leaves apart and remove choke with a spoon. Fill center and around leaves with shrimp mixture. Place each artichoke on a serving plate and garnish with zucchini slices to serve.

Yield: 4 servings.

ASPARAGUS CHEDDAR DISH

Power: HIGH
Microwave Time: 9½ to 12½ Minutes

- ¼ cup butter or margarine
- 3 slices bread, cubed
- 2 (16-ounce) cans asparagus pieces, drained
- 2 eggs, beaten
- 2 tablespoons dry white wine
- 1 teaspoon Worcestershire sauce
- 1½ cups shredded Cheddar cheese

Place butter in a 1½-quart casserole. Microwave at HIGH 30 seconds to melt. Stir in and toss bread cubes to coat. Microwave at HIGH 3 to 4 minutes or until crisp. Stir several times during microwaving. Place on a paper towel when crisp.

Place asparagus in a mixing bowl. Mash to break up slightly. Remove any tough parts. Add eggs, wine, and Worcestershire sauce. Stir well. Stir in cheese.

Pour into a greased 1½-quart casserole. Microwave at HIGH 4 minutes. Sprinkle bread cubes over top. Microwave at HIGH 2 to 4 minutes. Let stand 2 minutes before serving.

Yield: 6 servings.

CREAMED ASPARAGUS TUNA

Power: HIGH
Microwave Time: 9½ to 10½ Minutes

- 2 tablespoons butter or margarine
- 2 tablespoons all-purpose flour
- ⅔ cup evaporated milk
- 1 (14½-ounce) can asparagus spears, drain and reserve liquid
- 1 (7-ounce) can tuna fish, drained
- ¼ cup chopped pimiento
- ¼ teaspoon salt
- ¼ teaspoon onion salt
  Dash of pepper
  Dash of ground nutmeg
  Baked pastry shells or toast

Microwave butter in a 4-cup glass measure at HIGH 30 seconds. Blend in flour and milk. Stir drained liquid from asparagus spears into milk mixture. Microwave at HIGH 3 minutes. Stir mixture at 1 minute intervals until thickened.

Add asparagus, tuna fish, pimiento, salt, onion salt, pepper, and nutmeg. Microwave at HIGH 6 to 7 minutes. Stir mixture after 3 minutes. Serve in baked pastry shells or over toast.

Yield: 4 to 6 servings.

FRESH ASPARAGUS

Power: HIGH
Microwave Time: 5 to 7 Minutes

   1 pound asparagus
  ¼ cup water

Arrange prepared asparagus spears in a flat casserole with tougher stem ends toward the outside. Add ¼ cup water. Cover with plastic wrap. Microwave at HIGH 5 to 7 minutes.

Let stand, covered, 3 to 5 minutes before serving.

Yield: 2 to 4 servings.

BAKED BEANS

Power: HIGH/MEDIUM-HIGH
Microwave Time: 17 to 18 Minutes

   1 large onion, chopped
   6 slices bacon, diced
  ½ teaspoon chili powder
  ⅛ teaspoon pepper
   2 (1-pound) cans pork and beans
  ¼ cup firmly packed brown sugar
  ¼ cup beer
   1 tablespoon prepared mustard

Combine onion, bacon, and seasonings in a 2-quart casserole. Cover with paper towel. Microwave at HIGH 5 minutes.

Stir in remaining ingredients. Microwave at MEDIUM-HIGH 12 to 13 minutes. Stir once during microwaving. Let stand, covered with paper towel, 2 to 3 minutes before serving.

Yield: 6 to 8 servings.

BAKED BEANS FOR TWO

Power: HIGH
Microwave Time: 12 to 13 Minutes

   3 slices bacon, diced
   3 tablespoons chopped onion
   1 (11-ounce) can pork and beans
   2 tablespoons dark corn syrup
   **2 tablespoons firmly packed
       brown sugar**
   1 teaspoon dry mustard

Place bacon in a small glass casserole. Cover with paper towels. Microwave at HIGH 3 minutes. Remove bacon and drippings. Set bacon aside. Return 1 tablespoon of drippings to the casserole and add onion. Microwave at HIGH 1 minute.

Combine beans, syrup, brown sugar, and mustard with the onion. Place bacon pieces on top of beans. Cover with paper towel. Microwave at HIGH 8 to 9 minutes. Let stand, covered, 1 to 2 minutes.

Yield: 2 servings.

FAVORITE GREEN BEAN CASSEROLE

Power: MEDIUM/HIGH
Microwave Time: 18 to 23 Minutes

   **3 (10-ounce) packages frozen
       French-style green beans**
  **½ cup pasteurized process cheese
       spread**
   **1 (10¾-ounce) can cream of
       mushroom soup, undiluted**
   **1 (4-ounce) can water chestnuts,
       drained and sliced**
   **1 (3-ounce) can French fried onion
       rings**

Pierce the packages of beans and place side-by-side on paper plates in microwave oven. Microwave at MEDIUM 6 to 8 minutes to thaw. Turn each package over and rotate once. Drain, if necessary.

Combine beans, cheese spread, soup, and water chestnuts in a 1½-quart casserole. Spread onion rings over top. Cover with waxed paper.

Microwave at HIGH 12 to 15 minutes. Let stand, covered, 6 to 10 minutes before serving.

Yield: 6 to 8 servings.

FRESH LIMA BEANS

Power: HIGH/MEDIUM
Microwave Time: 14 to 20 Minutes

- 4 **cups fresh shelled beans**
- ¼ **to ½ cup water**
- 2 **tablespoons bacon drippings**
- 1 **teaspoon salt**

Combine all ingredients in a 2-quart glass casserole. Stir well. Cover with plastic wrap. Microwave at HIGH 2 to 4 minutes. Stir well. Microwave, covered, at MEDIUM 12 to 16 minutes. Stir well 2 or 3 times and add more water, as necessary, during cooking.

Let stand, covered, 5 minutes before serving.

Yield: 4 servings.

Micronote: Some cooks prefer to cook fresh lima beans and peas in large quantities the old-fashioned way and reheat them as needed, using the microwave oven.

SNAP BEANS WITH BACON

Power: HIGH/MEDIUM
Microwave Time: 17 to 23 Minutes

- 2 **slices bacon**
- ¼ **cup chopped green onion**
- 1 **pound fresh green beans, stringed and snapped**
- ¼ **cup water**
- ½ **teaspoon salt**

Arrange bacon in a 1½-quart casserole. Cover with paper towel. Microwave at HIGH 2 to 3 minutes. Remove bacon and set aside.

Add onion, beans, and water to drippings. Stir to combine. Cover. Microwave at HIGH 5 minutes. Stir well. Microwave at MEDIUM 10 to 15 minutes, covered, or until beans are desired tenderness.

Stir in bacon and salt. Toss to combine. Let stand, covered, 2 minutes.

Yield: 4 to 5 servings.

BROCCOLI BALLS ★

Power: HIGH
Microwave Time: 16½ to 20 Minutes for 4 servings

- 2 **(10-ounce) package frozen chopped broccoli**
- ¾ **cup butter or margarine**
- 6 **eggs, beaten**
- 2 **cups stuffing mix**
- 3 **green onions, chopped**
- ½ **cup grated Parmesan cheese**
- ½ **teaspoon salt**
- 1 **teaspoon celery seed**
- 1 **tablespoon lemon juice**
- 4 **to 5 tomatoes, sliced**
- ½ **to 1 cup grated Swiss cheese (optional)**

Pierce package of broccoli several times. Place each one on a paper plate. Microwave (one at a time) at HIGH 5 to 6 minutes. Drain. Microwave butter at HIGH 1½ to 2 minutes to melt in a 2-quart glass casserole. Stir in eggs, stuffing mix, onions, Parmesan cheese, salt, celery seed, lemon juice, and broccoli.

Using an ice cream scoop, form mixture into balls, or pack in muffin tins. Freeze. Remove to a suitable container for the freezer after the balls are frozen.

For serving, place frozen broccoli balls on a thick tomato slice. Place 4 at a time in an 8- x 8-inch glass dish. Cover. Microwave at HIGH 10 to 12 minutes. Rotate the dish ¼ turn at 3 minute intervals.

Before serving the tomato, peeling may be gently pulled away.

For garnish, grated Swiss cheese may be sprinkled on top of broccoli balls during the last ½ to 1 minute of cooking time.

Yield: 15 to 20 servings.

BROCCOLI-CAULIFLOWER SCALLOP

Power: HIGH
Microwave Time: 27½ to 34 Minutes

      2 (10-ounce) packages frozen
         broccoli spears
      1 (10-ounce) package frozen
         cauliflower
      1 (3-ounce) can mushroom slices
      ¼ cup butter or margarine, divided
      3 tablespoons all-purpose flour
   1½ cups milk
      1 cup cubed processed American
         cheese
      ⅛ teaspoon pepper
      1 cup herb-seasoned bread
         stuffing mix

Pierce packages of broccoli several times with fork and place on paper plates. Microwave at HIGH 8 to 10 minutes. Pierce package of cauliflower with a fork and place on paper plate. Microwave at HIGH 6 to 8 minutes.

Drain mushrooms, reserving liquid.

Microwave butter in a 4-cup glass measure at HIGH 1 minute to melt. Reserve 2 tablespoons. Stir flour into remaining 2 tablespoons of butter until smooth. Microwave at HIGH ½ to 1 minute. Stir in milk and liquid from the mushrooms. Microwave at HIGH 3 to 5 minutes, stirring at 1 minute intervals, until thickened.

Add cheese and pepper to the mixture. Stir. Microwave at HIGH 1 minute to melt the cheese. Add mushroom slices. Stir.

Drain broccoli and cauliflower. Arrange broccoli and cauliflower in alternate rows in a 12- x 8-inch glass baking dish. Pour cheese sauce over broccoli and cauliflower. Microwave at HIGH 4 minutes. Rotate the dish ½ turn. Microwave at HIGH 4 more minutes.

Combine reserved melted butter and stuffing mix for topping. Sprinkle over casserole mixture. Allow casserole to stand for 4 to 5 minutes before serving.

Yield: 6 to 8 servings.

BROCCOLI-ONION CASSEROLE ★

Power: HIGH
Microwave Time: 14 to 18 Minutes

      2 (10-ounce) packages frozen
         chopped broccoli
      1 (16-ounce) can whole onions,
         drained
      1 (10¾-ounce) can cream of celery
         soup, undiluted
      ½ teaspoon seasoned salt
      4 slices processed American cheese
      ⅓ cup nut-like cereal
      2 tablespoons butter or margarine,
         melted

Take broccoli out of packages and place in a 2-quart casserole. Cover. Microwave at HIGH 6 to 8 minutes. Drain.

Stir in onions, soup, and seasoned salt. Spread evenly in casserole. Top with cheese slices.

Combine cereal and butter. Spread over cheese-topped broccoli mixture.

Microwave at HIGH 8 to 10 minutes or until thoroughly heated. Rotate dish ½ turn after 5 minutes of microwaving. Let stand, covered with waxed paper, 2 to 3 minutes before serving.

Yield: 6 to 8 servings.

BROCCOLI-TOMATO CUPS

Power: HIGH
Microwave Time: 10 to 14 Minutes

      1 (10-ounce) package frozen
         chopped broccoli
      6 whole fresh tomatoes
      ¾ cup soft bread crumbs
      1 teaspoon salt
      ⅛ teaspoon pepper
      2 tablespoons butter, melted
      ½ cup grated Parmesan cheese

Place unwrapped broccoli in a 1½-quart casserole. Cover with plastic wrap. Microwave at HIGH 6 to 8 minutes. Let stand, covered, 2 minutes. Drain well.

Cut a slice off the stem end of each tomato. Scoop out the pulp. Set aside. Combine the drained broccoli, bread crumbs, salt, pepper, and the melted butter and as much of the tomato pulp as needed to fill 6 tomatoes.

Fill the tomatoes with the stuffing mixture. Arrange around the inside outer edge of a round glass baking dish. Cover with waxed paper. Microwave at HIGH 4 to 6 minutes. Sprinkle cheese over top. Let stand, covered, 2 minutes before serving.

Yield: 6 servings.

DILLED BRUSSELS SPROUTS

Power: HIGH/MEDIUM
Microwave Time: 21 to 24 Minutes

- 2 (10-ounce) packages frozen brussels sprouts
- 6 slices bacon
- ½ cup minced onion
- 1 (8-ounce) carton commercial sour cream
- ¼ cup milk
- 1 teaspoon salt
- ½ teaspoon dillweed
- ¼ teaspoon hot sauce
    Paprika

Remove brussels sprouts from package and place in a 2-quart casserole. Cover with plastic wrap. Microwave at HIGH 10 to 12 minutes. Drain.

Place bacon in a flat glass dish. Cover with a paper towel. Microwave at HIGH 5 minutes. Cool and crumble.

Place the onion in dish with bacon drippings. Cover with waxed paper. Microwave at HIGH 2 minutes. Add sour cream, milk, bacon, salt, dillweed, and hot sauce. Pour over brussels sprouts. Sprinkle with paprika.

Microwave at MEDIUM 4 to 5 minutes or until thick and hot.

Yield: 4 to 6 servings.

CARROT CASSEROLE

Power: HIGH
Microwave Time: 18 to 21 Minutes

- 12 carrots, pared
- ¼ cup water
- 1 teaspoon salt
- ¼ teaspoon dry mustard
- 3 tablespoons all-purpose flour
- ½ teaspoon dillseed
- ⅛ teaspoon pepper
- 1 small onion, chopped
- 2 cups shredded sharp Cheddar cheese
- 1 (10¾-ounce) can cream of celery soup, undiluted
- ½ cup cracker crumbs
- ¼ cup butter or margarine, melted

Slice carrots lengthwise. Combine carrots and water in a 1½-quart casserole. Cover with plastic wrap. Microwave at HIGH 10 to 12 minutes, or until carrots are almost tender. Let stand 1 or 2 minutes. Drain and remove carrots.

Combine salt, mustard, flour, dillseed, and pepper in a small bowl. Combine onion and cheese in a separate bowl.

Grease the 1½-quart casserole. Arrange alternate layers of carrots, soup, flour mixture, and cheese mixture. Toss cracker crumbs and melted butter together and spread on top.

Microwave at HIGH, uncovered, 8 to 9 minutes. Let stand 2 minutes before serving.

Yield: 8 servings.

GINGERED CARROTS

Power: HIGH
Microwave Time: 7 to 10 Minutes

     8 carrots, sliced
     3 tablespoons butter or margarine
     1 tablespoon firmly packed brown
        sugar
     1 teaspoons cornstarch
    ½ teaspoon salt
    ¼ teaspoon ground ginger
    ¼ cup orange juice

Combine carrots and butter in a 1½-quart
casserole. Cover. Microwave at HIGH 6 to 8
minutes, or until carrots are tender.
     Combine remaining ingredients in a
small bowl. Blend until smooth. Stir into
carrots. Cover. Microwave at HIGH 1 to 2
minutes, or until mixture boils.
     Yield: 4 to 6 servings.

ORANGE-SAUCED CARROTS

Power: HIGH
Microwave Time: 12 to 13½ Minutes

     3 cups sliced carrots
    ¼ cup water (optional ¼ cup
        orange juice)
     1 tablespoon firmly packed brown
        sugar
   1½ teaspoons cornstarch
    ⅔ cup orange juice
     1 tablespoon butter or margarine
    ¼ teaspoon salt
    ⅛ teaspoon ground ginger
    ⅛ teaspoon ground cloves
        Orange slices or parsley

Place sliced carrots and water or orange
juice in a 1½-quart glass casserole. Microwave at HIGH 9 to 10 minutes or until
carrots are tender. Stir once after 5 minutes.
     Combine brown sugar and cornstarch;
blend in orange juice, butter, salt, ginger,
and cloves. Stir mixture into carrots. Microwave at HIGH, uncovered, 2 minutes. Stir.
Microwave at HIGH 1 to 1½ minutes more.
Garnish with orange slices or parsley.
     Yield: 4 servings.

CARROT RING

Power: HIGH/MEDIUM-HIGH
Microwave Time: 18 to 19 Minutes

     5 cups grated raw carrot
     2 tablespoons water
     4 eggs
     2 cups evaporated milk
    ⅔ cup soft bread crumbs
     1 teaspoon salt
    ¼ teaspoon pepper
     1 tablespoon lemon juice
     1 cup slivered blanched almonds

Combine carrot and water in a 2-quart
casserole. Cover with plastic wrap. Microwave at HIGH 3 to 4 minutes. Let stand,
covered, 1 or 2 minutes. Drain.
     Beat eggs in a large bowl. Stir in milk,
bread crumbs, salt, pepper, lemon juice,
almonds, and carrots. Pour mixture into a
greased 9-inch microwave ring mold.
     Microwave at MEDIUM-HIGH 10 min-
utes. Rotate dish ½ turn. Microwave at
MEDIUM-HIGH 5 minutes. Let stand 5
minutes before removing from mold.
     Yield: 8 to 10 servings.

CAULIFLOWER ITALIANO

Power: HIGH
Microwave Time: 5 to 6 Minutes

     1 head of cauliflower, broken into
        flowerettes
     1 small onion, finely chopped
     2 tablespoons water
     2 tomatoes, peeled and cubed
     1 cup commercial Italian salad
        dressing
    ¼ cup grated Parmesan cheese

Combine cauliflower pieces and onion in a
2-quart casserole. Add water. Cover with

plastic wrap. Microwave at HIGH 5 to 6 minutes or until tender-crisp. Let stand 3 or 4 minutes. Drain.

Combine cauliflower, onion, tomatoes, and salad dressing in the 2-quart casserole. Toss well to coat with dressing. Sprinkle cheese over tossed vegetables. Serve hot or chilled.

Yield: 4 servings.

CAULIFLOWER MOUNTAIN

Power: HIGH
Microwave Time: 8 to 9 Minutes

> 1 **medium-sized head of cauliflower**
> ½ **cup mayonnaise**
> 1½ **teaspoons prepared mustard**
> ½ **teaspoon dry mustard**
> 2 **ounces sharp Cheddar cheese, shredded**

Place whole head of cauliflower, stem end down, in an 8-inch glass pie plate. Cover with plastic wrap. Microwave at HIGH 7 to 8 minutes or until tender.

Mix mayonnaise, prepared mustard, and dry mustard in a bowl. Pour mayonnaise mixture over top of cooked cauliflower. Sprinkle with shredded cheese. Microwave at HIGH 1 minute to melt cheese.

Yield: 4 servings.

COMPANY CELERY

Power: HIGH/MEDIUM-HIGH
Microwave Time: 12 to 15 Minutes

> 1 **large bunch celery, cut in 1-inch pieces**
> 2 **tablespoons water**
> ¼ **cup butter or margarine**
> ¼ **cup all-purpose flour**
> ½ **teaspoon salt**
> ⅛ **teaspoon pepper**
> 1 **cup half-and-half**
> 3 **green onions, chopped**
> 1 **(2-ounce) jar pimiento pieces, drained**
> ¼ **pound Swiss cheese, shredded**

Place celery and water in a 2-quart casserole. Cover with plastic wrap. Microwave at HIGH 4 minutes. Let stand, covered, 1 minute, then drain.

Place butter in a 2-cup glass measure. Microwave at HIGH 1 minute. Stir in flour, salt, pepper, and half-and-half. Blend well. Add onion and pimiento pieces. Pour over drained celery.

Cover with plastic wrap. Microwave at MEDIUM-HIGH 6 to 8 minutes. Stir well. Top with shredded cheese. Microwave, uncovered, at MEDIUM-HIGH 1 to 2 minutes.

Yield: 6 servings.

SOUTHERN CREAMED CORN

Power: HIGH
Microwave Time: 5 to 7 Minutes

> 6 **to 8 ears fresh corn**
> ¼ **to ½ cup water**
> 1 **teaspoon sugar**
> ½ **cup butter or margarine, melted**
> 1 **tablespoon cornmeal**

Cut corn off the cob and scrape well to remove all the milk. Place cut corn in a 1½-quart casserole. Add needed amount of water, sugar, butter, and cornmeal. Stir well.

Cover with plastic wrap or glass lid. Microwave at HIGH 2 minutes. Stir well and rotate dish ½ turn. Microwave at HIGH 3 to 5 minutes. Stir well. Let stand, covered, 2 or 3 minutes before serving.

Yield: 4 to 6 servings.

Micronote: The amount of starch in corn varies, thus amount of water may also vary. Add smaller amount to begin with, then add more during stirring if necessary.

CORN PUDDING

Power: HIGH/MEDIUM-HIGH
Microwave Time: 22 to 24 Minutes

       2   **eggs**
       2   **tablespoons sugar**
       2   **tablespoons all-purpose flour**
       1   **(16-ounce) can cream-style corn**
       1   **cup milk**
     ¼   **teaspoon salt**
     ⅛   **teaspoon pepper**
       2   **tablespoons butter or margarine**

Beat eggs well in a large bowl. Stir in sugar and flour. Add corn, milk, and seasonings. Combine well. Pour mixture into greased 1½-quart casserole. Dot with 2 tablespoons butter.

Microwave at HIGH 4 minutes. Rotate ¼ turn. Microwave at MEDIUM-HIGH 18 to 20 minutes, rotating ¼ turn at 5 minute intervals. Center will be soft, but will firm after standing 2 or 3 minutes.

Yield: 4 to 6 servings.

CHEESE AND CORN SOUFFLÉ

Power: HIGH/MEDIUM
Microwave Time: 23 to 26 Minutes

     ¼   **cup butter or margarine**
     ¼   **cup all-purpose flour**
     ⅓   **cup milk**
       1   **(16-ounce) can cream-style corn**
     ¼   **teaspoon salt**
     ⅛   **teaspoon garlic salt**
     ½   **teaspoon Worcestershire sauce**
   1½   **cups shredded Cheddar cheese**
     ½   **cup shredded Provolone cheese**
       5   **eggs**

Place butter in a 1½-quart casserole. Microwave at HIGH 1 minute. Blend in flour. Add milk and stir well. Stir in corn, salt, garlic salt, and Worcestershire sauce. Microwave at HIGH 3 to 4 minutes, stirring at 1 minute intervals. Add cheeses. Microwave at HIGH 1 minute.

While corn is cooking, separate eggs. Beat whites until stiff. Beat yolks lightly and stir in some of the hot corn mixture. Combine the yolks and hot corn mixture. Cool slightly, then fold whites into the corn mixture.

Pour soufflé mixture into a 2½-quart ungreased casserole. Microwave at MEDIUM 10 minutes. Rotate dish ½ turn. Microwave at MEDIUM 8 to 10 minutes. Serve immediately.

Yield: 6 to 8 servings.

SQUAW CORN

Power: HIGH
Microwave Time: 11 to 13 Minutes

       1   **pound ground chuck**
     ¼   **cup chopped onion**
     ¼   **cup chopped green pepper**
       1   **(10¾-ounce) can tomato soup, undiluted**
       1   **(16-ounce) can cream-style corn**
     ¼   **pound sharp cheese, shredded**
       1   **cup crushed corn chips**

Place ground beef, onion, and green pepper in a 1½-quart casserole. Microwave at HIGH 5 to 6 minutes. Stir several times to break meat apart. Drain, if necessary.

Add remaining ingredients except corn chips. Cover with waxed paper. Microwave at HIGH 6 to 7 minutes. Let stand, covered, 3 minutes.

To serve, sprinkle top with crushed corn chips.

Yield: 4 servings.

EGGPLANT CASSEROLE

Power: HIGH
Microwave Time: 14 to 16 Minutes

       1   **large eggplant, peeled and sliced**
     ⅓   **cup milk**
   1¼   **cups herb-seasoned stuffing mix, divided**
       1   **(10¾-ounce) can cream of mushroom soup, undiluted**
       1   **egg, slightly beaten**
     ½   **teaspoon salt**
       2   **tablespoons butter or margarine, melted**

Place eggplant in a 2-quart casserole. Cover with plastic wrap. Microwave at HIGH 7 minutes. Drain.

While eggplant is cooking, combine milk, ¾ cup stuffing mix, soup, egg, and salt. Blend well and stir in drained eggplant. Return mixture to the 2-quart casserole.

Combine butter and remaining stuffing mix. Sprinkle over eggplant mixture. Cover with waxed paper.

Microwave at HIGH 7 to 9 minutes. Let stand, covered, 3 to 5 minutes.

Yield: 4 servings.

EASY EGGPLANT CASSEROLE

Power: HIGH/MEDIUM-HIGH
Microwave Time: 13 to 14 Minutes

    4   cups diced eggplant
    2   tablespoons water
    ½   teaspoon salt
    2   eggs, well beaten
    ¾   cup shredded sharp Cheddar
        cheese

Combine eggplant, water, and salt in a 1½-quart casserole. Cover. Microwave at HIGH 5 minutes. Stir well after 2 minutes. Let stand, covered, 2 or 3 minutes. Drain, if necessary.

Combine eggs and cheese. Stir into drained eggplant. Cover. Microwave at MEDIUM-HIGH 8 to 9 minutes. Rotate dish ¼ turn at 3 minute intervals. Let stand, covered, 3 to 5 minutes.

Yield: 4 servings.

OYSTER EGGPLANT TREAT

Power: HIGH
Microwave Time: 16 to 19 Minutes

    1   small onion, chopped
    1   small eggplant, peeled and
        sliced
    2   tablespoons water
    ½   teaspoon salt
    2½ cups cracker crumbs, divided
    3   eggs, well beaten
    1   (10½-ounce) can oyster soup,
        undiluted

Place onion, eggplant, water, and salt in a 1½-quart casserole. Cover with waxed paper. Microwave at HIGH 6 to 7 minutes. Stir once during microwaving. Let stand, covered, 3 or 4 minutes. Drain.

Add 1½ cups cracker crumbs, eggs, and oyster soup. Spread remaining crumbs on top. Microwave at HIGH 10 to 12 minutes. Rotate dish ½ turn after 6 minutes. Let stand, covered, 3 to 5 minutes.

Yield: 4 servings.

ZESTY EGGPLANT BAKE

Power: HIGH
Microwave Time: 20 to 24 Minutes

    1   large eggplant, peeled and diced
    2   tablespoons water
        Salt and pepper to taste
    1   small onion, diced
    2   tablespoons butter or margarine
    ¾   cup milk
    ½   cup shredded sharp Cheddar
        cheese, divided
    1   cup cracker crumbs, divided

Combine eggplant and water in a 1¾-quart casserole. Add salt and pepper. Cover with waxed paper. Microwave at HIGH 8 minutes. Drain and mash.

Combine onion, butter, milk, half of cheese, and ¾ cup of cracker crumbs in a bowl. Reserve ¼ cup cheese and ¼ cup cracker crumbs. Add eggplant to first mixture and pour into a greased 1½-quart casserole. Cover with waxed paper. Microwave at HIGH 6 to 8 minutes. Stir. Sprinkle reserved cheese and crackers over top of casserole. Cover with waxed paper. Microwave at HIGH 6 to 8 minutes. Let stand, covered, 3 to 5 minutes.

Yield: 4 servings.

CREAMED ONIONS WITH PEANUTS

Power: HIGH
Microwave Time: 13 to 15 Minutes

>   16 small whole onions
>   3 tablespoons all-purpose flour
>   3 tablespoons butter or margarine
>   ¼ teaspoon salt
>   1⅔ cups milk
>   ½ cup salted peanuts, chopped and
>   divided
>   ¼ cup pimiento pieces, drained
>   1½ cups sliced mushrooms
>   ½ cup bread crumbs
>   2 tablespoons chopped parsley

Peel onions and roll in flour. Place in 1-quart casserole. Stir in butter, salt, and milk. Cover with plastic wrap. Microwave at HIGH 5 minutes.

Stir well. Add ¼ cup peanuts, pimiento, and mushrooms. Cover. Microwave at HIGH 4 to 5 minutes. Top with remaining peanuts, bread crumbs, and parsley. Microwave, uncovered, at HIGH 4 to 5 minutes.

Let stand, covered, 3 minutes before serving.

Yield: 6 to 8 servings.

STUFFED VIDALIA ONION ★ ★

Power: HIGH
Microwave Time: 6 to 7 Minutes

>   1 large Vidalia onion
>   1 tablespoon butter
>   ¼ teaspoon salt
>   ⅛ teaspoon pepper
>   1 cup herb-seasoned stuffing mix
>   ¼ cup beef broth

Place a piece of plastic wrap large enough to cover stuffed onion in a 1½-quart casserole. Slice onion crosswise into 3 layers. Place bottom slice of onion on plastic wrap.

Place butter in a 4-cup glass measure. Microwave at HIGH 20 seconds to melt. Stir in salt, pepper, stuffing mix, and beef broth. Place a little less than ½ of the stuffing mixture on onion slice in casserole.

Add center slice of onion. Top with most of remaining stuffing mixture, reserving 1 tablespoon. Top mixture with third onion slice. Spread remaining stuffing mixture over onion. Pull up corners of plastic wrap. Tie with string.

Microwave at HIGH 6 minutes. Let stand 6 to 8 minutes before serving.

Yield: 1 to 2 servings.

Micronote: Any large sweet onion may be used. Larger onions or more onions will require longer microwaving time.

WALNUT-STUFFED ONION

Power: HIGH
Microwave Time: 6 to 8 Minutes

>   6 medium-sized white onions
>   2 cups dry bread crumbs
>   6 tablespoons butter, melted
>   ¾ cup chopped walnuts
>   Dash of oregano
>   Butter

Peel onions and hollow out, leaving a ½ inch thick shell.

Combine bread crumbs, 6 tablespoons melted butter, walnuts, and oregano. Stuff onion shells with mixture. Dot tops with small pieces of butter. Place stuffed onions in an 8-inch round glass casserole. Cover with plastic wrap.

Microwave at HIGH 6 to 8 minutes. Let stand, covered, 2 to 3 minutes before serving.

Yield: 6 servings.

FRESH BLACK-EYED PEAS

Power: HIGH/MEDIUM
Microwave Time: 14 to 20 Minutes

>   4 cups fresh shelled peas
>   ¼ to ½ cup water
>   2 tablespoons bacon drippings
>   1 teaspoon salt

Combine all ingredients in a 2-quart casserole. Stir well. Cover with plastic wrap. Microwave at HIGH 2 to 4 minutes. Stir well. Microwave, covered, at MEDIUM 12 to 16 minutes. Stir well 2 or 3 times and add small amount of water during cooking, if necessary.

Let stand, covered, 5 minutes before serving.

Yield: 4 servings.

Micronote: Because of the starch in fresh beans and peas, adding small amounts of water and cooking on a lower power produces a better quality vegetable. Older, more mature peas and beans should be cooked in the conventional way.

BAKED POTATOES

Power: HIGH
Microwave Time: See below

1 to 6 (6- to 8-ounces each) baking potatoes

Rinse potatoes and pat dry. Prick potatoes several times with a fork. Place potatoes on a double-layer of paper towels. (If baking more than 2 potatoes, arrange in a circle.)

Microwave at HIGH according to the times below.

Let stand 3 to 5 minutes before serving.

Number of Potatoes	Minutes at HIGH
1	4 to 6
2	6 to 8
4	8 to 10
6	12 to 13

IRISH POTATO CASSEROLE

Power: HIGH
Microwave Time: 20 to 25 Minutes

8 medium-sized white potatoes, thinly sliced
1 teaspoon salt
¼ teaspoon pepper
1 onion, sliced
1 (10¾-ounce) can cream of mushroom soup, undiluted
1½ cups milk

Place half of potatoes in a 12- x 8-inch glass baking dish. Sprinkle with salt and pepper. Add half the sliced onion.

Combine soup and milk. Pour half over the onion and potato. Top with remaining potato slices, onion slices, and the soup mixture.

Cover with waxed paper. Microwave at HIGH 20 to 25 minutes. Rotate dish ½ turn after 10 minutes. Let stand, covered, 3 to 5 minutes.

Yield: 6 to 8 servings.

BACON POTATO SUPPER

Power: HIGH
Microwave Time: 27 to 28 Minutes

6 potatoes, peeled and quartered
¼ cup water
½ teaspoon salt
6 slices bacon
1 (10¾-ounce) can cream of potato soup, undiluted
1 (8-ounce) carton French onion dip
1½ teaspoons seasoned salt
3 tablespoons butter
Parsley

Combine potatoes, water, and salt in a 2-quart casserole. Cover. Microwave at HIGH 15 minutes. Let stand 5 minutes. Drain.

Place bacon on a paper plate or microwave roasting rack placed in a 12- by 8-inch casserole. Cover with paper towel. Microwave at HIGH 5 to 6 minutes. Cool slightly. Crumble and reserve.

Combine soup, onion dip, seasoned salt, and butter in a bowl. Microwave at HIGH 2 minutes. Pour over potatoes. Cover with waxed paper.

Microwave at HIGH 5 minutes. Sprinkle crumbled bacon over potatoes. Let stand, covered, 2 minutes before serving. Sprinkle with parsley.

Yield: 6 servings.

FAVORITE POTATO CASSEROLE

Power: HIGH
Microwave Time: 14½ to 18 Minutes

- ½ cup butter or margarine
- 1 onion, chopped
- 1 (2-pound) bag frozen nugget potatoes
- 1 (10¾-ounce) can cream of mushroom soup, undiluted
- 1 (8-ounce) carton commercial sour cream or plain yogurt
- 1 cup shredded Cheddar cheese
- ¼ teaspoon dillweed
  Parsley
  Paprika

Place butter in a glass 9-inch pie plate. Microwave at HIGH 1 minute to melt. Stir in onion. Cover with waxed paper. Microwave at HIGH 1½ to 2 minutes.

Combine onion and remaining ingredients except spices in a 2-quart glass baking dish. Sprinkle with dillweed, parsley, and paprika. Cover with waxed paper. Microwave at HIGH 12 to 15 minutes.

Yield: 6 to 8 servings.

CHEESE POTATOES

Power: HIGH
Microwave Time: 20 to 24 Minutes

- 5 medium-sized white potatoes, peeled and thinly sliced
- 1 tablespoon all-purpose flour
- 1 teaspoon salt
- ⅛ teaspoon pepper
- ¼ cup chopped onion
- 1 (10¾-ounce) can Cheddar cheese soup, undiluted
- ½ cup milk
- 1 tablespoon butter or margarine

Arrange potato slices in a 3-quart casserole. Sprinkle flour, salt, pepper, and onion over potatoes. Mix soup with milk and pour over potatoes. Dot with butter.

Cover with waxed paper. Microwave at HIGH 20 to 24 minutes. Rotate dish ¼ turn

at 5 minute intervals. Let stand, covered, 4 to 5 minutes before serving.

Yield: 5 to 6 servings.

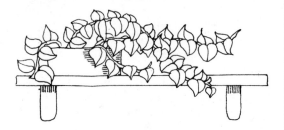

HASH BROWN POTATOES AU GRATIN

Power: HIGH/MEDIUM-HIGH
Microwave Time: 8 to 10 Minutes

- ½ cup water
- 1 chicken bouillon cube
- 2 cups frozen shredded hash brown potatoes
- 1 small carrot, grated coarsely
- 2 green onions, chopped
- ⅛ teaspoon pepper
- 1 tablespoon butter or margarine
- 4 slices processed American cheese

Combine water and bouillon cube in a 1-cup glass measure. Microwave at HIGH 1 to 2 minutes to boil.

Spread potatoes in a 1½-quart casserole. Pour bouillon over potatoes. Then gently mix in carrot, onion, and pepper. Dot with butter.

Cover with waxed paper. Microwave at HIGH 3 minutes. Stir gently. Microwave at HIGH 2 minutes.

Spread cheese slices over top. Microwave at MEDIUM-HIGH 2 to 3 minutes or until cheese melts.

Yield: 3 to 4 servings.

Potatoes are a natural choice for microwaving and are good served plain or with butter, sour cream, bacon chips, chives, or other toppings. (See p.185.)

ELEGANT HASH BROWNS

Power: HIGH
Microwave Time: 8 to 10 Minutes

> 1 (6-ounce) package hash brown
>   potatoes with onions
>   Boiling water
> ½ cup chopped green onions
> 4 ounces sharp Cheddar cheese,
>   shredded and divided
> ½ teaspoon salt
> 3 tablespoons butter or margarine

Place potatoes in a bowl. Cover with boiling water. Let stand 5 minutes. Drain.

Layer one-half each of potatoes, onions, cheese, salt, and butter in a 2-quart casserole. Repeat with remaining potatoes, onions, salt, and butter.

Cover with waxed paper. Microwave at HIGH 6 to 8 minutes. Sprinkle with remaining cheese. Cover. Microwave at HIGH 2 minutes. Let stand, covered, 3 to 5 minutes before serving.

Yield: 4 to 6 servings.

SPINACH BALLS

Power: HIGH
Microwave Time: 13 to 20 Minutes for 10 to 12 balls

> 1 (10-ounce) package frozen
>   spinach
> 1 cup herb-seasoned stuffing mix
> 1 medium-sized onion, finely
>   chopped
> 3 eggs, beaten
> 2 tablespoons butter or margarine,
>   softened
> ⅓ cup grated Parmesan cheese
> ½ teaspoon garlic powder
> ½ teaspoon ground thyme
> 1½ teaspoons monosodium
>   glutamate

Combine ground chuck and rice as a filling for a nutritious main dish—Beef Stuffed Green Peppers (p.124). You will enjoy the crisp texture and bright color of this old favorite even more when it is microwaved.

With a fork, punch holes in spinach box and place on a paper plate. Microwave at HIGH 5 to 6 minutes. Drain well. Mix remaining ingredients in a large bowl. Add drained spinach. Shape into walnut-size balls.

Arrange 10 balls at a time on a paper plate or serving platter suitable for microwaving. Microwave at HIGH 3 to 4 minutes. Serve immediately.

Yield: 30 to 35 balls.

Micronote: Cooked Spinach Balls can be frozen. Thaw and heat in microwave when ready to serve. To thaw and heat 10 balls, microwave at MEDIUM 3 to 5 minutes, or until heated.

SPINACH CASSEROLE
(Quajado de Spinica)

Power: HIGH
Microwave Time: 8 to 10 Minutes

> 1 (10-ounce) package frozen
>   chopped spinach
> 2 eggs, beaten
> 2 tablespoons milk
> ¼ cup cottage cheese
> ¼ cup grated sharp Cheddar cheese
> ⅛ teaspoon salt
> 1 cup herb-seasoned stuffing mix

Pierce package of spinach several times. Place on paper plate. Microwave at HIGH for 3 minutes, or until spinach can be separated.

Combine eggs, milk, cottage cheese, Cheddar cheese, salt, stuffing mix, and spinach.

Spread mixture evenly in a greased 1- to 1½-quart glass casserole. Microwave at HIGH 5 to 7 minutes. Let stand 2 to 3 minutes before serving.

Yield: 4 servings.

CRUNCHY BAKED ACORN SQUASH

Power: HIGH
Microwave Time: 13 to 16 Minutes

> 2 medium-sized acorn squash
> ¼ cup butter or margarine, melted
> ¼ cup firmly packed brown sugar
> ¾ cup chopped pecans
> ¾ cup flaked coconut

Pierce each squash with a fork. Place in a flat glass baking dish. Microwave at HIGH, 8 to 10 minutes. Let stand 4 to 5 minutes.

Combine butter, sugar, pecans, and coconut in a bowl.

Cut squash in half. Remove seeds and place squash, cut side up, in a flat glass baking dish. Spread each squash with half the coconut mixture.

Cover with waxed paper. Microwave at HIGH 5 to 6 minutes or until bubbly. Let stand, covered, 2 minutes before serving.

Yield: 4 servings.

STUFFED SQUASH

Power: HIGH
Microwave Time: 8½ to 12½ Minutes

> 4 medium-sized yellow squash
> 2 tablespoons butter or margarine
> ½ teaspoon salt
> Dash of pepper
> ½ cup dry bread crumbs
> ¼ cup grated Parmesan cheese

Pierce each squash once or twice with a fork and place in an 8-inch glass baking dish. Cover with plastic wrap. Microwave at HIGH 6 to 8 minutes. Let stand 1 or 2 minutes. Cut in half lengthwise. Scoop out center of squash. Set pulp aside, leaving squash shells in glass dish.

Place butter in a glass bowl. Microwave at HIGH 30 seconds to melt. Stir in squash pulp, salt, pepper, bread crumbs, and grated cheese. Fill squash shells with stuffing mixture. Microwave at HIGH 2 to 3 minutes.

Yield: 4 to 6 servings.

SQUASH CASSEROLE

Power: HIGH
Microwave Time: 29 to 30 Minutes

> 4 cups sliced fresh yellow squash (substitute 2 cups mashed, canned or frozen)
> ½ cup water
> 1 egg, beaten
> ⅓ cup skim milk
> ¼ cup butter or margarine, melted
> ¾ cup herb-seasoned stuffing mix
> ½ cup onion, finely chopped
> ¼ teaspoon salt
> Dash of pepper

Topping:

> ½ cup crushed herb-seasoned stuffing mix
> 1 teaspoon wheat germ
> 2 tablespoons butter or margarine, melted

Place sliced squash and water in a 1½- to 2-quart casserole. Cover. Microwave at HIGH 16 minutes or until tender. Stir squash once after 8 minutes. Allow squash to stand while combining remaining ingredients. Blend together egg, milk, butter, stuffing mix, onion, salt, and pepper.

Mash squash. Stir into bread stuffing mixture. Microwave at HIGH, uncovered, 8 minutes.

For Topping, combine crushed stuffing mix, wheat germ, and butter.

Stir casserole. Sprinkle on the topping mixture. Microwave at HIGH 5 minutes. Allow 5 minutes standing time before serving.

Yield: 6 servings.

CHICKEN ZUCCHINI

Power: HIGH
Microwave Time: 11 to 13 Minutes

- 2 whole chicken breasts
- 3 cups sliced zucchini
- 1 onion, sliced
- 1 clove garlic, minced
- 2 tablespoons all-purpose flour
- 2 teaspoons chicken bouillon
granules
- ½ teaspoon salt
- ¼ teaspoon thyme
- 2 tomatoes
- 1 cup seasoned croutons

Bone chicken breasts. Cut into bite-size pieces. Place in 2-quart casserole. Cover with waxed paper. Microwave at HIGH 5 minutes.

Add zucchini, onion, garlic, flour, bouillon granules, salt, and thyme. Blend well. Cover with waxed paper. Microwave, covered, at HIGH 5 to 6 minutes. Stir once or twice during microwaving.

Cut tomatoes in wedges. Arrange over cooked chicken. Microwave at HIGH 1 to 2 minutes or until tomatoes are heated. Garnish with croutons to serve.

Yield: 4 to 6 servings.

SPICY ZUCCHINI-TOMATO BAKE

Power: HIGH
Microwave Time: 12 to 14 Minutes

- 3 (1-pound) cans tomato wedges,
drained
- 3 medium-sized zucchini, sliced
- 1 small onion, chopped
- 6 slices bread, crumbled
- ¼ cup sugar
- ¼ teaspoon salt
- ⅛ teaspoon cayenne pepper
- 4 tablespoons butter or margarine,
melted
- 2 tablespoons firm butter or
margarine

Combine tomato wedges, zucchini, onion, bread crumbs, sugar, salt, pepper, and 4 tablespoons melted butter in a large bowl. Pour into a greased 2½-quart casserole. Dot

with pieces of remaining butter.

Microwave at HIGH 12 to 14 minutes. Rotate dish ½ turn after 7 minutes of microwaving. When cooked, mixture will set into a soft custard and zucchini will be slightly crunchy.

Yield: 4 to 6 servings.

ZUCCHINI-TOMATO BAKE

Power: HIGH
Microwave Time: 6 to 8 Minutes

- 2 cups thinly sliced zucchini
- 1 tomato, thinly sliced
- 1 medium-sized onion, thinly
sliced
- ½ teaspoon salt
- 3 tablespoons grated Parmesan
cheese, divided
- 3 slices bacon, cooked

Layer half the zucchini, tomato, and onion in a greased 1½-quart casserole. Sprinkle with half of the salt and cheese. Repeat. Crumble bacon coarsely over top. Microwave at HIGH 3 to 4 minutes. Rotate dish ½ turn. Microwave at HIGH 3 to 4 minutes.

Yield: 4 servings.

SWEET POTATOES

Power: HIGH
Microwave Time: 11 to 13 Minutes

- 1 (29-ounce) can small whole
sweet potatoes, drained
- ¼ cup butter or margarine
- 1 teaspoon ground cinnamon
- ¼ cup firmly packed brown sugar
- ½ cup crushed pineapple, drained

Place potatoes in 1½-quart casserole. Microwave butter at HIGH 1 minute in 2-cup glass measure. Stir in remaining ingredients. Pour over sweet potatoes. Cover with waxed paper. Microwave at HIGH 10 to 12 minutes. Let stand, covered, 2 to 3 minutes.

Yield: 4 servings

CRUSTY SWEET POTATO CASSEROLE

Power: HIGH
Microwave Time: 8 to 10 Minutes

    4   to 6 medium-sized sweet
          potatoes, cooked
    1   teaspoon salt
    ¼   teaspoon ground mace
    1   egg, slightly beaten
    ⅓   cup crushed pineapple, drained
    ⅛   teaspoon ground ginger
    2   tablespoons butter or margarine
    1   tablespoon orange juice
    ⅓   cup finely chopped, unsalted
          peanuts
    ⅓   cup flaked coconut
    2   tablespoons firmly packed
          brown sugar

Peel and mash sweet potatoes. Combine sweet potatoes, salt, mace, egg, pineapple, ginger, butter, and orange juice in a 1½-quart glass casserole. Microwave at HIGH 5 to 6 minutes.

Combine peanuts, coconut, and brown sugar. Sprinkle over casserole. Microwave at HIGH 3 to 4 minutes. Serve hot.

Yield: 6 servings.

TASTY ORANGE YAMS ★

Power: HIGH
Microwave Time: 8½ to 10½ Minutes

    ¼   cup butter or margarine
    ¾   cup firmly packed brown sugar
    2   teaspoons orange rind
    4   cups canned yams, drained and
          liquid reserved

Place butter in a 1½-quart glass bowl. Microwave at HIGH 30 seconds. Stir in brown sugar, orange rind, and ½ cup liquid from yams. Stir until sugar is moistened.

Add yams to sugar mixture. Microwave, uncovered, at HIGH 4 minutes. Stir lightly to coat yams with glaze. Rotate dish ¼ turn. Microwave at HIGH 4 to 6 minutes.

Yield: 4 servings.

SWEET POTATO SOUFFLÉ

Power: HIGH
Microwave Time: 17 to 19 Minutes

    ½   cup butter or margarine, divided
    3   eggs, beaten
    3   cups cooked mashed sweet
          potato
    1   cup sugar
    1   cup milk
    1   teaspoon ground nutmeg
    ½   teaspoon ground cinnamon
    ½   cup seedless raisins
    ¼   cup orange juice
    1   cup corn flakes, crushed
    ½   cup chopped nuts
    ½   cup firmly packed brown sugar

Place ¼ cup butter in a 2-quart casserole. Microwave at HIGH 30 seconds. Add eggs and sweet potato to butter. Stir to combine. Add sugar, milk, nutmeg, cinnamon, raisins, and orange juice.

Cover with waxed paper. Microwave at HIGH 15 to 16 minutes or until firm.

Combine remaining ¼ cup of butter and other ingredients in a bowl. Sprinkle over soufflé. Microwave, uncovered, at HIGH 2 minutes. Let stand, covered, 2 to 3 minutes before serving.

Yield: 6 to 8 servings.

SWEET POTATO SURPRISE

Power: HIGH
Microwave Time: 8 to 9 Minutes

    1½ cups cubed ham
    1   (29-ounce) can whole sweet
          potatoes, drained
    1   tablespoon butter or margarine
    ⅓   cup dark corn syrup
    ¼   cup crunchy peanut butter
    ¼   cup orange juice

Place ham in round glass baking dish. Slice sweet potatoes and arrange on top of ham.

Place butter in a 1-quart glass bowl. Microwave at HIGH 30 seconds to melt. Stir in corn syrup, peanut butter, and orange juice. Pour over sweet potato and ham mixture. Microwave at HIGH 4 minutes.

Rotate ½ turn. Microwave at HIGH 4 minutes. Let stand, covered, 2 to 3 minutes before serving.
Yield: 4 to 6 servings.

MAIN DISH TOMATO

Power: HIGH
Microwave Time: 3 to 4 Minutes

  1 large, firm ripe tomato
  ⅛ teaspoon garlic salt
  2 tablespoons chopped onion
  ¼ pound ground chuck
  ¼ cup herb-seasoned stuffing mix
  1 tablespoon chopped parsley
  1 egg, beaten
     Dash of pepper

Cut a slice off the stem end of tomato. Scoop out pulp. Place pulp in a small glass baking dish.
Combine garlic salt, onion, ground beef, stuffing mix, parsley, egg, and pepper in a bowl. Fill tomato shell with mixture. Place the stuffed tomato in dish containing the tomato pulp. Cover with waxed paper. Microwave at HIGH 3 to 4 minutes. Let stand, covered, 2 minutes before serving.
Yield: 1 serving.
Micronote: Add 2 to 3 minutes microwaving time for each additional tomato to be cooked.

CORN-STUFFED TOMATOES

Power: HIGH
Microwave Time: 5½ to 6½ Minutes

  6 ripe tomatoes
  6 tablespoons butter or margarine
  2 cups cooked whole kernel corn, drained
  2 tablespoons minced onion
  8 to 10 sprigs parsley, minced
  1 teaspoon salt
     Dash of pepper
  ¼ cup fine bread crumbs
  2 tablespoons butter or margarine

Cut a slice off stem end of each tomato. Scoop out pulp. Place shells in a flat glass baking dish.
Place butter in a 1-quart glass bowl. Microwave at HIGH 30 seconds to melt. Stir in corn, onion, parsley, salt, and pepper. Fill the tomato shells with this mixture. Top with the bread crumbs. Place about 1 teaspoon of butter on top of each tomato.
Microwave at HIGH, uncovered, 5 to 6 minutes or until piping hot.
Yield: 6 servings.

FANCY STUFFED TOMATOES

Power: HIGH
Microwave Time: 13 to 17 Minutes

  4 large ripe tomatoes
  6 slices bacon, diced
  ¼ cup chopped onion
  1 (10-ounce) package frozen chopped spinach
  ½ cup commercial sour cream
  ½ cup grated Mozzarella cheese
  ¼ teaspoon dried basil

Cut a slice off stem end of tomatoes. Scoop out pulp.
Place bacon in a flat glass casserole. Cover with paper towel. Microwave at HIGH 4 to 5 minutes. Remove bacon with a slotted spoon. Set aside.
Stir onion into bacon drippings. Cover with paper towel. Microwave at HIGH 2 minutes.
Pierce spinach package with a fork. Place package on a paper plate. Microwave at HIGH 3 to 4 minutes. Drain well.
Add spinach to the onion. Stir in bacon, sour cream, cheese, and basil. Fill tomato shells with this mixture.
Place stuffed tomatoes in a glass casserole. Cover with waxed paper. Microwave at HIGH 4 to 6 minutes. Let stand, covered, 1 minute.
Yield: 4 servings.

SUMMER VEGETABLE COMBO

Power: HIGH
Microwave Time: 10 to 12 Minutes

  1   medium-sized zucchini or
        yellow squash, sliced
  ½   cup chopped onion
  1   green pepper, chopped
  2   medium-sized tomatoes,
        chopped
  1   teaspoon salt
  ⅛   teaspoon pepper
  ¼   cup butter or margarine

Arrange vegetables in layers in a 1-quart greased casserole. Sprinkle with salt and pepper. Cut butter in small pieces, and place on top.

Cover with plastic wrap. Microwave at HIGH 10 to 12 minutes or until done as desired.

Yield: 4 servings.

Micronote: For a low-calorie meal, use diet margarine. Vary the vegetables and the amount to enjoy single portions of fresh, summer vegetables, cooked as they are available.

SUMMER VEGETABLE SIZZLE

Power: HIGH
Microwave Time: 4½ to 5½ Minutes

  ¼   cup salad oil
  2   cups summer squash, cut in
        pieces
  1   zucchini, cut in pieces
  1   onion, sliced
  1   tablespoon Worcestershire sauce
  1   tablespoon soy sauce
  ½   teaspoon garlic powder
  ½   teaspoon ground ginger

Microwave ¼ cup oil in a 9½-inch browning dish at HIGH 1½ minutes. Add squash, zucchini, and onion to the hot oil.

Mix Worcestershire sauce, soy sauce, garlic powder, and ginger in a small container. Pour mixture over vegetables. Microwave at HIGH 3 to 4 minutes or until vegetables are tender.

Yield: 4 to 6 servings.

WILTED GREENS

Power: HIGH
Microwave Time: 9 to 11 Minutes

  6   slices bacon, cut in 2-inch pieces
  ½   cup chopped green onion
  ¼   cup red wine vinegar
  ¼   cup water
  1   tablespoon sugar
  ¾   teaspoon salt
  6   cups fresh greens (spring or leaf
        lettuce, spinach, mustard
        leaves, or a combination)
        Radishes, sliced

Place bacon on microwave roasting rack in a 12- x 8-inch baking dish. Cover with paper towel. Microwave at HIGH 5 to 6 minutes or until crisp. Remove bacon. Crumble and set aside.

Stir onion into bacon drippings. Cover with waxed paper. Microwave at HIGH 2 to 3 minutes. Add vinegar, water, sugar, and salt. Microwave at HIGH 2 minutes or until boiling.

Place torn lettuce in a large bowl. Pour the hot dressing over the greens and toss lightly. Add crumbled bacon and radishes. Serve immediately.

Yield: 4 to 6 servings.

Micronote: Dry one or two slices of bread quickly for crumbs or toppings. Place the bread on a paper towel. Microwave at HIGH 1½ minutes. Turn slices over after half the cooking time. After standing, the bread slices will become crisp and dry and can be easily crushed.

SPECIAL MICROWAVE OVEN USES

These are among some of the most functional and important ways in which to use a microwave oven. In addition to all the primary cooking functions it can perform, a microwave can also be used to do the following:

- *Speed barbecue or outdoor grill cooking.*
- *Blanch small quantities of vegetables for freezing.*
- *Cook small quantities of fruits and vegetables for quick jellies, conserves, and relishes.*
- *Prepare gifts and special treats quickly.*

BARBECUING—
MICROWAVE STYLE

The grill and your microwave can be combined to add even more enjoyment to meals prepared outdoors. The microwave oven can be used to quickly defrost meat and poultry. If the meat will be marinated, it needs only partial defrosting.

Partially cooking large roasts or quantities of ribs, either beef or pork, in the microwave oven before placing on the grill can cut the total cooking time in half.

For real convenience, and grilled steaks to serve any time, follow this technique:
• While the charcoal grill is hot, quickly sear a quantity of steaks, chops, or patties. Leave them rare and allow them to cool.
• Wrap in plastic wrap or freezer paper. Seal, label, and freeze for use later.
• To prepare for serving, remove wrapper from frozen meat and arrange on a microwave roasting rack. Microwave at MEDIUM to defrost and heat.

Size	Doneness	Time
1-inch thick steak or chop	Rare	1 minute per side
1-inch thick steak or chop	Medium	1½ minutes per side
Four ¾-inch thick patties	Medium	1 to 1½ minutes per side

BARBEQUED RIBS—
MICROWAVE STYLE

Power: HIGH
Microwave Time: 17 to 23 Minutes
Grill Time: 45 to 50 Minutes

4 to 6 pounds	spareribs
⅓ cup	lemon juice
1½ tablespoons	seasoned salt
½ teaspoon	paprika
½ teaspoon	pepper
1 cup	beef broth
¼ cup	Worcestershire sauce
¼ cup	wine vinegar
¼ cup	salad oil
½ teaspoon	hot sauce
¼ teaspoon	garlic powder
1 teaspoon	dry mustard
¼ teaspoon	chili powder
½ teaspoon	salt

Place ribs on microwave roasting rack in flat casserole. Brush ribs with lemon juice. Combine seasoned salt, paprika, and pepper and sprinkle over ribs. Cover and set aside.

Combine the remaining ingredients in a 4-cup glass measure. Microwave, covered with plastic wrap, at HIGH 2 to 3 minutes. Stir well and let stand about 2 hours to develop flavor.

When ready to microwave, baste ribs well with sauce. Microwave at HIGH 15 to 20 minutes. Turn and baste frequently. Complete cooking on a hot grill for 45 to 50 minutes.

Yield: 4 to 6 servings.

MARINADES FOR MEATS

Before barbecuing your steak or chops, you may wish to marinate meat to enhance its flavor.

TERIYAKI MARINADE

- ½ cup soy sauce
- ½ cup brandy
- 1 (1-inch) piece gingerroot, minced
- ¼ cup catsup
- 1 tablespoon prepared mustard
- 1 teaspoon Worcestershire sauce
- ¼ cup firmly packed brown sugar

Combine all ingredients. Marinate meat several hours in refrigerator.

Yield: 1½ cups.

BEEF WINE MARINADE

- ¼ cup salad oil
- ¼ cup dry vermouth
- ¼ cup soy sauce
- 1 teaspoon prepared mustard
- ½ teaspoon dry mustard
- 1 clove garlic, minced
- ¼ teaspoon pepper
- ½ teaspoon salt
- 2 teaspoons Worcestershire sauce

Place all ingredients in blender and process on Blend for 2 minutes. Marinate meat in refrigerator for several hours, turning meat frequently.

Yield: approximately 1 cup.

MARINADE FOR MEAT

- ½ cup wine vinegar
- 1 cup salad oil
- ½ cup grated onion
- 1 clove garlic, crushed
- 1 tablespoon Worcestershire sauce
- 3 pounds meat, pork or beef

Combine vinegar, oil, onion, garlic, and Worcestershire sauce in a large glass bowl. Mix well; add meat and stir. Let stand in refrigerator overnight, turning the meat occasionally.

Yield: about 8 servings.

OIL AND VINEGAR MARINADE

- ½ cup salad oil
- ⅓ cup wine vinegar
- 1 clove garlic, minced
- ½ teaspoon salt
- ¼ teaspoon pepper

Combine all ingredients in a jar; cover. Shake well and chill. Shake well before pouring over meat for marinating.

Yield: ¾ cup.

SOY-SESAME MARINADE

- ¼ cup chopped onion
- ¼ cup soy sauce
- 1 tablespoon firmly packed light brown sugar
- 1 tablespoon sesame seed
- 1 tablespoon salad oil
- 1 teaspoon salt
- 1 teaspoon freshly squeezed lemon juice
- ¼ teaspoon pepper
- ¼ teaspoon ground ginger

Combine all ingredients; stir until well-blended. Use to marinate beef or lamb before grilling.

Yield: ½ cup.

THE FREEZER AND
A MICROWAVE OVEN

Home food preservation has become a very important necessity in the last few years. Many people with only limited spaces are growing vegetables for their personal use.

With a bumper crop, many people find it impossible to consume all the vegetables they produce, so they give them away to friends. Whether you receive the vegetables as gifts or grow them yourself, you often want to freeze some for use at a later time. By using a microwave oven, it is possible with a minimum of time and effort to blanch small quantities of fresh vegetables.

MICROWAVE BLANCHING TECHNIQUES
- Blanch only 1 quart or 1 pound of vegetables at a time.
- Wash, peel, and slice or dice to prepare.
- Place vegetables in a 2½-quart casserole or bowl. (*Do not add salt.*)

MICROWAVE BLANCHING CHART

Vegetable	Quantity	Amount of Water	Minutes at HIGH*
Asparagus	1 pound	¼ cup	2½ to 4
Beans, Green	1 pound	⅓ cup	4 to 5
Broccoli	1 pound	⅓ cup	3½ to 4
Carrots	1 pound	¼ cup	4 to 5
Cauliflower	1 head	⅓ cup	4 to 5
Corn-on-the-cob	4 ears	None	3½ to 4½
Corn, Whole Kernel	4 cups	None	4 to 5
Peas	4 cups	¼ cup	4 to 5
Spinach	½ pound	None	1½ to 2
Squash	1 pound	¼ cup	3 to 4

*These times are approximate. The vegetables are properly blanched when evenly bright in color.

- Cover with casserole lid or plastic wrap.
- Microwave at HIGH following times on blanching chart.
- Stir well halfway through blanching.
- Vegetables should be very bright in color when ready.
- At completion of blanching time, *immediately* plunge into ice water to stop cooking procedure.

- Spread vegetables in a single layer on towel to drain.
- Blot with paper towels to remove excess moisture.
- Package in 1-pint freezer containers, sealable freezer bags, or wrap in freezer paper.
- Seal, label, and freeze up to 1 year.

Wash, peel, slice, or dice

Cover

Stir halfway through blanching

Plunge into ice water

Drain and blot

Place in freezing containers

FREEZING COOKED FOODS FOR MICROWAVING

With a microwave oven and a freezer, there will never be any need to throw leftovers away. With proper packaging for the freezer and a microwave oven to heat them, these foods can become planned-overs.

Prepare double batches of favorite foods in a safe-for-microwave casserole. Cook them either conventionally or in the microwave oven. When they are cooled, place in the freezer until they hold their shape. Then, remove the frozen food from the casserole. Package in plastic wrap or freezer paper. Seal, label, and freeze.

Use sealable freezer bags for individual portions or package single servings in plastic wrap. Either of these packages can go directly into the microwave oven to serve as a container for defrosting and heating.

DEFROSTING AND HEATING COOKED FOODS

- Remove freezer wrapping from the food, if desired.
- Return the food to the casserole used for cooking and shaping.
- Cover loosely with plastic wrap.
- Microwave at MEDIUM to defrost and heat.
- Stir casseroles, soups, stews, and vegetables once during microwaving to combine heated and unheated portions.
  Follow these times for heating cooked foods:
- Allow about 1½ to 2 minutes for heating per cup of food, after defrosting.

Quantity	Minutes at MEDIUM
4 cups	5 to 6
6 cups	7 to 8
8 cups	10 to 12

- Allow to stand 3 to 5 minutes after microwaving for the temperature to even out within the food.

MICROWAVING TIME FOR HOME FROZEN VEGETABLES

The very special vegetables below are simple to prepare in the microwave. Most home frozen vegetables should be microwaved the same way as the commercially prepared types. If the vegetables are packaged in a rigid plastic container or a plastic freezer bag, microwave them for a short period of time to defrost slightly. Remove the freezer wrapping and place the vegetables in a small, flat casserole. Cover the container and microwave at HIGH power. Follow the times below or those suggested on commercially packaged frozen food.

Vegetable	Quantity	Water Added	Minutes at HIGH Power
Beans, Green diagonal cut	2 to 4 servings	None	5 to 6
Beans, Lima	2 to 4 servings	None	6 to 7
Corn, cut off cob	2 to 4 servings	¼ cup hot water	4 to 5
Corn, on cob	1 ear	None	4 to 4½
	2 ears		6 to 7
	4 ears		10 to 11
Okra	2 to 4 servings	2 tbsp. hot water	6 to 7
Peas, Black-eyed	2 to 4 servings	¼ cup water	8 to 10
Peas, Green	2 to 4 servings	2 tbsp. hot water	4½ to 5½

MICROWAVE GIFT IDEAS

This is one situation where the microwave oven can be a real time and energy saver. Use it to quickly prepare a custard for a sick friend, minted nuts for a 'hostess' gift, or to quickly bake a 2-layer cake for a moving-in neighbor.

The following recipes make very appropriate Christmas gifts.

CAKE FROM A MIX

Power: HIGH
Microwaving Time: 10 to 12 Minutes

  1 (18½- to 20-ounce)
       pudding-added cake mix
       Commercial frosting (optional)

Prepare the mix according to package directions. Pour the batter into a greased 10-inch microwave plastic fluted tube pan. Microwave at HIGH 10 to 12 minutes. Rotate every 3 to 4 minutes during microwaving. Place directly on the counter to cool 5 minutes before removing from the pan. Glaze with a commercially prepared frosting, if desired.

Yield: 10 to 12 servings.

MINTED NUTS

Power: HIGH
Microwave Time: 5 to 7 Minutes

  1   cup sugar
  ⅓   cup water
  ⅛   teaspoon salt
  1   tablespoon light corn syrup
  6   large-size marshmallows
  ¼   teaspoon peppermint extract
  3   cups pecan halves

Combine sugar, water, salt, and corn syrup in a large mixing bowl. Cover with waxed paper. Microwave at HIGH 5 to 7 minutes or until mixture reaches a soft ball (235°).

Add marshmallows. Stir until they are dissolved. Add peppermint; stir well. Add pecans and stir with a circular motion until every nut is coated. Mixture should harden slightly. Drop each pecan onto a cookie sheet. Cool.

Yield: 3 cups pecan halves.

Micronote: If mixture hardens while dropping, return bowl to the microwave oven. Microwave at HIGH 1 to 2 minutes, then let stand a few seconds to firm slightly.

SUGAR-GLAZED PEANUTS

Power: HIGH
Microwave Time: 5 to 6 Minutes

- 1 **cup firmly packed light brown sugar**
- 1 **teaspoon ground cinnamon**
- 1 **pound shelled peanuts**
- ½ **cup butter or margarine**

Toss together sugar, cinnamon, and peanuts in a 1½-quart glass casserole. Dot butter over the mixture. Microwave at HIGH 5 to 6 minutes.

Immediately pour mixture onto aluminum foil to coat all the peanuts. Serve warm or cold.

Yield: 4 cups.

SALTED PEANUTS

Power: HIGH
Microwave Time: 5 to 6 Minutes

- 1 **cup raw shelled peanuts**
   Cold water
- ½ **teaspoon salt**

Pour peanuts into colander or wire basket and wet thoroughly. Sprinkle with salt. Pour into small casserole or pie plate. Microwave at HIGH 5 to 6 minutes, stirring at 2 minute intervals. Peanuts will be crisp when cool.

Yield: 1 cup peanuts.

JELLIES, JAMS, CONSERVES

Yes, these can be prepared in the microwave oven. For large quantities of these you may prefer to use the conventional kettle method; but for small quantities of certain fruits, the microwave oven is a cool, relatively easy method of cooking.

It will usually be necessary to add pectin for microwave jellies and jams because the

moisture will not evaporate quickly enough for the natural pectin to develop.

To microwave jellies and jams use the following techniques:
- Use fresh, high quality or select frozen fruits.
- Prepare fruit according to recipe directions.
- Combine fruit and other ingredients in a 3- to 4-quart casserole or heat-proof mixing bowl. Using a dry pot holder, handle carefully.
- Cover if the recipe specifies.
- Stir according to the directions.
- Pour into prepared containers. Seal with hot lids.
- Store as recommended.

AMBROSIA CONSERVE

Power: HIGH
Microwave Time: 19 to 21 Minutes

- 1 **orange, peeled and sectioned**
- 2 **(20-ounce) cans crushed pineapple, drained**
- 3 **cooking apples, pared, cored, and chopped**
- 1 **(6-ounce) bottle fruit pectin**
- 2 **tablespoons lemon juice**
- 5 **cups sugar**
- 1 **(7-ounce) package flaked coconut**
- 1 **cup seedless raisins**

Combine orange sections, pineapple, apple, pectin, and lemon juice in a 3-quart casserole. Stir well. Cover with waxed paper.

Microwave at HIGH 10 to 12 minutes or until boiling. Stir once or twice during cooking. After mixture comes to a full boil, stir in sugar.

Microwave at HIGH 8 minutes or until mixture reaches a full boil. Time for 1 minute of boiling. Remove from oven and stir in coconut and raisins. Ladle into hot, sterilized jars and seal.

Yield: 6 to 8 (6-ounce) jars.

SPECIAL APPLE RELISH

Power: HIGH
Microwave Time: 20 to 25 Minutes

4 cups chunky applesauce
1 cup chopped, dried peaches
1 (20-ounce) can crushed
   pineapple, drained
1 cup sugar
2 tablespoons lemon juice
¾ cup seedless raisins

Combine all ingredients in a 3-quart casserole. Cover with waxed paper. Microwave at HIGH 20 to 25 minutes, stirring well several times.

Spoon into hot, sterilized jars and seal. Serve with pork, beef, or poultry.
Yield: 7 to 8 (6-ounce) jars.

CARROT CONSERVE

Power: HIGH
Microwave Time: 19 to 23 Minutes

1 (32-ounce) package carrots,
   finely chopped
2 oranges, peeled and sectioned
⅓ cup lemon juice
½ teaspoon salt
1 (1¾-ounce) package powdered
   fruit pectin
4 cups sugar
½ cup blanched almonds, chopped

Combine carrots, orange sections, lemon juice, salt, and pectin in a 3-quart casserole. Stir well. Cover with waxed paper. Microwave at HIGH 12 to 15 minutes. Stir once or twice during microwaving.

Add sugar to mixture. Stir well. Cover again with waxed paper and microwave at HIGH 6 to 7 minutes or until mixture begins to boil; then time for 1 minute of boiling. Stir in chopped almonds. Pour into hot, sterilized jars and seal.
Yield: 6 (6-ounce) jars.

CRANBERRY CHUTNEY

Power: HIGH
Microwave Time: 10 to 12 Minutes

4 cups fresh cranberries
2 oranges, thinly sliced
¼ cup wine vinegar
1 cup firmly packed dark brown
   sugar
¼ teaspoon ground ginger
1 cup mixed candied fruit
6 whole cloves

Combine all ingredients in a 3-quart casserole. Cover with waxed paper. Microwave at HIGH 10 to 12 minutes or until thickened. Stir once during microwaving.

Pour into hot, sterilized jars and seal. Store in the refrigerator until served.
Yield: 8 to 9 (6-ounce) jars.

GRAPE JELLY FROM FROZEN CONCENTRATE

Power: HIGH
Microwave Time: 15 to 19 Minutes

1 (6-ounce) can frozen grape juice
   concentrate, thawed
1 (1¾-ounce) package powdered
   fruit pectin
2 cups hot tap water
3¾ cups sugar

Combine thoroughly thawed concentrate, pectin, and water in a 3-quart casserole. Cover with waxed paper. Microwave at HIGH 8 to 10 minutes or until bubbles form around edge of mixture. Stir well after 4 minutes.

Add sugar. Stir well. Cover with waxed paper. Microwave at HIGH 6 to 8 minutes, stirring once, until mixture reaches a rolling boil. When boiling begins, time for 1 minute of hard boiling. Skim off foam. Pour into hot, sterilized jars and seal while hot.
Yield: 5 to 6 (6-ounce) jars.

STEP-BY-STEP GUIDE
FOR YOUNG MICROWAVERS

Because a microwave oven is easy and safe for youngsters to use, encourage them to learn to do the following:
• Prepare simple meals on their own.
• Make their own snacks and treats.
• Heat already cooked food for fast meals.
• Cook easy-to-prepare and fast cooking foods.

TIPS TO HELP
YOUNG MICROWAVERS
• Go over the controls of the microwave oven explaining its basic operation. Show children how to use it correctly.
• Show youngsters which utensils are good to use for microwave cooking. You might want to mark cups, mugs, bowls, and other similar dishes so they will be easy to identify.
• Point out ways in which they can use heat-resistant glass measuring cups and mixing bowls for thawing, heating, and cooking.
• Keep a supply of paper cups, bowls, and plates on hand as they are easy to use as containers for soups, sandwiches, and

some desserts. Heavy-duty plastic wrap makes an easy-to-use throwaway cover.
• As a special treat, cook your youngsters' special favorites (either microwave or conventional). Package them individually for the freezer. Seal, label, and freeze for children to thaw or heat as desired in the microwave.

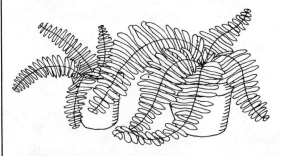

SOME FOODS THAT
YOUNG MICROWAVERS
CAN PREPARE
Many of the recipes in *Microwave Cooking Made Easy* may be prepared by almost anyone in the family. However, to get your young microwaver started, you might suggest that he try one of the following kid-tested favorite recipes.

HOT APPLESAUCE

Power: HIGH
Microwave Time: 1 to 2 Minutes

  ½ cup applesauce (individual
       serving)
     Ground cinnamon or red hot
       candies

Microwave applesauce at HIGH 1 to 2 minutes in a 1-cup glass measure or individual serving dishes suitable for microwaving.
  Garnish with cinnamon or a few red hot candies.
  Yield: 1 serving.
  Micronote: Increase the microwaving time to 2 to 4 minutes for 4 to 6 servings.

PLAIN BAKED APPLE

Power: HIGH
Microwave Time: 1 Minute

  1 large baking apple
     Brown sugar
     Cinnamon candies
     Raisins
     Other flavorings (optional)

Core apple to within ½ inch of end. Remove about ½ inch of skin from around stem end.
  Mix brown sugar, candies, raisins, and other flavorings as desired, and place in opening. Place apple in a custard cup or other round dish. Cover with waxed paper. Microwave at HIGH 1 minute.
  Yield: 1 serving.

CARAMEL CHEWS

Power: HIGH
Microwave Time: 3½ to 4 minutes

  28 caramels
   3 tablespoons butter or margarine
   2 tablespoons water
   1 (3-ounce) can chow mein
        noodles
   1 cup roasted peanuts
   1 (6-ounce) package semisweet
        chocolate morsels
   2 tablespoons water

Mix caramels, butter, and water in a large, deep glass mixing bowl. Microwave at HIGH 1½ to 2 minutes. Stir well and continue to microwave at HIGH about 1 minute. Stir well to combine caramels, water, and butter into a smooth mixture. Add noodles and peanuts. Drop by rounded teaspoonfuls onto a greased cookie sheet.
  Place chocolate morsels and water in a 4-cup glass measure. Microwave at HIGH about 45 seconds. Remove from oven and stir the mixture well. Microwave at HIGH about 15 seconds more; then stir to dissolve rest of chocolate. Spread over each chew. Chill until firm.
  Yield: 30 pieces.

CEREAL CANDY

Power: HIGH
Microwave Time: 5 to 6 minutes

  1 cup sugar
  1 cup light corn syrup
  1 cup peanut butter
  6 cups wheat or corn flake cereal

Combine sugar and corn syrup in a large glass bowl. Microwave at HIGH 5 to 6 minutes or until bubbly. Stir in peanut butter. Add cereal and blend well, being careful not to crush cereal. Drop by teaspoonfuls onto waxed paper. Let stand in refrigerator to chill before serving.
  Yield: 4 to 5 dozen pieces.

FAST TOASTED
CHEESE SANDWICH

Power: MEDIUM-HIGH
Microwave Time: 15 to 20 Seconds

  2 slices toast, prepared
       conventionally
  1 slice cheese

Arrange cheese between toast slices. Place on paper plate. Microwave at MEDIUM-HIGH 15 to 20 seconds or until cheese melts. Serve immediately.
  Yield: 1 serving.

APPENDIX

COOKING MEASURE EQUIVALENTS

Metric Cup	Volume (Liquid)	Liquid Solids (Butter)	Fine Powder (Flour)	Granular (Sugar)	Grain (Rice)
1	250 ml	200 g	140 g	190 g	150 g
¾	188 ml	150 g	105 g	143 g	113 g
⅔	167 ml	133 g	93 g	127 g	100 g
½	125 ml	100 g	70 g	95 g	75 g
⅓	83 ml	67 g	47 g	63 g	50 g
¼	63 ml	50 g	35 g	48 g	38 g
⅛	31 ml	25 g	18 g	24 g	19 g

EQUIVALENT MEASUREMENTS

3 teaspoons .... 1 tablespoon
2 tablespoons... 1 fluid ounce
4 tablespoons .... ¼ cup
5 tablespoons plus 1 teaspoon .... ⅓ cup
8 tablespoons... ½ cup
16 tablespoons .... 1 cup
1 cup.. 8 fluid ounces
2 cups .... 1 pint (16 fluid ounces)
⅛ cup... 2 tablespoons
⅓ cup.. 5 tablespoons plus 1 teaspoon
⅔ cup... 10 tablespoons plus 2 teaspoons
¾ cup..12 tablespoons
Few Grains (or dash)... less than ⅛ teaspoon
Pinch............................... as much as can be taken between tip of finger and thumb.

INDEXES

RECITES

Chicken Summer Vegetable
  Duo, 157
Chicken, Sweet-and-Sour, 156
Chicken Teriyaki, 156
Chicken Tetrazzini, 159
Chicken Zucchini, 189
Chicken Zucchini Casserole, 156
Cordon Bleu, Easy, 150
Curried Two-in-One Dinner, 157
Curry, Peanut-Chicken, 153
Hot Brown Sandwich, 48
Livers, Saucy Chicken, 46
Sweet 'n Sour Peglegs, 46
Chili
  Chili Beef Casserole, 121
  Chili-Cheese Dip, 40
Chocolate
  Brownies, 80
  Cakes
    Cherry-Brownie Pudding
      Cake, 66
    Chocolate Cake, 67
    Chocolate-Covered Cherry
      Roll, 66
    Chocolate Fudge Cake
      Deluxe, 67
    Cocoa Cola Cake, 68
    Fudge Surprise Cake, 68
    Mississippi Mud Cake, 69
    Self-Iced Chocolate Cake, 68
    Upside-Down Christmas
      Wreath Cake, 71
  Candies
    Double Fudge, 74
    Marshmallow Fudge, 75
    Real Chocolate Fudge, 74
  Cookies
    Chocolate Chip Bars, 80
    Chocolate-Mint Bars, 80
    Creme-Filled Chocolate
      Cookies, 81
    Crunchy Peanut Butter-
      Chocolate Squares, 84
    Fudge-Filled Peanut Butter
      Bars, 84
  Crust, Chocolate Wafer, 140
  Frostings
    Chocolate Cola Icing, 68
    Cocoa Fudge Frosting, 66
    Fudge Frosting, 67
    Fudge Icing, 69
  Hot Chocolate, Southern, 51
  Mousse, Yogurt Chocolate, 87
  Pies
    Chocolate Peanut Pie, 141
    Chocolate Pie, 141
    Fantastic Chocolate Pie, 141
    Fudge Nut Pie, 142
  Pudding, Chocolate, 86, 87
  Sauce, Chocolate, 164

Chowders. *See* Soups.
Cider, Hot Spicy, 51
Clam Chowder, 169
Coconut
  Crust, Coconut, 140
  Filling, Coconut, 61, 62
  Pie, Hawaiian Coconut Icebox, 142
  Pie, Old-Fashioned
    Coconut Custard, 143
Coffee
  Bars, Warm Coffee, 81
  Coffee, Irish, 51
  Coffee, Spiced, 51
  Parfait, Coffee, 90
  Pie, Coffee, 143
Conserves. *See* Jellies.
Consommé. *See* Soups.
Cookies
  Apple-Nut Squares, 78, 79
  Apricot-Almond Bars, 79
  Brownies, 80
  Chocolate Chip Bars, 80
  Chocolate Cookies, Creme-Filled, 81
  Chocolate-Mint Bars, 80
  Coffee Bars, Warm, 81
  Crunch Squares, 82
  Fudge-Filled Peanut Butter Bars, 84
  Ginger-Mincemeat Bars, 82
  Graham Cracker Bars, 82
  Lemon Bars, 82
  Peanut Butter Bars, 83
  Peanut Butter-Chocolate Squares,
    Crunchy, 84
  Pumpkin Bars, 84
  Quick Breakfast Bars, 56
  Raisin or Date Mumbles, 85
  Three-Layer Bars, 83
  Wheat Germ-Carrot Bars, 85
Coquille St. Jacques, 107
Corn
  Corn, Southern Creamed, 181
  Corn, Squaw, 182
  Dippers, Corn, 42
  Pudding, Corn, 182
  Quiche, Fresh Corn-Cheese, 96
  Soufflé, Cheese and Corn, 182
  Tomatoes, Corn-Stuffed, 191
Cornbread, Fancy, 55
Cornish Hens
  Brown Game Hens, 162
  Succulent Cornish Hen, 163
Crab
  Crab Bisque, 170
  Crab Deluxe, 105
  Crabmeat Appetizer, Hot, 43
  Crabmeat Be-Gones in Bacon, 45
  Crabmeat-Broccoli Casserole, 105
  Crabmeat Canapés, Hot, 44
  Crabmeat Eleanor, 104
  Crabmeat Supreme, 43

MICROWAVE TERMS AND USES

CHARTS

THE Magazine For You
if You Share Our Interest
in the South.

SOUTHERN LIVING
features articles to help make
life for you and your
family more comfortable,
more stimulating, more fun...

SOUTHERN LIVING is about your home and how to make a more attractive, more convenient, more comfortable place to live. Each issue brings you dozens of decorating and remodeling ideas you can adapt to your own surroundings.

SOUTHERN LIVING is about gardening and landscaping and how to make the outside of your home just as attractive as the inside. In addition to gardening features, you'll find a monthly garden calendar pinpointing what to plant and when, plus a "Letters to our Garden Editor" section to answer your own particular questions.

SOUTHERN LIVING is about good food and entertaining, with recipes and menu ideas that are sure to delight your family and friends. You'll discover recipes with a Southern accent from some of the South's superlative cooks.

SOUTHERN LIVING is about travel and just plain fun. Every new issue offers an information-packed monthly calendar of special events and happenings throughout the South, plus features on the many fascinating places of interest the South has to offer.

To find out how you can receive SOUTHERN LIVING every month, simply write to: SOUTHERN LIVING, P. O. Box C-119, Birmingham, AL 35283.